To Sue

One of the truly
great and special
Blue Devils —
Go Duke!

John
Moore

D1467139

The Blue Divide

Duke, North Carolina,
and the Battle on Tobacco Road

JOHNNY MOORE

&

ART CHANSKY

TRIUMPH
BOOKS

Copyright © 2014 by Johnny Moore and Art Chansky

No part of this publication may be reproduced, stored in a retrieval system, or transmitted in any form by any means, electronic, mechanical, photocopying, or otherwise, without the prior written permission of the publisher, Triumph Books LLC, 814 North Franklin Street, Chicago, Illinois 60610.

Library of Congress Cataloging-in-Publication Data

Moore, Johnny, 1955–
    The blue divide: Duke, North Carolina, and the battle on tobacco road / Johnny Moore, Art Chansky.
        pages cm
    ISBN 978-1-60078-986-1 (hardback)
1. Duke Blue Devils (Basketball team)—History. 2. North Carolina Tar Heels (Basketball team)—History. 3. Duke University—Basketball—History. 4. University of North Carolina at Chapel Hill—Basketball—History. 5. Sports rivalries—North Carolina—History. 6. College sports—North Carolina—History. I. Chansky, Art. II. Title.
    GV885.43.D85M67 2014
    796.323'6309756—dc23

                                                                    2014018817

This book is available in quantity at special discounts for your group or organization. For further information, contact:

Triumph Books LLC
814 North Franklin Street
Chicago, Illinois 60610
(312) 337-0747
www.triumphbooks.com

Printed in U.S.A.
ISBN: 978-1-60078-986-1
Design by Alex Lubertozzi
Photos courtesy of Robert Crawford unless otherwise indicated

To all the coaches and their staffs, players and their families, and generations of students and fans who have participated in or witnessed firsthand undoubtedly the greatest rivalry in the history of college basketball.

————————————

This book is dedicated to the love of my life, Robin, and my wonderful daughters, Beth and Sarah.
—Johnny Moore

————————————

To the relatives and special friends from both sides of the Blue Divide, who root like hell for their teams but never let Duke-Carolina come between us. You know who you are!
—Art Chansky

Contents

Foreword

Coming to Durham from Los Angeles in the fall of 1982, I was well aware of how good the basketball program was at the University of North Carolina. The Heels were coming off a national championship in the spring, and everybody knew Dean Smith. Carolina was the gold standard.

What I didn't understand was the depth of dislike between Duke and Carolina. I didn't really get at the time how Duke always felt slighted and what a measuring stick the Tar Heel program was for Duke fans. It hit me in 1985 in the Carmichael Auditorium locker room.

The year before, we lost a crushing game on the road in double overtime, and those of us in the locker room were reduced to tears. The next year in 1985, I was a junior, and Duke was highly ranked going into Carmichael to play the final Duke-Carolina game in that building.

We won.

This time we were all happy and celebrating in the locker room when we noticed some of the older guys standing around with tears in their eyes—tears of joy. One of us remarked, "Hey, crying was last year. You guys know we won, right?" Johnny Moore from our sports information office stopped us and said, "You don't understand. We haven't won here in 19 years. Gminski, Banks, Spanarkel, Armstrong, DeVenzio, Denton. Those guys never won here."

Wow. That one stuck with me.

Moore's statement was added to two other stories in my memory bank from the prior year when Duke beat No. 1 North Carolina in the ACC Tournament. I don't remember the score of many games, but I remember the score of that 1984 Duke-Carolina game because when we returned to Durham I saw it on bumper stickers on every car that said "Duke Blue 77–Carolina Blue 74." We players were insulted. At that time Carolina didn't print up bumper stickers over beating Duke. This shouldn't be such a big deal, and we needed to make it a more normal occurrence.

The second memory was following that 77–74 win in the ACC Tournament. That was another joyous locker room, and several members of Duke's administration came into the locker room to join in. Duke chancellor Kenneth Pye, who was like Winston Churchill to me, came up, shook my hand, and said, "Son, you see Carolina blue like a bull sees red." It remains the coolest compliment I have ever received. The problem was: it wasn't really true. As a player, I wanted to defeat North Carolina because they were so good—not because of some Hatfield and McCoy feeling of hatred. If you beat Carolina, it said something really good about you, that you were capable of beating anyone. But beating Carolina had different meaning to many of the people around us.

The Dean E. Smith Center opened in January of 1986, and I had the good fortune to play in the first game in the building. Both teams were undefeated and title favorites, and the buildup to the game was massive. We walked into the building and we had never played anywhere that big. It was all light blue. Carolina beat Duke 95–92 that day, and after the game somebody lamented our foul trouble and that we didn't get a good whistle. Johnny Dawkins said, "What did you expect? Did you think we were getting calls in here? They just named the building after their coach!"

Today the rivalry is expertly packaged and marketed with beautiful montages set to music that are evocative of greatness and the dislike between the competitors. But that doesn't change the fundamental nature of Duke-Carolina. As a broadcaster I have been fortunate to gain a different and more informed perspective of each program. Both sides have been very kind to announcers coming in to learn about their programs—whether it was Hubert Davis going to a Duke practice or me going over to a Carolina practice. Duke and Carolina not only recruit the same type of player, but they often recruit the same players. So the player that Duke fans dislike intensely would have been loved in a Duke uniform and vice versa. When you get an inside view, you see the quality people in each program, that the programs are more alike than they are different, and the incredible respect and admiration for the competitors in both programs.

Any objective view of these two programs clearly reveals that they are two of the best organizations in sports, not just college basketball. And the two programs feed off each other. Each program has been elevated by the other and has reached heights it would not have reached without each other. Sure, there are cycles where Duke will win six out of seven, or Carolina will win six out of seven, but the most amazing stat I saw last season was that with all the games the two had played over the years there was one point separating them in total score.

I understand desperately wanting to win and being devastated when you lose. But I don't understand any suggestion of hatred in this rivalry. Hating to lose and hating your opponent are two different things. There is nothing to hate about Duke, and nothing to hate about Carolina. Nothing.

When I step back and think about this rivalry, the two words that come to me first are "respect" and "grateful." I am grateful to have played in these games, to have competed against Dean Smith's teams with great players like Michael Jordan, Sam Perkins, Brad Daugherty, and Kenny Smith. And I couldn't have more respect for the Carolina program and the people who have worn the uniform and walked the sideline. Even today at 50 years old, I am still asked what it was like to play in the Duke-Carolina game. No disrespect intended, but people don't ask me what it was like to play against N.C. State, Wake Forest, or Virginia. They ask what your record was against Carolina and how you played. Even if Duke won a title or went to the Final Four, you were still judged by your performance in games against Carolina, and I know it's the same for UNC.

I am honored and grateful to have been a small part of the greatest rivalry in college basketball—Duke vs. Carolina.

—Jay Bilas
ESPN college basketball analyst
Duke forward, 1982–86

Introduction

Strangest Blue Collaborators

Why in Blue Heaven and Hell would we, Johnny Moore and Art Chansky, collaborate on a Duke-Carolina book? Whenever a book is written about Duke or Carolina basketball, it is usually authored by an alumnus or a fan of one school or the other. No matter how unflappable they might think they are, there will be a bias in the book for one shade of blue.

That was the point of writing *The Blue Divide*.

We have been friendly rivals for more than 35 years—since Johnny was the assistant sports information director at Duke and Art was sports editor of the *Durham Morning Herald* after graduating from UNC. Moore went on to become the producer of the Duke radio and TV networks and publish *Blue Devil Weekly*, and Chansky left the newspaper business to write books.

Johnny went to Guilford College, where he was trained in his profession, but has been a lifelong Duke fan since he grew up in a divided household. His mother loved Carolina and thought Billy Cunningham was the greatest player ever. His father was a die-hard Dukie. The family attended the Duke-Carolina football game in 1959, a 50–0 shellacking by the Tar Heels on Thanksgiving Day. Five-year-old Johnny cried all the way home while being comforted by his mother, who was trying not to smile too much.

He has hated Carolina ever since the Tar Heels ruined his Thanksgiving dinner.

Art grew up in Boston and went south for college because older siblings of two high school friends were at Duke, and that's all they talked about. Duke didn't have a journalism school, so Art picked Carolina. He knew little about the rivalry until arriving in Chapel Hill. Though he became an instant Tar Heel fan, he was mesmerized by his first visit to Cameron Indoor Stadium as a writer for the *Daily Tar Heel*.

Johnny knew he would have trouble with Art in 1977 when he went to the home of Duke football coach Mike McGee in Hope Valley the Saturday night after the Blue Devils had lost in Durham to the Liberty Bowl-bound Tar Heels 16–3. McGee was perhaps Duke's greatest football player ever, winning the Outland Trophy under Bill Murray, but as a coach, he was struggling to make the Blue Devils relevant again in football.

Johnny was to escort his coach to the home of Duke athletic director Tom Butters, who was either going to fire McGee or give him a new contract. When Johnny walked in, Art was sitting at the McGee's kitchen table, waiting for the news so he could break the story in Sunday's edition. What kind of reporter is already in the kitchen before the SID?

McGee got a three-year contract, but one year later—after UNC had rallied to deal Duke a heart-breaking 16–15 loss in Chapel Hill—the exact same scenario unfolded. Johnny showed up to take McGee to Butters' home. Art was at the kitchen table, knowing that McGee was getting fired because he had a three-year contract. So why meet with Butters?

The fired McGee used the money from the last two years of his contract to get a doctorate from UNC, where he had already earned a master's! He later became athletic director at Cincinnati, Southern Cal, and the University of South Carolina. Johnny and Art still laugh about those two Saturday nights in November.

We have remained the friendliest of adversaries ever since.

Over occasional breakfasts or beers (not at the same time), Johnny would spin story after story about what he knew (firsthand) about Duke athletics, especially the basketball programs built by Bill Foster and Mike Krzyzewski. A student of history, he had also learned plenty about Vic Bubas' teams of the 1960s and still talks about the day he was at one of McGee's football practices attended by the late Wallace Wade, the legendary Duke coach and one of Johnny's drinking buddies during Wade's later years.

Art, who had already written five books on Carolina basketball and Dean Smith, said, "Johnny, you have to write these stories. You can't keep them to yourself."

"I know," he said. "But where would I start? I'm a radio and TV guy now."

"I'll help you," Art said, "because I don't know shit about producing a TV show."

So, after talking about it, we did it. It's not a point-counterpoint, but a true collaboration of what we both know about Duke and Carolina basketball. Each chapter begins with a personal vignette from one of us. Johnny writes about Coach K as the leader, and Art writes about Dean as the teacher. The goal was to tell stories readers have never heard and elaborate on the ones they want to know more about.

We hope you like the book and that it ends up on your favorite bookshelf.

—Johnny Moore and Art Chansky

Chapter 1

2014: A Storm Is Brewing

The game had just been snowed out, and Art Chansky was on WCHL radio speculating as to why Duke could not navigate the eight miles over to Chapel Hill for the 9:00 PM tip-off. "If their bus couldn't get to campus, all the team had to do is tweet out that they needed eight four-wheel drive vehicles in front of Cameron by 6:00…drivers get to sit behind the Duke bench for the game," Chansky said. "I don't think Mike Krzyzewski wanted to play this game in front of 22,000 Carolina students."

Two minutes after Chansky got off the air, his cell phone rang. Johnny Moore, the longtime radio and TV producer for Duke athletics, was on the other end, half laughing and half pissed off. "You hung around Dean Smith for too long," Moore said. "That's the way he always thought about things like this. What's the angle? Honestly, no one over here is that smart. Trust me, they just couldn't get to the damn Dean Dome, okay?"

—JM and AC

The February 12, 2014, renewal set for 9:00 PM in the Dean Smith Center marked just another Duke-Carolina week with all the typical media hype and fan frenzy. All the prized jerseys, balls, and hardware on display—at the Dean Dome and Carolina Basketball Museum at UNC and at Cameron Indoor Stadium and the Schwartz-Butters Athletic Center at Duke—were under heavy security. Call it prank-avoidance mode.

Then two major winter storms were forecast to collide over North Carolina with the bull's-eye on the Research Triangle that is between Raleigh, Durham, and Chapel Hill. Travel alerts for roads and airports began on Monday, more than 48 hours before the game. "I was watching the forecast," recalled UNC's veteran Media Relations boss Steve Kirschner, "and it looked like a storm was on the way and would get here sometime Wednesday. But how bad could it be? Duke is only eight miles away, and I am sure the officials will try to get here early if there is any question."

To concerned media and fans who called, Kirschner basically outlined the ACC's short-sighted policy that the game must be played if the officials and visiting team can make it safely. Screw the fans; they can stay home and watch on TV, bolstering the ratings and allowing advertising rates to jump the next season. Alumni and fans in attendance pay their schools. TV pays the ACC, which distributes the money to its member schools.

As it turned out, Duke being close enough to bus over two hours before the game ultimately caused the problem. Any other opponent, save N.C. State, would have already been in town the day before, staying at a local hotel, and would have been off the roads.

At about 11:00 that morning, Kirschner walked from the basketball suite to his office in the next building and nearly got frostbite. It was that cold. He thought to himself, *If it does snow, it will freeze right away*. When snow began falling an hour later, he yelled to basketball sports information director Matt Bowers to look out the window and see how quickly the cars in the parking lot were turning white.

The calls and emails were now flooding in at both schools. But the response was the same—the game would go on as scheduled, reciting the ACC policy if need be. The media was having its own problems driving to the Smith Center. Several members of the press corps got close enough before hitting traffic snarls that they left their cars and walked for an hour just to get there.

Dick Vitale's plane was unable to land at Raleigh-Durham International Airport. After circling for more than an hour, a runway was sufficiently cleared, and Vitale's Southwest Airlines flight from Tampa, Florida, touched down in early afternoon. But no one was there to get him, and no cabs were going to Chapel Hill because of the mess on Interstate 40.

Dan Shulman and Jay Bilas, the former Duke star who was becoming the new voice of basketball for ESPN, were staying at the Sheraton, four miles from the Smith Center, and it took them two hours to drive there. Tim Brando and color analyst Dan Bonner of the Raycom network had a similarly arduous journey to the arena from their hotel.

All the media that did get to the Dean Dome were royally fed by Bullock's BBQ, whose truck made it in mid-afternoon and led to later cynicism about Duke's travails. Bullock's is located within a mile of the Duke campus, and a picture of their truck sitting outside of the Smith Center was tweeted and re-tweeted hundreds of times. If Bullock's could get there, why couldn't the Blue Devils?

Both basketball programs had plenty of history with winter weather travel. UNC played a game at Providence in 1978, a day after a blizzard shut down the city, and the governor of Rhode Island allowed Carolina's plane to land. Five weeks later, ironically, Duke defeated Villanova in Providence to reach the Final Four the day after a second snowstorm socked the city.

The Tar Heels trekked to Maryland twice within 15 years when a blizzard fell on the nation's capital. Each time the ACC wanted those televised games to be played despite knowing the ominous forecast, and the conference foolishly made UNC travel.

Two of the greatest weekends in Duke basketball history came amidst unlikely snowstorms in Greensboro, North Carolina, site of the ACC Tournaments both years. Before the Blue Devils, who had finished last in the ACC the previous four seasons, won the 1978 ACC Championship, Duke coach Bill Foster deadpanned at the sparsely attended press conference the prior day, "They said it would be a snowy day in Greensboro before Foster ever played for the ACC title."

Two years later one of the worst storms in North Carolina history dumped more than two feet of snow on the middle of the state, and Duke again reached the ACC final. Only half the people with tickets to the sold-out Greensboro Coliseum made the Saturday night game, and most of those arrived via heavy-duty pickups and sturdy four-wheel drive vehicles. Duke edged Maryland to win its second ACC title in three years, and again Foster quipped, "Just another snowy day in Greensboro."

Snow had already been a problem in 2014. Just two weeks before the Tar Heels were to play Duke, the ACC told UNC its game at Georgia Tech would go on as scheduled and to leave for Atlanta early enough to beat the winter storm that was forecast. The snow actually beat the Tar Heels there.

Roy Williams, his coaching staff, players, managers, Kirschner, Bowers, and Roy's wife Wanda boarded one of the last planes to land at Hartsfield Airport just after midnight. And they caught *the* last MARTA train into the city before the subway closed, which would have forced them to find a hotel near the airport at 1:00 in the morning.

As it were, after emerging from the train stop, they were still four blocks from their hotel. Toting their suitcases and duffel bags of uniforms, they all trudged through the ice and snow that had caused the worst gridlock on the eight-lane I-75/85 in Atlanta history that afternoon. ESPN cancelled its telecast when its trucks could not get there, but the game was played as scheduled. Mostly Georgia Tech students, who could walk to the on-campus McCamish Pavilion, showed up. The Tar Heels were able to go home the next day with their second of what would be 12 straight victories.

• • •

Kirschner got his most sobering phone call at about 2:30 when his wife, Jeanne, called his cell phone on the way to pick up their daughter, Emilie, from school. She said she was on Estes Drive, and cars, unable to get up the hill or having slid down it, were stopped in every direction. With Jeanne growing up in Philadelphia and Kirschner in Connecticut, both had childhoods full of snowstorms. So when Jeanne said, "This is really bad," it was the first indication the game was in jeopardy. Ninety minutes later Jeanne and Emilie made it home safely in what is usually a 10-minute trip.

With schools letting out early, several members of the Duke basketball staff had ventured out to pick up their children. After dropping them at home, they began the treacherous drive back, which now took two hours.

Duke assistant Steve Wojciechowski lived just two miles from Cameron on the east side of Durham. The normal five-minute drive from his home to his office had become an adventure with cars strewn all over Morreene Road. Twice, Wojo had to drive through ditches just to keep moving forward.

Apparently, between noon and 3:00, everyone in the Triangle Area got in their cars and tried to make it somewhere—either home or to pick up their children. This caused North Carolina's own unprecedented gridlock because the snow was forecast for later in the day, and most businesses were closing early. Schools let out when the snow began, which kept hundreds of fretting parents from fetching their kids in anywhere close to a timely fashion.

By mid-afternoon on February 12, Smith Center director Angie Bitting had already been on the phone hourly with the Duke operations staff. She was assured the Blue Devils were coming and in fact planned to be there by 6:00 PM, an hour early. Instead, the Duke team should have left later because by 7:00 most everyone had gotten to where they were going, and the roads were icy but clear.

After governor Pat McCrory declared a state of emergency, urging everyone to stay off the roads, Kirschner put out a second statement, saying the game was still on but recommended everyone stay home unless they could walk to the Smith Center. This triggered two eventualities. First, the statement implied that any of the 28,000 students who lived on or close to campus would be welcome to come and cheer on the Tar Heels. When the prospect of such an historic event reached Twitter and other social media, Carolina fans with tickets began either selling them on StubHub or calling the UNC ticket office directly, offering them to anyone who could get there.

Images of the famous 2000 game against Maryland came to mind, when a similar storm kept the regular crowd home, and students took advantage of the open seating to suffocate the court, helping the Tar Heels upset the No. 22-ranked Terrapins. Former Tar Heel guard Ed Cota gave the home crowd the ultimate compliment. "It sure felt like we were at Cameron or something," Cota said.

Around 4:00 Kirschner called Duke associate athletic director Jon Jackson, his friend for more than 25 years, and asked him for a status report. While Jackson said the team was still planning to come, Kirschner heard less conviction in his voice. Jackson told him of reports that the 15-501 Highway Duke would travel to Chapel Hill was impassable with vehicles either stuck in traffic or abandoned and that the Duke bus had yet to arrive to pick up the team, which had hoped to leave within the hour.

Ah, the Duke team bus.

That was the next indication the game was in limbo. The charter company used by Duke had called to say its bus was stuck on Highway 147 but would keep trying to reach campus. When Roy Williams heard that and was informed that the Twitter world was now saying Duke did not want to play in front of 22,000 UNC students, he quipped, "Tell them we'll send our bus to get them." Both schools, however, use the same bus service.

Finally, just before 5:00 PM Kirschner called Duke's basketball sports information director Matt Plizga, who said that the bus had yet to arrive and half the Blue Devils and coaches were having trouble getting there for the pregame meal. Rodney Hood, a transfer from Mississippi State, was scared to death driving from his apartment. "I'm not used to this snow," Hood said later, "and there were cars everywhere."

In Durham County alone, the Sheriff's Department had already reported 52 traffic accidents. And the fact that UNC was situated on a hill (with a Chapel) was not making the Duke party feel any better about the trip over. Almost any approach to the Smith Center included driving up an incline, and Franklin Street, Airport Road, and Manning Drive were all littered with cars that were stuck like a scene from the movie *The Day The Earth Stood Still*. "Steve, I don't think we can get there," Plizga said to Kirschner. "And if we do, what if we can't home after the game?"

Within 10 minutes UNC athletic director Bubba Cunningham called Duke AD Kevin White, and they agreed to postpone the game. Since it was Duke that could not get to Chapel Hill, White had to contact the ACC to get official approval. The media that had arrived heard first and began tweeting out the news. Finally, UNC put out yet another statement, confirming the game was off.

The reaction was immediate on sports radio shows and social media: the Blue Devils were too chicken to come over and play in front of 22,000 raucous students, the only fans who could make it to the game on foot.

It went as far as a Duke fan, Jack Markham, seeking compensation from Duke in the amount of $827.95 for the lack of foresight by the university and the delayed postponement. Markham was on his way to Chapel Hill when he heard the news on the radio.

Markham, who lives in Southern Pines and has been a Duke fan since he was eight-years old, loves the Duke-UNC rivalry. He asked the school for $162 for the two tickets, $58 for lodging at the Red Roof Inn, $37.95 for an unused parking pass in the Smith-Bowles Lot, $170 in fuel costs for him and a friend who made the trip from Knoxville, Tennessee, and $400 in mental anguish. In his claim he stated that, "Duke was aware of the storm and had time to prepare." He also stated in the claim, "After years of loyalty and spending thousands of dollars on Duke tickets and paraphernalia, I'm eager to see how your organization treats its most true-blue supporters." The claim was sent to the university legal office, and nothing ever came of it.

Once the decision was made, Kirschner suggested that Williams be told and asked to call Krzyzewski to formalize the postponement and discuss rescheduling. Apparently, when the outbreak of the Gulf War cancelled the 1991 N.C. State game and with fans already in the Smith Center, Dean Smith and Wolfpack coach Les Robinson were not consulted on the decision. Kirschner did not want that to happen again.

The following night was eliminated because the roads would still be frozen. Duke and Carolina came to the same conclusion about when to play, even though it was to their mutual disadvantage because it set up a four-games-in-eight-days scenario for each team. The only real hole in the schedule this late in the season was the next Thursday, February 20. UNC had a game the previous Monday at Florida State and Duke the next night at Georgia Tech. Plus, it meant Duke would have to play UNC and Syracuse the following Saturday within 48 hours. But that was the best option available and should have proven to all the naysayers that the Blue Devils hadn't ducked the game.

In a matter of minutes, the February 20 date was agreed upon, though it would be the next day before a starting time of 9:00 PM could be confirmed by the TV networks. Eight days later, the snow was gone, and the roads were clear, but there would be a ticket gridlock, the likes of which UNC had never experienced before.

• • •

Considering how turbulent both seasons were from start to finish for both archrivals, a snow-out seemed appropriate.

Duke had lost three seniors—Seth Curry, Ryan Kelly, and Mason Plumlee—who represented more than 60 percent of the scoring average and more than 55 percent of the rebounding from its Elite Eight team of 2013. Plumlee averaged a double-double his senior year, and the first-round draft pick would make the NBA's All-Rookie first team. Curry and Kelly averaged 43 percent shooting from the three-point line.

So with only role players returning, it was a given that the 6'8" Hood and 6'8" Jabari Parker, the most celebrated recruit Krzyzewski has ever signed (which is saying something), got most of the attention before the first game. In fact, Hood was named a co-captain after showing what a great teammate he would be while practicing with the Blue Devils during his transfer season. Krzyzewski also granted *Sports Illustrated* writer Jeff Benedict extraordinary access to his relationship with Parker over the first half of the season.

After winning 11 of their first 13 against a typical Duke schedule of home and neutral site games, the Blue Devils stumbled on their first two true road trips at Clemson and Notre Dame, two teams that would not make the NCAA Tournament. He averaged 22.2 points in his first 12 games, but Parker went into a semi-slump for three weeks when he looked somewhat tired, out of shape, and/or sick. With all the buildup, he may have hit the infamous freshman wall earlier than most freshmen.

When Duke barely beat Virginia at home, it showed how under-rated the Cavaliers were and vulnerable the Blue Devils could be inside. If it wasn't for thin 6'9" sophomore Amile Jefferson staking claim to the other post position and averaging about seven points and seven rebounds, they would have had to rely on Parker's broad shoulders even more. Duke had some signature performances, none better than routing No. 18 Pitt on the road and losing in overtime at No. 2-ranked Syracuse in a schedule that wasn't nearly as challenging over the second half of the season as it was the first half.

Despite remaining a perennial lock for the NCAA Tournament, two prevailing subplots plagued the team all season: was it good enough to go very deep in the postseason and were Parker and Hood likely one-and-dones? By signing the nation's top high school recruiting class of 2014, Krzyzewski had suddenly become "Calipari Light." The coach who did not lose a single projected first-round draft pick early to the draft during his first 18 years at Duke was going to have four one-and-done players in four years—Kyrie Irving in 2011, Austin Rivers in 2012, and, as it turned out, Hood and Parker in 2014. Not exactly losing three or four a season like Kentucky's John Calipari but still atypical of Duke.

Was the 67-year-old Krzyzewski trying to hang one more banner in Cameron before his retirement sometime after he coaches the 2016 USA Olympic Team in Rio? With three more top 10 freshmen coming in the next season, he seemed to be going against his own philosophy. His 1991, 1992, 2001, and 2010 NCAA Champions were all supported by the old formula of experienced talent that it usually takes to win championships. The players who stayed at Duke for four years had the experience, but the true talent was in and out through a revolving door.

Carolina, on the other hand, was relying on Williams' proven formula that won national championships for the Tar Heels in 2005 and 2009 and might have won another in 2012 if two starters weren't felled by injuries in the postseason. After the Tar Heels crushed Duke 88–70 in the season finale at Cameron, Williams told his team, "You play like tonight, and we'll be playing on Monday night [in the NCAA title game]. Then John Henson sprained his right wrist in the ACC Tournament and Kendall Marshall broke his in the NCAA Tournament, and UNC did not reach the Final Four.

Even though Reggie Bullock surprised almost everyone by entering the 2013 NBA Draft as a junior, Williams kept building toward that tried and true combo of experience and talent. But nothing it seemed had gone as expected at UNC since the football and academic scandal broke in 2010. Ongoing external (NCAA) and internal (academic) investigations delighted the ABC (Anybody But Carolina) crowd that had waited 50 years for something *really* bad to happen in Chapel Hill. And it had arrived and seemed to take on a life of its own.

After NCAA allegations of impermissible benefits to a handful of football players resulted in the firing of head coach Butch Davis and the early retirement of athletic director Dick Baddour, the controversy morphed into a full-blown academic scandal that seemed like it would never end. (The NCAA later reopened its investigation, following Rashad McCants' allegations of academic fraud to ESPN's *Outside the Lines*.) And there was the P.J. Hairston saga.

Basketball players have screwed up at Carolina but always in a vacuum during the Dean Smith era and, until recently, the Roy Williams era. So when leading scorer and deadly three-point shooter Hairston did some really stupid things during the summer of 2013, he was thrown into the grinding mixer of bad publicity that was dogging UNC.

Hairston and fifth-year senior Leslie McDonald drove a rental car paid for by a Durham party planner. Plus Hairston was involved (but never charged) in an incident where marijuana and a gun were found outside the car he was driving. And when he was arrested for speeding in another illegally rented car, Williams had no choice but to suspend him indefinitely.

Hairston called Williams from the police station after being cited for driving 93 in a 65-mph stretch of I-85. Williams said to the 6'5" junior from the tough side of Greensboro, North Carolina, "Do not say a word, and when I am finished talking to you, hand the phone back to the person who let you make this call." Williams' words to Hairston remain private, but he acknowledged never having been madder at a player in his 26-year coaching career. Still, Carolina basketball was used to handing out praise and punishment within "the family," and Williams eventually fought for Hairston's reinstatement after the NCAA got involved. When UNC learned the NCAA would not reinstate Hairston, Williams helped him get placed with an NBA Developmental League team, where he recovered his projected status as a first-round draft pick.

Officially, Carolina basketball was no longer insulated from the rest of the athletic department, and all the bad news coming out from various media and the academic probes that followed kept trying to implicate Williams' program and even Smith's dating back to the 1990s. How long had all this alleged cheating been going on?

Hairston was never going to be reinstated by the NCAA—McDonald was after missing nine games—and Mary Willingham, a learning specialist on campus, went on CNN and said she tutored several basketball players from the 2005 NCAA Championship team who basically could not read.

Carolina officials rebutted Willingham's claims, saying an internal review found that more than 97 percent of the first-year student-athletes enrolled between 2004 and 2012 exceeded SAT and ACT thresholds as indicative of reading levels.

The school later asked researchers at the University of Virginia, the University of Minnesota, and Georgia State University to analyze the data independently, and Carolina administrators said their findings backed up the stance that the majority of the school's student-athletes "scored at or above college entry level on the SATA Reading Vocabulary subtest." The result was that, while Willingham had legitimate concerns, she had overstated her claims with faulty data.

The learning specialist and former top tutor to Carolina athletes, who had been moved from that position in 2010, eventually resigned at UNC but not before she teamed up with the faculty's Athletic Reform Group led by French history professor Jay Smith, who critics labeled anti-athletics and a borderline racist and believed that no students who fell below the university's standard admission requirements should be accepted. Smith, who as a tenured faculty could not be fired, and Willingham said they were collaborating on a tell-all book, but it had not come out before the one you are reading went to press.

An angry Williams privately called "bullshit" on what was being said by Willingham and Smith, who on national TV suggested UNC should voluntarily take down the 2005 and 2009 NCAA Championship banners because it "would be the honorable" thing to do. Publicly, Williams tried to work within the new reforms and speak-with-one-voice philosophy of new chancellor Carol Folt, new vice chancellor for communications Joel Curran, and athletic director Cunningham, who was in his second year.

On the court, Williams was holding his team together and doing one of the best coaching jobs of his career. The uncertain status of Hairston, who had practiced with the team and absolutely tore it up during scrimmages, left the Tar Heels in a state of basketball schizophrenia. They missed 26 free throws and lost at home to Belmont, missed 23 more and lost at home to Texas, played horribly and lost at UAB (coached by smart former Williams assistant Jerod Haase), played worse and lost their first two ACC games to doormats Wake Forest and Miami. Playing Jekyll to that Hyde, they were also the first college basketball team in history to defeat the preseason No. 1 (Kentucky), No. 2 (Michigan State), and No. 3 (Louisville) in the same season.

The players were simultaneously inspired by Hairston's absence and the minutes it gave them to raise their games but also frustrated when they could not generate enough offense without their suspended long bomber. If it weren't for the emergence of sophomore guard Marcus Paige, who became the Tar Heels' leading scorer and second-half assassin, there is no question they would have been Williams' second eligible team to miss the NCAA Tournament. Paige, an exemplary student and tremendous teammate, took over games in the second half, shocking Louisville with a career-high 32 points and surpassing that with 35 at N.C. State, including the coast-to-coast buzzer-beater that instantly silenced the State crowd that Tar Heel Nation had come to despise because of a few obsessive social media maniacs who clearly identified themselves as State students or fans and incessantly tweeted both true and false stories about Carolina athletics.

• • •

The postponement caused both teams to go an entire week without a game. The return to the court was a pretty big match-up for the Blue Devils as they faced Maryland at home for the last time as an ACC foe. In a classic ACC game that Krzyzewski called "vintage Cameron," Parker gave the Blue Devils the lead late in the game, but the ghosts of the old building played defense on Maryland's last possession.

With 18.8 seconds left, the Terps inbounded the ball, and Charles Mitchell attempted a hook shot that Parker blocked. But the ball came back to Mitchell, whose follow shot sat on the front of the rim for a full second before falling off. "I don't know how Charles' shot didn't go in," said Maryland coach Mark Turgeon. "Call it the Duke Gods."

Parker knew the Blue Devils had just stolen one. "You get out of rhythm," said Parker with a sly grin on his face, following the game while sitting in a chair in front of his locker and surrounded by reporters. "You are supposed to play two games a week. Suddenly you're not playing, and school is closed, so it knocks you off your rhythm. We tried to have an emotional practice on Friday. Next week we'll be playing basketball and going to class, the way it should be."

Earlier in the day, Carolina had beaten a physical Pittsburgh team 75–71 as James Michael McAdoo continued his late-season surge with a double-double—24 points and 12 rebounds. After the game the Tar Heels were still upset over the Duke game being postponed. "It's a little heartbreaking we couldn't play Duke," said sophomore Brice Johnson, who hit the game-clinching free throws against Pitt. "I was ready—all of us were ready—to play them. Knowing there were going to be a lot of students in here, we were extremely ready for that."

Carolina would jump on a charter flight to Tallahassee the next day for a game on Monday night with Florida State, winning 81–75 for its seventh consecutive victory. The Blue Devils flew out to Atlanta Monday evening and defeated Georgia Tech on Tuesday night 68–51 for their fourth straight win since losing the overtime thriller at Syracuse.

Everything was back in order, and on the charter flight home from Atlanta, Krzyzewski and his staff once again pulled out the folder marked "UNC" and began preparations for the rescheduled Thursday night game, which like Carolina was its third of four in an eight-day span.

On February 20, Duke arrived safely for the makeup game in Chapel Hill—well aware of what had been speculated about the team's failure to navigate the eight miles from Durham and face what would have surely been a historic student atmosphere in the snow-covered Smith Center eight days earlier.

Those kinds of accusations used to bother Krzyzewski, whose program had grown bigger than the rivalry, though he still treated it with the ultimate respect. Although Carolina was always the archrival, the Blue Devils' MO had long ago risen above any single game on the schedule. Winning the ACC championship and getting a favorable draw in the NCAA Tournament had become more important to Krzyzewski than any one opponent since he elevated his program to—and beyond—UNC's level. His goal was to make Duke a national brand, and he had succeeded.

Outside the Smith Center, a virulent air of anger was growing. Dozens of people with tickets were being denied access to the biggest game of the season, creating chaos unlike anything Carolina had ever experienced. The unique on-off status of the originally scheduled game left hundreds of tickets with voided bar codes for a variety of reasons.

Many fans had released or sold those tickets online and had been trying ever since the game was rescheduled to get them back. They were demanding solutions from the young worker bees behind the glass of the UNC ticket windows. Others with bad bar codes wanted to find out what happened. Combining that with the longer-than-usual line to pick up tickets at will call turned the scene into an unmanageable mob as the minutes ticked away toward the 9:00 tip-off.

UNC associate athletic director Paul Pogge was charged with trying to figure out exactly what caused more than 100 cases of "double ticketing." Pogge said many people had agreed to release their tickets to UNC or put them up for sale on ticket sites like StubHub when they thought the original game was being played and could not go. Since there was no time to mail in the actual tickets, their bar codes were voided before they had been resold and reissued electronically with new bar codes. Getting them back with bar codes that worked was next to impossible; besides, once the game was postponed and rescheduled, all Duke-Carolina tickets again became the hottest of the season—the singular reason why many people join the Rams Club Foundation at Carolina and give gobs of money each year.

Pogge did not mention the criminal intent that also played into the confusion. Undoubtedly, some people who had sold their tickets online or over the phone still had the originals, which they knew would bring top dollar outside of the Smith Center. Fans clamoring to see the game bought those bogus tickets. After being denied entrance, they went ballistic over losing three to four times the $75 face value and not getting in. Plus, they did not know the identity of who sold them the tickets to try to get their money back or describe them to the authorities. Although the Dean Dome was packed to the last row in the upper deck, plus standing room, there were two seats here and there that remained empty until someone without a seat spotted them.

"UNC had never had a situation like this since Desert Storm," Pogge said of the 1991 State game cancellation. "We didn't have a lot of experience, but we learned a lot that night. We tried to be proactive the next morning and sent out an email to all season-ticket holders, acknowledging what had happened. And it kept us from having to answer a lot of angry phone calls. Thank God we won."

• • •

For the first 30 minutes of the game, Pogge sweated over the reaction the next day because it looked like the unranked Tar Heels could not stay with the No. 5 Blue Devils. For starters, Carolina missed seven of its first eight free throws, accentuating a problem that had plagued the program since 2009, the last season UNC shot at least 70 percent from the foul line. The home team was lucky to be down only 37–30 at halftime.

The fans had done their part, standing and screaming since the Tar Heels came out of the home tunnel, following the giant Carolina blue flag. The "wine and cheese" crowd that few Duke teams have witnessed was again nowhere to be found. Clearly, though, there was trepidation in the air as the second half started.

Five minutes into the second half, Duke's lead had grown to 11 after a layup by Parker, but that was to be his last field goal until 21 seconds remained in the game. Carolina held Duke to a pair of free throws over the next nine minutes, mainly due to a 1-3-1 zone Williams had learned from Smith but not used very much over the years. Several coaching colleagues who could talk frankly to Williams had been imploring him to "change your defense once in a while." Obviously, the 1-3-1 wasn't in Duke's scouting report.

While holding the Blue Devils without a field goal, the Tar Heels scored six unanswered points to get back in the game, including dunks by McAdoo and J.P. Tokoto that revved the already raucous crowd to a new noise level. In three time-outs during the scoring drought, Krzyzewski admonished his team to play harder but could not come up with an offensive set that got the ball past the long-armed Tokoto and Johnson on the wings of the zone into the corners where the 1-3-1 is vulnerable.

Duke continued going aggressively to the basket and shooting long three-pointers when winning the chess game was needed. "They just kept switching," Duke guard Quinn Cook said. "We'd come down and we wouldn't know what they would be in. Their defense kept us on our toes."

Duke missed 13 consecutive shots and went scoreless for six minutes. The Blue Devils were just 11 for 31 in the second half, while Carolina drove to the basket and wound up making 50 percent from the floor and, more importantly, an atypical 13 of 17 from the free throw line. The more aggressive Tar Heels would go to the stripe 31 times compared to just 12 free throws for Duke.

McAdoo tied the score at 60, and Carolina took the lead for good on a jumper by McDonald, playing the best game of his shortened season with 21 points. Duke wound up scoring 15 points over the last 15 minutes of the game, as the Tar Heels rang up 34 to win 74–66, unleashing thousands of students onto the court to celebrate with the team. The pure emotion of this victory was all over the tear-stained face of a UNC female manager trying to get through the mob and enter the locker room. Parker passed in front of her with a look of despair that said he had just lost more than a basketball game.

Krzyzewski gave his team a tongue-lashing that could be easily heard by the waiting media through the cinder block wall of the visitors' dressing room, screaming about not playing with emotion and losing this game because they didn't play hard enough. "Not playing hard is no excuse!" he yelled.

In his press conference, Coach K joked that his team just didn't have "it...whatever the hell that is, we didn't have it." He was asked whether great players like Parker and Hood, who had already played two games in Madison Square Garden and drew the largest crowd in Carrier Dome history at Syracuse, still might be surprised by the intensity of their first Duke-Carolina game, especially on the road. "Maybe," Krzyzewski said. "I don't know, maybe."

In the Duke locker room, Parker sat half-stunned. He obviously thought he was ready to play and finished with 17 points and 11 rebounds. But he had committed a team-high five turnovers and in crunch time looked lost on the court and from the bench when taken out for several minutes. "We didn't have our emotions toward winning," Parker said, his body slumped over and his eyes red, looking exhausted. "They were more enthusiastic, they wanted to pull it through, energy was on their side, and we let them get it, especially on offensive rebounds [which the Tar Heels dominated in the second half].

"Their intensity level was really strong. We didn't match their intensity and we just didn't play together."

A week earlier at the press conference prior to the scheduled Duke-Carolina game, the Blue Devils had tried to play off the rivalry renewal as just another game, not any more important than any other on the ACC schedule. Parker said he knew about being in big games; they'd played in the Garden against Arizona and UCLA and at Syracuse.

When the media dispersed and left Parker sitting in the corner of the locker room by himself, he dropped his head into his hands and then took a deep breath, still looking at his shoes and saying to himself, "I had no idea."

This was not just another game, and he learned the hard way about the intensity level of Duke-Carolina.

The victory was more important for the Tar Heels, who kept their eventual 12-game winning streak going that solidified an at-large bid to the NCAA Tournament. And they avoided losing to Duke at home for the third straight season. The year before they had been blown out by the much better Blue Devils, but the program needed this win to assuage the bad taste from 2012, when Duke rallied from double-digits to upset the fifth-ranked Heels on the Austin Rivers three-pointer over Tyler Zeller as time ran out.

Shown over and over before each rematch, that shot made freshman Rivers a hero forever in Duke annals. However, the son of Doc Rivers never really meshed with the Duke style of play because he needed to have the ball in his hands to be more effective when that is not the principle of Duke's motion offense. Having been around the NBA all of his life, Rivers' dream was to play in the same league where his father coached. He turned pro after his freshman season, which ended after his team had suffered an embarrassing loss to No. 15 seed Lehigh in the NCAA Tournament.

• • •

Duke went on to win three of its last four regular-season games, beginning with the epic rematch against Syracuse in Cameron, which combined with the earlier 91–89 overtime victory by the Orange drew the largest TV audiences of the season, close to 8 million in total. The Blue Devils rebounded with one of their best performances and won after a controversial charging foul on Syracuse star C.J. Fair along the baseline. Hood had slipped in to block Fair's path as he laid in the potential tying basket, and official Tony Greene waived it off with the offensive foul call.

Syracuse coach Jim Boeheim erupted, creating the most-watched clip of the season as he ran onto the court with his suit jacket flapping to protest what he believed was the wrong interpretation of the new block-charge call. Despite his team only being down by two points with 10 seconds to play, Boeheim decided the outcome by drawing two technical fouls and an ejection, which gave Duke four free throws to wrap up the 66–60 win.

Most pundits, including ESPN's Bilas, who was working the game from the crow's nest in Cameron, thought Greene blew the call and Fair should have been awarded the basket and gone to the free throw line with a chance to put Syracuse ahead. After the game both coaches tried to lighten up what had been a volatile scene. "I guess people saw the old man still has a little fire," Boeheim said, smiling. Krzyzewski pulled out his old "Basketball Gods" line, recalling a similar call at the Carrier Dome that did not go in Duke's favor.

In the locker room, Parker was smiling after coming back with 19 points and 10 rebounds against the Orange in what had been the best atmosphere in Cameron all season. He was asked how it compared to what he had experienced two nights before in Chapel Hill. Parker rolled his eyes and smiled, confirming his newfound belief that nothing on the planet compared to a Duke-Carolina game.

Eleven days later Coach K and Parker were in a much worse place, namely at Wake Forest, where Krzyzewski was screaming at his team for a lackadaisical performance that led to an 82–72 loss to the far less talented Deacons whose coach Jeff Bzdelik would resign after the season. Krzyzewski saw it coming early.

During the first timeout of the game, he had his clipboard and was starting to draw up a play when he stopped, slammed the board on his thigh, and screamed at his team to: "Play some fucking defense; that's all you have to do. Play defense."

Duke may have taken Wake lightly and was looking ahead to the rematch with Carolina Saturday night in Cameron. The Blue Devils got it together but could never shake Wake. After Parker's slam put them ahead 66–59 with 5:44 remaining, the Deacons went on an unforgivable 17–0 run that gave them their sixth ACC win of the season. (Their first was over Carolina back in January.)

During the second half, Krzyzewski had suffered a dizzy spell not unlike what Roy Williams encounters several times each season. He laid down on the locker room floor while Wojciechowski handled the postgame press conference (good practice for being named the new Marquette coach after the season). "He has not been ill; he's actually in as good of shape as can be," Wojo said. "Just the emotion of the game, obviously we weren't playing as well as we needed, and there's a great emotional investment into the game. Maybe the emotion got the better of him."

The real culprit may well have been religion. A devoted Catholic, Krzyzewski had eaten only a bowl of soup early on Ash Wednesday, the first day of Lent, and fasted the rest of the day before busing to Wake Forest.

Krzyzewski walked out of Joel Coliseum under his own power, but he did not ride home with the team, instead driving with Duke AD Kevin White, who took Coach K directly to Duke Medical Center. Krzyzewski was checked out and released at 2:30 on Thursday morning—just in time to get ready for another game with North Carolina.

Meanwhile, the Tar Heels had clobbered Wake Forest 36 hours after the first Duke game and finished the regular season with three close victories at State (on Paige's heroics) and Virginia Tech and on McDonald's Senior Night against Notre Dame for their 12th consecutive victory—with only two against ranked teams (Duke and Pitt). Carolina and Duke were both 13–5 in the ACC and had clinched byes into the quarterfinals of the ACC Tournament. ESPN's *GameDay* was at Cameron for Senior Night for Andre Dawkins, Josh Hairston, and Tyler Thornton, who started with Hood and Parker, both believed to also be playing their last home game.

Cameron Indoor Stadium opened in 1940—prior to the birth of television—and was not built to handle the mass confusion that ESPN and TV have brought to the world of college basketball. The *GameDay* set took up so much room at midcourt that the players on both teams could not run a full layup line.

As always, celebrities were at the game, and most noticeable were Dallas Cowboys head coach Jason Garrett and quarterback Tony Romo. When asked why he and Romo were there, Garrett said: "Just a chance to be around Coach K and his staff and his program. I came down a few years ago to visit, and it's such a rich and fertile learning environment for someone who is interested in coaching and interested in developing your team. You would be hard-pressed to find a better program, a better organization than Duke basketball in this country. They have given me incredible access to what they do from being able to hang out in meetings to watching practice and picking the brain of Coach K and his staff on how they maintain this level of success."

UNC left the floor, and the Duke Senior Night ceremonies began with videos of each departing player and as much noise as Cameron could handle. Few expected the Tar Heels to be able to match their second-half performance in Chapel Hill and spring another upset.

The Blue Devils never trailed, shooting 51 percent from the field, 57 percent in the second half, and this time dominating Carolina on the boards 34–20. In what indeed turned out to be his final game at Cameron, Parker was unstoppable with 30 points in the 93–81 win. Hood was almost as good, scoring 24 points and hitting three key three-pointers. Jefferson completed his unsung regular season with eight points and eight rebounds, giving Duke some experience to join the high school talent Krzyzewski was again bringing in.

Parker also added 11 rebounds as part of his electric performance. "I just thought he had his best spirit to score tonight that he's had all season because they're really good, and at times he just wasn't going to be denied," Krzyzewski said. "And then, boom, boom, boom, you hit those threes, and that lead can go to double-digits quick."

Carolina could not stop Parker and Hood but had perhaps its best offensive game of the season, shooting just under 60 percent with four players in double figures. Paige had 24 points with most coming in the second half when he was driving through Duke for easy baskets to try to spark a comeback that the Blue Devils would not allow.

• • •

The snow game season did not end well for either team. Carolina lost the rematch with Pitt in its first ACC Tournament game and then had to rally to defeat Providence in the second round of the NCAA Tournament despite 36 points by the Friars' sensational senior guard Bryce Cotton. The Tar Heels then blew their final game of the season by squandering an eight-point lead with less than four minutes to play against Iowa State—who seemed vulnerable without injured star Georges Niang—losing a chance to face eventual national champion UConn in the Sweet 16 at Madison Square Garden.

With Hairston and all the other off-court distractions, the 24–10 record and the important win over Duke constituted a great season for Williams, who would have everyone returning except McDonald and McAdoo, a surprising entry in the NBA draft as a junior.

The Tar Heels had three top 20 recruits coming in, 6'0" Joel Berry, 6'7" Justin Jackson, and 6'6" Theo Pinson to join returning starters Paige, Tokoto, Kennedy Meeks, and sixth man Brice Johnson. Clearly, they were building toward Williams' goal of putting another team of experienced talent on the floor to compete with Duke.

Following the win over Carolina, the Blue Devils' season ended in embarrassing fashion. Duke would win just two more games, a controversial 63–62 victory against Clemson in the quarterfinals of the ACC Tournament and a 75–67 win against N.C. State in the semifinals. Despite their 13th appearance in the ACC Championship Game since 1998, the Blue Devils lost the game and their cool with Krzyzewski picking up a technical from Jamie Luckie for angrily throwing a pen at his bench during a timeout. Sophomore Rasheed Sulaimon uncharacteristically picked up a technical as well for questioning an official's call, something he had not done all year.

After Virginia claimed only its second ACC title, 72–63, Krzyzewski was summoned into a meeting by John Clougherty, the head of ACC officials. Luckie had told Clougherty that he felt Krzyzewski tried to show him up by throwing the pen. "I just wanted Mike to understand what happened," Clougherty said. "We had a good talk; he understood and headed to his press conference."

The Blue Devils closed out the 2014 season in shocking fashion, losing to 14-seed Mercer at the PNC Arena in Raleigh. Although unknown and a double-digit underdog, Mercer had only one freshman on its roster against a Duke team that had yet to find a leader. Mercer had scouted Duke brilliantly, going inside repeatedly for easy baskets and getting to the foul line 15 more times. The Bears hit five three-pointers compared to Duke's 15 but won 78–71 by pounding the boards and making 11 more free throws. It was Duke's third one-and-done from the NCAA Tournament in eight years and Krzyzewski's fifth overall. Carolina fans were quick to point out that in 24 NCAA Tournaments Roy Williams had never lost his opening game.

Head down with tears in his eyes, Parker tried to find words to describe possibly playing his final game in a Duke uniform. His one season was a highlight of dunks and great offensive plays, an undefeated slate at home with wins over No. 1 Syracuse and North Carolina but no banners.

He was struggling with the fact that—besides a *Sports Illustrated* cover story and all the other publicity—he hadn't really made his mark as a Duke player. Now he was going on to the NBA, which he made official on April 17, the day after the annual Duke basketball banquet. The next day Hood announced he would also be leaving for the NBA, which Krzyzewski had unwittingly revealed when praising Hood late in the season and saying he wished "we had Rodney for more than one year."

While the Duke players were dealing with the abrupt end of the season, their coach stopped by the victors' locker room to congratulate Mercer on playing so well: "You guys have a hell of a basketball team," Krzyzewski said. "I love the game, and you guys play the game really, really well, and your coach coaches it well. If we had to lose, I'm glad we got beat by a hell of a basketball team, so good luck to you." That provided extra meaning for the Mercer squad. "Coach K is one of the most famous basketball coaches ever and for him to just come in here and tell us we're a great basketball team—that's pretty unbelievable to tell you the truth," said Mercer senior Daniel Coursey.

Just three days following the end of the season, the world did continue to spin on its axis as Luke Kennard called Krzyzewski and Wojo and told them he would be attending Duke beginning in 2015. The

6′6″ shooting guard from Franklin, Ohio, averaged 40 points and 10.4 rebounds as a junior and was named Associated Press Mr. Basketball and the Gatorade Player of the Year. He had narrowed his choices to Ohio State, Kentucky, Louisville, Michigan, UNC, Duke, and Florida. "Being around Coach K and the players—how the program was run—I could tell it was a very special place and I could see myself fitting in there," he explained. "I felt at peace with my decision. Duke was the best fit for me."

It would be a year before Duke fans got to see Kennard, having to settle for the top recruiting class in the country in 2014–15. All four players coming in were ranked among the top 35 led by No.1 Jahlil Okafor, a 6′10″ center; No. 5 Tyus Jones, a 6′1″ guard; No. 12 Justise Winslow, a 6′5″ forward; and No. 34 Grayson Allen, a 6′4″ shooting guard, who won the McDonald's All-American slam dunk contest.

At the ensuing 2014 McDonald's All-America Game, Okafor and UNC recruit Jackson shared MVP honors. The Duke-Carolina beat goes on, as it has for more than 50 years.

Chapter 2

Old-School
Recruiting Battles

*A*rt *Heyman did not return to Duke until 1973—10 years after he played his last game for the Blue Devils—because he felt snubbed by the school after leading the Blue Devils to their second ACC championship and first Final Four his senior year. He left Durham as Duke's all-time leading scorer and with All-American honors. But Duke did not retire his No. 25 jersey.*

Nicknamed "The Pest" for the aggressive way he played on the court and the trouble he got into off the court, Heyman felt disrespected by his alma mater. And to make matters worse, Duke had become an also-ran in the ACC by 1973, four years after his beloved coach Vic Bubas had retired.

Heyman stood in the runway between the end zone bleachers and the student section, which was not even full, watching the game between Duke and seventh-ranked N.C. State, whose 5'7" sophomore point guard Monte Towe was brazenly driving down the lane for a layup or dishing off to his All-American teammate David Thompson, who would score 31 points on the Blue Devils that night.

The Pest was infuriated with how easily Towe got into the lane against Duke. "That little pissant," Heyman said, "if he had tried to do that against us, the first time someone would have leveled him with a forearm, just knocked the shit out of him. He never would have tried it again."

Heyman was also surprised that State was so good. When he played for Duke, the Wolfpack was on probation because of recruiting violations, several of their players were involved in a point-shaving scandal, and their coach, Everett Case, was nearing retirement. Duke's biggest rival at that time was Wake Forest. "Who else is good in the ACC now?" asked Heyman, who had been in New York for the past 10 years and lost touch with ACC basketball.

He was told that North Carolina was considered the best program in the ACC and Dean Smith considered the best coach. "Dean Smith!" Heyman chortled. "He was the biggest joke when I played. Everyone wanted him fired!"

Heyman's jersey was finally retired in 1990 by Duke athletic director Tom Butters, who said, "There is no denying this honor is long overdue. I cannot speak to why it wasn't done during his playing career."

—AC

As Duke and Carolina fought fiercely in bandbox gyms in the shadow of king football, basketball got serious in 1959–60 when Duke hired an energetic young coach named Vic Bubas to compete against the legend in Chapel Hill, Frank McGuire, whose 1957 team had gone undefeated and won the national championship in storybook fashion—beating Michigan State and Kansas with Wilt Chamberlain, in Kansas City no less. Both games were on consecutive nights and in triple overtime.

McGuire had an Underground Railroad pipeline that carried high school stars from New York down to Tobacco Road, and that looked to be continuing in the spring of 1959 when the Irishman lured rivals from contiguous towns on Long Island. Larry Brown was considered the top lead guard in New York when he played for UNC alumnus Bob Gersten at Long Beach. Bull-like Art Heyman, a 6′5″ forward, was the best player in all of New York, putting up record numbers for neighboring Oceanside.

They had a classic game in February of 1958 at Long Beach, when the 5′10″ Brown scored 45 points (compared to Heyman's 29) and led his team to an upset. McGuire was in attendance and afterward he offered UNC scholarships to both players. Brown was a year older and had to attend prep school to beef up his grades, so this odd couple of greatness planned to enroll at Carolina together in the fall of 1959. The schoolboy rivals would finally be teammates.

Brown and Heyman would be the heart and soul of another flashy juggernaut for the Tar Heels, who had lost to Maryland in the 1958 ACC Championship Game (denying their return to the NCAA Tournament) and were upset by Navy in a first-round game the following year after backing into the NCAAs due to a probation that kept ACC champ N.C. State out. Freshmen were not eligible in those days, so it would be the 1961 season before Brown and Heyman could play for the UNC varsity.

But Heyman never made it to Chapel Hill, triggering the first of many controversies involving the two Jewish antagonists from the Island.

Upon moving to Duke from Everett Case's staff at N.C. State, Bubas was aware that McGuire and Heyman's stepfather were at odds. McGuire was known as the Godfather, and it was a given that when parents sent their sons to play for him that there were no questions asked; they were lucky to be going to college and lucky to be playing for McGuire. Bill Heyman was an engineer and asked what most other parents did not, such as would his stepson take the classes he wanted and how much study time he would have.

McGuire was insulted and on the Heymans' last recruiting trip to Chapel Hill in June of 1959, the coach and stepfather nearly came to blows at the old University Motel. Returning from the movies with a Carolina player, Art long claimed that he stopped the near fistfight before the first punch was thrown. "I had to step between them," Heyman said years later. "My stepfather called Carolina a basketball factory, and McGuire didn't like that. They were about to start swinging at each other."

No punches were thrown, but the Heymans went back to New York, knowing that Art's recruitment was again open. Had he not gone to the movies and left his stepfather alone with McGuire, the argument may never have started, and Heyman may have gone on to several national championships with Brown at UNC while Duke would have missed out on its first recruit under its young coach.

Bubas had been watching Heyman play summer league games on Long Island and already taken Heyman's parents to dinner to pitch them on why "Artie" would be better off at Duke. He was the player around whom Bubas could build the Blue Devils into a national power, and the coach answered all the academic questions cleanly. Since a national letter of intent was not binding in the eyes of the Atlantic Coast Conference until July 1, Heyman signed a second letter with Duke. And when his plane landed at Raleigh-Durham Airport in early September, he hopped in a cab to Durham, not Chapel Hill.

Jack Horner, *Durham Morning Herald* sports editor and a long-time Blue Devils apologist, began writing columns hailing Bubas' first recruiting coup and publishing letters he received from Tar Heel alumni accusing the new Duke coach of dirty tricks. One regrettable letter written by Gersten, Brown's high school coach, implied Duke paid Heyman's parents to sway their son away from UNC. Because of academic problems with the three other recruits in McGuire's supposed 1960 freshman class, Brown was the only star player to enroll at UNC that fall. It marked the start of a turbulent period in the rivalry and foretold the end of McGuire's days at North Carolina.

Long before they were coined the Cameron Crazies, Duke students could be entertaining and edgy with opponents. McGuire was a particular foil due to his stature with his impeccable dress and his Irish brogue. The students who sat behind the UNC bench greased their hair with Brylcreem like McGuire and wore fashionable string ties around their necks. They taunted McGuire and the Tar Heels but usually went back to their dorms unhappy, as Carolina won 12 of the last 15 games McGuire coached against their team before Heyman arrived. But they knew better days were ahead with the recruit Bubas had stolen from UNC.

As Duke fans delighted in the high-strung and immensely talented Heyman playing for the Blue Imps (as the freshmen were called in those days), McGuire and Carolina seethed over the defection. Because all freshmen had to play on freshman teams in 1960, Brown and Heyman competed at that level while anticipation grew for their varsity match-up as sophomores.

Back then, the freshmen from the Big Four schools—Duke, North Carolina, N.C. State, and Wake Forest—played each other three times, once at each home venue and then one on the road somewhere in the state of North Carolina.

Before the Duke freshmen swept UNC in their home-and-home series, they had a game in Siler City, North Carolina, on December 9, 1959, the first time Brown and Heyman faced each other wearing their college uniforms. Bucky Waters was in his first season as an assistant at Duke and coached the freshman team. "We drove down in cars, and I had Art ride with me," Waters recounted. "I told him I had no idea what was coming tonight from the Carolina team, but he needed to be prepared, knowing the feeling of hatred they had for him in walking away from their program. If they can bring you down any way, as a person, as a player, that's going to please them. You have to be ready for whatever they throw at you. It's going to challenge you, but you cannot buckle under and let your emotions get the best of you."

Sure enough, in the first minute of the game the taunting of Heyman began. "I'm sitting on the bench and I'm hearing, 'You Christ-killer, you monkey Jew-boy' from the Carolina guys at Art, and I called timeout in the first minute," Waters recounted. "I looked at Art and said, 'We knew this was coming but didn't think it would be this bad.' After having a minute or so to think about it, I called a second timeout and brought the guys back to the bench. I said to Art and the rest of them, 'Here's the answer to what they are doing—you just kick their ass, show them how good you really are, and don't get down on their level.'"

The game continued, and the Blue Devils and Heyman handled the insults and dealt out their own brand of abuse as they took a commanding lead. At halftime UNC freshman coach Ken Rosemond chastised his players for not playing aggressively enough on defense, and they responded with a more determined effort in the second half.

Toward the end of the game that Duke won 88–70, Heyman got into it with UNC's Dieter Krause, a tough guy McGuire had signed late after three others from his freshman class failed to gain admission to Carolina. "I had promised Art I would get him out before something happened," Waters said. "I was getting ready to take him out and remind him to not gloat when he came off the court. We had spread the floor, and Art came out of the corner to catch the ball at the top of the key. Dieter was right behind him and looked like he had a javelin in his hand; his fist nailed Art across the jaw, and Art went down hard."

Krause, a 6'5", 200-pounder from Norfolk, Virginia, who is a retired Lieutenant Colonel in the U.S. Army after a 28-year military career and two tours of Vietnam, remembers it differently than Waters. In fact, Krause said that when he bodied up to Heyman, it was Heyman who took the first swing. "Maybe because I was being more aggressive on defense," Krause recalled years later, "a fist came at me and missed, and instinctively, I counter-punched and connected and hit him in the face. Mayhem broke out, and I was on the floor trying to protect my head."

"I'm in my early 20s," Waters said. "I didn't even try to hold my players back. I headed right for Rosemond. I got him by the lapels of his jacket and threw him up on the scorer's table. His ass was hitting all sorts of toggle switches, and buttons and horns went off, and I told him exactly what I thought of a coaching staff that would stoop that low to do that to one of our players."

When things finally calmed down, Heyman was taken to the Siler City Hospital where he received six stitches—five outside his mouth and one inside.

Duke won the game but looked like it lost the war because of Heyman's bandaged jaw. Heyman had scored 34 points, while Krause led Carolina with 20. Larry Brown had 17 points, and the future mayor of Charlotte and North Carolina gubernatorial candidate Richard Vinroot scored two.

"After the game I called Coach Bubas and told him what happened and was very honest with him," Waters said. "He told me to call him when I got back to Durham. When I did, he said Coach Cameron wanted to see us at 8:00 the next morning."

Waters sat anxiously in Cameron's office as the Duke athletic director leaned back in his chair puffing on a pipe. "I knew I was going to get fired for the way I handled things," Waters said. "He asked me to tell him what happened. He asked me to repeat what the players were saying to Art. He paused for a really long second after I finished talking, tapped his pipe out in the ashtray, and said there was a lot he liked about me, but that was not the way we handled things at Duke… and not to let it happen again."

Since the game was off-campus and not under the jurisdiction of either school, perhaps the UNC players went after Heyman because there was really nothing anyone could do about it. No one had ever turned his back on McGuire as Heyman did in switching to the archrival. McGuire, who died in 1994, denied having anything to do with Heyman and in fact never again referred to the Duke star by his name.

Meanwhile, Bubas' first varsity team lost three times to the nationally ranked Tar Heels by a combined 74 points. But by the end of the season, both the UNC and N.C. State programs were under scrutiny from the North Carolina State Bureau of Investigation for involvement in a point-shaving scandal that had migrated down the East Coast from New York. Several players at both schools, including Carolina juniors Doug Moe and Lou Brown, had been interrogated about calls and visits they had with "agents" of well-known gambling figures.

It was a distraction, and six days after the Tar Heels had ended the regular season with a 75–50 win at Duke, the teams met again in the semifinals of the 1960 ACC Tournament. With UNC All-American and ACC Player of the Year Lee Shaffer getting into foul trouble, the Blue Devils somehow stunned No. 16 Carolina 71–69, snapping a six-game losing streak to UNC. The Blue Devils went on to win the conference title the next night over Wake Forest. It was another foreshadowing of the seismic shift coming.

When Larry Brown and Heyman moved up to their respective varsities, the old prep combatants and now bitter college competitors started a much more famous fight in Durham on February 4, 1961. A capacity crowd at steamy Duke Indoor Stadium plus a regional television audience witnessed the seminal moment in the basketball rivalry, elevating it above football.

The brawl began with only seconds left in the game and Duke leading 81–75 and Heyman having scored 36 points on 11 field goals and 14 free throws. In those days the benches at Duke were on the baselines under the baskets.

Trying to score in a hurry, Brown dribbled the length of the court, as time was running out and Bubas was yelling to his defense not to foul. Spitting at each other was a part of the game in the 1950s, and as Brown drove along the baseline Heyman spit at him and grabbed him for what would be an obvious—and perhaps intentional—foul. Brown threw the ball at Heyman and began swinging. The UNC players came off their bench and jumped Heyman, forcing him to the floor before he fought his way out of the pile and started swinging wildly at anyone who came near him. By that time players from both teams along with dozens of fans were on the court, and the 10 Durham policemen in attendance were powerless to stop the isolated skirmishes popping up everywhere. "I was a freshman…sitting behind the Carolina bench," UNC alum Charlie Schaffer said. "Larry and Art started it, but then everyone got involved, and the fight lasted a good 10 minutes before they could break it up."

Heyman was ejected for starting the fight, an error by the officials that was corrected in a statement by the ACC the following week after watching the game film. Brown stayed in the game and sunk two free throws to make the final score 81–77, which avenged Duke's earlier loss to the Tar Heels in the 1960 Dixie Classic when Heyman was held to 15 points on 5-of-15 shooting by UNC's Moe, now a senior and considered one of the best defenders in the ACC.

Carolina won the rematch in Chapel Hill in overtime with both Brown and Heyman suspended by the ACC for their part in the fight at Duke. But McGuire had pulled the Tar Heels out of the 1961 ACC Tournament after they received a postseason ban from the NCAA for alleged recruiting violations by the head coach.

Late that summer, a little more than four years after he had authored what is still the greatest story in the Tar Heel state's glorious sports history, an embattled McGuire resigned to coach Chamberlain and the Philadelphia Warriors of the NBA. Duke went on to win the next seven match-ups, as Bubas schooled new UNC coach Dean Smith, who had been McGuire's unknown assistant for three years and was given a mandate to clean up the program.

McGuire left UNC basketball on six-month NCAA probation while the emerging point-shaving scandal forced the abolishment of the popular Dixie Classic due to the unscrupulous characters who showed up in Raleigh over the holidays. The eight-team event between Christmas and New Year's was the brainchild of N.C. State coach Everett Case, who in 1949 had opened the 12,000-seat William Neal Reynolds Coliseum on his campus. What better way to showcase the four major programs in the area than invite four prestigious outside teams and have the national press corps converge on Case's new domain? Cincinnati and Oscar Robertson, the first African American to ever play in the Dixie Classic, finished third in 1959 on the way to the Bearcats' second of six straight Final Fours.

Cancelling the Dixie Classic angered thousands of fans, many of whom had packed Reynolds Coliseum for three days in late December since the event began in 1949. Raleigh merchants, who benefitted during the post-Christmas period from the influx of fans, claim they lost thousands in expected income. But mostly it ended an almost fabled tradition. "It's like the State Fair; it's part of the people," former Wake Forest coach Bones McKinney said.

UNC consolidated university president Bill Friday had reports that shady characters were threatening the ballplayers from State and Carolina and, according to Friday, several men had been spotted with guns in their jackets while attending the games. "In our minds we were dealing with protection of human life of an innocent college kid that, because he had exceptional skills, had gotten all his fame," Friday said of his 1961 decision. "Forces were preying upon these young men that were bigger than they could handle. You believe that threat to be real. That's what the difference was. I really did believe these [gamblers] would hurt these kids. That being said, you weren't left with any alternative."

As part of the residue, UNC's Smith and N.C. State's Case had their 1962 schedules reduced to 16 games and were limited to signing only two recruits from outside of the four-state ACC footprint, as Friday sought to minimize the influence of gamblers now under federal investigation. Duke had escaped any such scrutiny, as the front men for the gamblers usually offered money to shave points only to poor kids who played for state schools.

Taking over a program in turmoil, Smith had to re-recruit Brown, a rising junior, and Billy Cunningham, who had graduated late from high school, spent one semester at home, and enrolled in classes at UNC in January of 1961. Despite McGuire's attempts to make him eligible for the varsity, Cunningham was still facing a full freshman year. It was Smith's good fortune that McGuire had moved on to pro basketball rather than one of several other schools that were pursuing him because Brown and Cunningham might have easily followed. As it was, McGuire's departure did cost Carolina two highly recruited prospects, Judd Rothman and Billy Lawrence, who both decided to attend college in New York instead of playing for Smith, who released them from their scholarships.

Smith had coached Brown as an assistant during his sophomore season and figured his starting point guard would stay. But late in the summer, Smith wound up in the kitchen of Brown's modest home on Long Island, trying to convince him to return to school. "Coach McGuire was bigger than life, and the relationship I had with Coach Smith as an assistant was much different," Brown recalled. "All of a sudden, Frank is gone, and Dean takes over. It was like my whole life changed, and I was ready to run."

Smith developed an ally in Brown's mother, Ann. "I was going to leave school, and my mom said, 'You're staying. This is the man I want you to be with.' Fortunately, my mom liked Coach Smith because going back to Carolina was the best thing that ever happened to me."

Brooklyn-born Cunningham landed in Chapel Hill because his father—a tough, Irish New York city firefighter—had known McGuire's sister for years. After meeting McGuire the older Cunningham knew where his son was going to college. "My father said I was going to a Catholic school or to play for Coach McGuire," remembered Cunningham, whose family drove him 12 hours to see Chapel Hill. "I never visited another school, never thought about another one."

Cunningham was home in the summer of 1961 and also thought about not going back to finish his freshman year. But because he had already spent five months in Chapel Hill and liked the town, Cunningham returned to complete his freshman courses as Smith's first varsity team struggled to an 8–9 record. An instant star as a sophomore in the fall of 1962, he led the ACC in rebounding and was second in scoring to Duke's Heyman, who, as Bubas had promised, was now the star of a program that had remained nationally ranked since early in the 1961 season.

Bubas went on to sign Kentuckian Jeff Mullins, who never lost to UNC in 10 games against the Tar Heel freshmen and varsity, and a bevy of high schools stars—most notably Pennsylvanians Jack Marin and Steve Vacendak, Bob Verga from New Jersey, and Mike Lewis from Missoula, Montana, who would all have a part in leading the Blue Devils to three more ACC championships and trips to the NCAA Final Four, going three straight seasons without losing to Carolina.

Smith needed better talent to play with Cunningham and he had signed a skinny kid from Washington, D.C., who was electrifying crowds during freshman games at Woollen Gym by averaging 36 points from all over the floor. Bobby Lewis had not considered Carolina and in fact did not even know Smith had written to him until he watched UNC upset Notre Dame in South Bend on TV behind Cunningham's scoring and rebounding. After that game Lewis went through a shoe box of unopened letters from college coaches and found one from Smith. "Good luck in your senior year," Smith had written in his standard recruiting language. "When it comes time to look at colleges, I hope you will consider Chapel Hill."

Wanting to meet Cunningham, Lewis scheduled a springtime recruiting visit to UNC with his mother and fell in love with the school. Ironically, Bubas and Duke, only eight miles away, had also written to Lewis but did not follow up because they deemed the 6'3" jumping jack too small to play forward and not a guard due to shaky ballhandling.

Lewis became Smith's first big time recruiting catch, and it was helped by his mother having dinner with Smith after her son went out on the town with Cunningham. Unlike McGuire, who had been insulted by any academic questions from parents, Smith talked about the importance of getting a degree. Lewis committed to UNC the next morning.

So now there were two bona fide stars in the program, but they would play only one varsity season together. Smith needed someone to replace Cunningham, voted the 1965 ACC Player of the Year in a landslide, after he graduated. Carolina had gone 15–9 and finished second in the ACC in Cunningham's senior season, but the Tar Heels were still chasing Duke for victories and recruits.

Smith, who admitted to copying Bubas' recruiting methods of assigning his assistant coaches to different regions of the country and personalizing the approach to each family, got a measure of revenge in 1964 for UNC losing Heyman. He snatched heralded schoolboy hero Larry Miller from Duke's Pennsylvania recruiting hotbed. Duke already had seniors Marin from Farrell, Pennsylvania, Vacendak from Scranton, and Bob Reidy from Allentown in the program, which was signing star players from the Keystone State long before Bubas arrived, dating all the way back to Dick Groat, Joe Belmont, and Ronnie Mayer.

The Miller coup was set up by UNC freshman coach Rosemond, who made dozens of trips to Catasauqua, Pennsylvania, before the rules limited recruiting visits.

Rosemond spent afternoons drinking beer with Miller's father, a third-shift factory worker, and when Larry came home from school, he always heard the same message: "If you went to Duke, you'd be going all that way and still be 10 minutes from heaven," Rosemond joked.

Miller laughed at that until he decided to visit Chapel Hill on Jubilee Weekend in the spring of 1964. Beautiful weather, rock and roll bands, and the Southern coeds in knee-length skirts turned Miller's head and his heart toward UNC. "I hung out with Billy Cunningham and Bobby Lewis that weekend," Miller said. "They asked me if I wanted to go to the movies or go to a party. I said to them, 'Are you kidding?'"

Miller had dozens of suitors, including McGuire, who had resigned from the Warriors when the franchise announced it was being sold and moving to San Francisco. Several schools were courting McGuire to be their new head coach, and he decided to start recruiting before he knew where he was going. Miller was one of his first targets. "He said it would be either LaSalle or South Carolina," Miller said of McGuire's phone call, "and then [in typical McGuire fashion] he asked to speak to my mother."

By then Miller had it down to two schools from Tobacco Road. He was in tears the week before at a Holiday Inn in Allentown, Pennsylvania, when Bubas took the scholarship out of his coat pocket and placed it on the table with a pen. "I was crying because Vic Bubas was a wonderful person and I really liked him and Bucky Waters," Miller said years later. "But I couldn't sign. It was a very emotional thing."

Miller told Bubas and Smith that he wanted his future college coach to attend his high school graduation and would telephone the winner a few days before. "I called Coach Smith, and he came up. I was excited about going to the ACC," Miller said. "Another ACC coach had told me that wherever I went, the pendulum would swing toward that school."

Some high school stars chose already established programs because they would be playing for a winning team. Miller, as Heyman had done five years earlier, liked the idea of starting something on his own. And Lewis was already in the program, putting up big numbers as a freshman.

Smith actually rebuilt UNC basketball on the foundation of in-state players, 7'0" Rusty Clark from Fayetteville, 6'8" Bill Bunting from New Bern, and 6'7" Joe Brown from Valdese, plus 6'4" guard Dick Grubar from Schenectady, New York, and Gerald Tuttle from London, Kentucky.

Clark's goal was to go to medical school, and he was recruited heavily by both Bubas and Davidson coach Lefty Driesell. But UNC made Clark a candidate for the prestigious Morehead Scholarship, which he eventually accepted. Bunting's father had gone to Duke, and his son was leaning in that direction until he read about Clark. At barely 200 pounds, Bunting knew that with Clark at Carolina he would not have to play center for the Tar Heels. Bubas worked the Duke connection hard, but in the end, Chapel Hill was a better fit for Bunting.

Plus, Carolina already had Lewis and Miller. The homegrown North Carolina talent that enrolled the next year not only allowed the "L&M Boys" to play their natural positions of small forward and shooting guard, it gave Smith a dominating lineup that delivered his first ACC championship and the school's first trip to the Final Four in 10 years. The Tar Heels did it by defeating Duke three times, the last in the 1967 ACC Tournament Championship Game at the then-9,000-seat Greensboro Coliseum.

However, the next time a heralded recruit decided between Duke and Carolina, the Blue Devils won out. Dick DeVenzio, a shifty southpaw guard from Ambridge, Pennsylvania, liked UNC, but his father, who was also his high school coach, preferred the more established Bubas. Of course, neither of them knew that Bubas would retire from coaching after DeVenzio's sophomore season or that both father and son would wind up wishing they had made a different decision because of Duke's next coach.

Smith felt confident about his chances of landing DeVenzio. Larry Brown had joined the UNC coaching staff, was only nine years older than DeVenzio, and had been the same kind of pass-first guard at Carolina that DeVenzio was at Ambridge High School. And the two hit it off on Brown's recruiting visits to his home during that 1967 season, when the Tar Heels unseated the Blue Devils as ACC champions and reached Smith's first Final Four.

In fact, Smith and Brown thought they also would get Austin Carr, a talented scoring guard from Washington, D.C., who had more than 2,000 points in high school and thus was a perfect complement to assist-maker DeVenzio. After returning from the Final Four in Louisville that spring, Smith and Brown planned to sign up their back-court of the future, even though both players were still being heavily recruited by Duke and Notre Dame, respectfully.

Their plan was to fly to Washington on a Saturday morning, sign Carr, and then drive to Pennsylvania and sign DeVenzio that night. When they arrived in the nation's capital, Carr was not at home and (they later learned) had been taken to a hotel suite by Notre Dame coach Johnny Dee. Carr eventually signed with the Fighting Irish, averaged 35 points over his career (51 in seven NCAA Tournament games), and was the first pick in the 1971 NBA Draft.

Meanwhile, the night before, Bubas and Waters had visited the DeVenzio family, arguing that UNC was guard-heavy with Grubar and rising sophomores Eddie Fogler and Jim Delany, not to mention Charlie Scott, who could play both guard and forward. When the Carolina coaches arrived at the DeVenzio home that evening, Dick opened the door. He was in tears when he said, "I'm going to Duke, I'm going to Duke" and closed the door.

After the Blue Devils upset second-ranked Carolina in 1969 behind sophomore DeVenzio's 13 points and 11 assists, Smith said, "This game was decided two years ago when Dick DeVenzio picked Duke over North Carolina."

Imagine if DeVenzio and/or Carr had gone to UNC and played for two seasons with Scott, who had became UNC's first black scholarship athlete after backing off his commitment to Davidson and Driesell due to a racial incident at a restaurant near campus. Bishop McDuffie, Scott's coach at Laurinburg Prep, had actually called Duke, Princeton, and West Virginia to see if they wanted to recruit Scott, but Carolina had swooped in and gained a commitment from the 6′5″ superstar, whom Smith always called "Charles" because that was Scott's preferred first name. Charles starred at UNC and paved the way for other minority athletes in all sports.

DeVenzio and Raleigh's Randy Denton, who played for Enloe High School and former Duke standout Howard Hurt, headed the last top-rated recruiting class Bubas signed. Denton, the curly haired 6'10" forward, was also a prime target of Smith, who had by then established his program's inside game with Clark and Bunting. After Bubas retired, Smith owned in-state recruiting among all of the Big Four schools. He never lost another five-star high school senior from North Carolina with the exception of David Thompson, who went to State and was later the subject of an NCAA investigation that landed both the Wolfpack and Duke on probation.

While Denton made an All-ACC team for three straight years, DeVenzio never clicked with Bucky Waters. After Waters was named to succeed Bubas, DeVenzio actually became a friend of UNC basketball and eventually a secret recruiter for the Tar Heels. He was player host on Duke campus visits for George Karl and Mitch Kupchak, both of whom he told to go to Carolina. DeVenzio was a youth coach and the first former athlete to try to organize a union for college players until his death from colon cancer at age 52.

Duke tried hard to reestablish its recruiting presence in Pennsylvania, but Smith beat the Blue Devils for DeVenzio's former Ambridge teammate Dennis Wuycik and cat-quick guard Steve Previs from Bethel Park a year before Karl, the cocky kid from Penn Hills, followed them. Bubas' last recruiting class settled for 5'10" Pat Doughty from Tempe, Arizona, who never played, 6'2" Robbie West from South Orange, New Jersey, whose claim to fame was a buzzer-beater that upset the third-ranked Tar Heels his senior year, and 6'4" Stu Yarborough of Durham, who eventually married Bubas' oldest daughter, Vicki. None of them turned into star players, and UNC took a stranglehold on the rivalry, winning 16 of 17 meetings over one stretch.

Freshmen became eligible for the 1972–73 season, and UNC signed Kupchak, Maryland landed John Lucas, and Virginia wooed "Wondrous Wally" Walker. Duke struck out on every high school star it recruited, largely due to the unpopular Waters, who had returned to Durham after four successful seasons as head coach at West Virginia.

Waters quit suddenly in September of 1973, Neill McGeachy coached the Blue Devils for one interim season, and Bill Foster came from Utah in 1974. Not surprisingly, Duke recruiting remained an abject failure until 1976, when Foster signed Jim Sparnarkel out of Hudson Catholic in New Jersey, where he had played with Mike O'Koren, who picked the Tar Heels the following season over Duke and Notre Dame.

The Blue Devils' best player in the mid-1970s was a lightly recruited guard from Houston named Tate Armstrong, a scoring machine as a junior when he averaged 24 points a game and was first team All-ACC for the last-place, 13–14 Dukies. Armstrong also made the 1976 Olympic team coached by Dean Smith, who admired how he had made himself into a great player.

However, Armstrong played sparingly for the USA's Gold Medal team with UNC's Kupchak, Phil Ford, Walter Davis, and Tom LaGarde and vowed to prove Smith wrong for keeping him on the bench during the Summer Games in Montreal. Armstrong also vowed to snap Duke's three straight last-place finishes in the ACC and he got the Blue Devils off to an 11–3 start before breaking his wrist while scoring 33 points in a victory at Virginia. Armstrong spent the rest of the season rehabbing his injury and preparing for the 1977 NBA Draft, when he was a first-round pick of the Chicago Bulls.

Literally and figuratively, Duke's biggest recruit of the decade was 6'11" Mike Gminski, who graduated high school a year early and jump-started Foster's three-year run in the top 10 before he left Duke for South Carolina in 1980. Gminski was also interested in UNC and, with the Tar Heels' success of the 1970s, would have gladly accepted a scholarship offer. But even after averaging 40 points and 20 rebounds his last year in high school in Monroe, Connecticut, he got no such offer. As it turned out, Carolina mistakenly judged Gminski as too slow afoot to be an impact player in the ACC.

Following his official visit to Chapel Hill, the G-man received a letter from Smith's chief assistant Bill Guthridge, saying that pursuing UNC was not in his best interest. Gminski and his family always held a grudge about that decision, and after signing at Duke, he proved Carolina terribly wrong by becoming one of the dominating forces in the history of the ACC. Gminski was ACC Rookie of the Year as a freshman, averaging a double-double (15 points and 11 rebounds), made first-team All-ACC for the next three seasons, and was the 1979 ACC Player of the Year. His career averages were 19 points and 10 rebounds.

He long ago acknowledged that the best thing to ever happen to him was not going to Carolina, which played without an All-Conference big man for Gminski's last three seasons at Duke. He went on to have a 14-year NBA career and become one of the most respected basketball analysts on TV.

Gminski also played on three NCAA Tournament teams at Duke, which lost a heartbreaker to Kentucky in the 1978 National Championship game in St. Louis. His front line mates in that three-year run were Gene Banks, who picked Duke over UNC, and 6'7" Kenny Dennard, from King, North Carolina, who like Gminski was not offered a scholarship by the Tar Heels and held it against them throughout his college career. Carolina already had O'Koren at power forward, and Dennard actually decided on Duke during his official visit to Clemson, which was playing Duke in football that weekend. Dennard found himself rooting for the Blue Devils, who pulled out an 18–18 tie on the sixth field goal of the game, Vince Fusco's 57-yarder as the clock went to double-zero. Dennard was hooked on Duke.

But the most important recruit for the Duke basketball program perhaps in its glorious history was Banks, the nation's top prep player in 1977. Since the doors opened at lily-white schools like Duke to accept African American student-athletes, the Blue Devils had yet to hit on a big time black basketball player.

But that ended with the successful recruitment of Eugene Lavon Banks of Philadelphia. Banks had an incredible prep career. He was named All-State three times, a first-team All-American two times, and led West Philadelphia High School to a 79–2 record.

It was a recruiting war for Banks, the powerful 6'8" forward, between Duke, North Carolina, Penn, Notre Dame, and UCLA. "Penn had me locked up at one time," Banks explained. "Tim Smith from my high school had already gone to Penn, so I knew a lot about the school. I already liked the Big Five, playing in Philadelphia, so I knew I could go to Penn. After the recruiting started, UCLA really had me. I liked Coach [Gene] Bartow a lot, the visit was great, L.A. was awesome, I got a tour of the Playboy Mansion, which was off the hook, and Marques Johnson was great on my visit."

Banks liked North Carolina as well. He remembers Dean Smith coming to his home and impressing his mother. But the school up the road had already caught his eye. "I really enjoyed my visit to Duke," he said. "The black community, the students that were there were very connected. It wasn't a whole lot, but it was just enough. Out of all my visits, it seemed to be more intimate than all the other schools, and that's what I liked about it.

"The only real thing I knew about Duke was Tate Armstrong, Coach Foster, and the fact that I knew if I came to Duke, I could help to make them a national power. There was just a feel. I know people think I talk a lot of bullshit, but there was a spiritual feel about the whole visit to Duke. At UCLA there were all kinds of offers and jobs waiting for my stepdad Walt in Los Angeles. My best friends had stuff locked up that I didn't even know about. They were doing deals behind my back that I wasn't going to know about until I signed. Then I found out about them, and it turned me off on UCLA."

The recruitment of Banks by the Blue Devils was always an intriguing affair, including the day he signed his national letter of intent. Foster had used up all of his face-to-face visits with Banks, but on Signing Day, he was intent on getting the letter of intent before Banks changed his mind. Since they couldn't meet face-to-face, Foster and Banks agreed by phone that Foster would leave the letter in Banks' mailbox first thing the next morning.

Foster flew to Philadelphia and borrowed the big Cadillac of his friend and owner of the Philadelphia 76ers, drove into West Philadelphia, and left the letter of intent in Banks' mailbox. Banks retrieved it, sat down at the kitchen table with his mom, signed his name, and put it back in the mailbox with Foster sitting around the corner watching from his car. After Banks left for school, Foster returned to the mailbox, got out the letter of intent, looked at the signature, and headed back to Durham a very happy man.

Legend has it, Notre Dame coach Digger Phelps was sitting just down the street watching the letter exchange and hoping to get one last chance to talk with Banks or maybe catch Foster in a recruiting violation. "Every coach was trying to get a chance to see me one more time even after I told them I was going to Duke," Banks said. "I had to end up staying at friends' homes a lot to get away from all of them trying to see me at school and at home."

Banks was also one of the first student-athletes with lower SAT scores than Duke normally accepted. A street smart and intelligent young man, Banks did not test well but ended up graduating from Duke on time and was a class speaker at his graduation. "He sold himself to the school," Foster explained. "The admissions office was charmed by him. Gene was the type of guy that did a lot of things that endeared him to people. Duke wanted people who could contribute to the school in many different ways. He could and he did."

It didn't take long for Banks to understand the Duke-Carolina rivalry either. After arriving on the Duke campus as a freshman, he decided to head over to Chapel Hill and Granville Towers to visit with some of the Carolina guys he had made friends with on his recruiting visit. When he received a very cool welcome from Phil Ford and all the Tar Heel players, he knew he was now their enemy.

Chapter 3

New-School Recruiting Battles

In a radio commentary during the late summer of 2013, I praised UNC coach Roy Williams for fighting his way through a difficult year, in which he not only got past a serious health scare, worried about the NCAA probation and academic scandal that was getting closer to the legacy of Carolina basketball, but also continued to coach at the highest level and remain competitive in the cutthroat world of college recruiting.

As an aside, I tossed in a one-liner about how Williams could keep luring top players into his program—even without the benefit of walking around all summer in a USA Basketball shirt (like Krzyzewski). "I heard that commentary and appreciate what you said about me," Williams told me one morning that week. "And when I heard the line about the USA Basketball shirt, I laughed so hard I nearly drove my car off the road."

—AC

When he arrived at Duke, Mike Krzyzewski recruited against Dean Smith for a number of players, most notably Michael Jordan from Wilmington, North Carolina. But while the Jordan family agreed to have dinner with South Carolina coach Bill Foster at the governor's mansion in Columbia in the summer of 1980, Michael never seriously considered Duke's fledgling program under Coach K. Krzyzewski's good luck letter hangs prominently in Jordan's glass-enclosed display case in the Carolina Basketball Museum next to the Smith Center.

Duke had a far better chance with a local star from Southern Durham High School named Curtis Hunter. "Curtis was right there in Durham, and we both recruited him really, really hard," Roy Williams said of his days as a UNC assistant, "and we were fortunate to get him."

When Hunter chose the Tar Heels, Duke took David Henderson from Drewry, a small town in northeastern North Carolina, away from N.C. State. Neither player made All-Conference during their careers, but Henderson was far more productive than the oft-injured Hunter.

Henderson was in the freshman class that turned Duke's program around with five other freshmen, none of whom considered the Tar Heels because Krzyzewski had decided to broaden his recruiting base after missing on every five-star recruit he went after during his first year in Durham. Mark Alarie was from Arizona, Jay Bilas was from California, and Johnny Dawkins was from Washington, D.C. Weldon Williams from Illinois was a career reserve, and Bill Jackman from Nebraska transferred after his freshman year. Most significantly, this freshman class showed Krzyzewski that he did not have to go after every player UNC recruited but that he could still have a national program.

Dawkins was the key recruit for Krzyzewski. Duke had never had a player quite like Dawkins. A gym rat that could score at will, hitting jumpers or driving the ball. He relished scoring, wanting to try and set the school record each and every night that he played.

He was a coveted player in the D.C. area. Georgetown coach John Thompson made him the youngest player to be placed on an Olympic Festival team, and Maryland's Lefty Driesell used all his charm to woo the Mackin High School star.

For some reason Dawkins just didn't like Thompson, and when Driesell stood in front of his players and told Dawkins they would love to have him as part of the team, Adrian Branch and his teammates shook their heads no—they didn't need another shooting guard.

Bobby Dwyer, a former Wake Forest guard and assistant for Krzyzewski at Army and Duke, did a great job of staying on Dawkins.

Gun-shy over recruiting misses his first year, Krzyzewski also offered a scholarship to another point guard, Jo Jo Buchanan, saying whoever committed first would get it. Fortunately for Duke, Buchanan, who was plagued by injuries, picked Notre Dame.

Alarie was a different story. With the early commitment from Bilas—on a napkin at a restaurant—Krzyzewski wasn't sure he needed "another Bilas" when Blue Devil assistant coach Chuck Swenson wanted the head coach to stop by Phoenix on a West Coast recruiting trip and watch Alarie's Brophy Prep team take on 6'11" Brad Lohaus.

Swenson talked Krzyzewski into making the visit, and when the 6'7" Alarie pinned a Lohaus shot against the square on the backboard, Krzyzewski was sure he didn't need another Bilas. He wanted and needed Alarie.

The one recruit Duke did go head-to-head for with Carolina was Danny Ferry, the son of an NBA general manager who had grown up in the Tar Heels' heydays of the 1970s. Ferry rooted for them because former UNC star Mitch Kupchak played for the Washington Bullets when Ferry's father was their GM and he was a ball boy for the team. Since Dean Smith had a long friendship with Morgan Wootten, who coached Ferry's DeMatha High team, the smart money was on the ballyhooed Ferry wearing Tar Heel blue. "This is really a compliment to Coach Wootten because Morgan got so much out of his players," Williams said. "There was some talk that maybe Danny was as good as he was going to be. Eddie Fogler used the terminology, 'Has Danny Ferry been milked, and is there anything left?' But I thought Danny was one of the great all-around players I had seen at that time."

By then Duke had escaped the ACC cellar, and Krzyzewski had produced two NCAA Tournament teams. And he had a starting position open after forward Danny Meagher graduated in 1985. Ferry liked that because he had told both coaches that he did not want to play center in college. Krzyzewski emphasized to Ferry that Duke did not have a system that "numbered" its players by position; i.e., the center was not the "5 man." The Blue Devils ran more of a motion offense where all five players kept moving around the front court, never posting up under the basket and remaining stationary.

Meanwhile, Smith told Ferry he would be a forward because Carolina was loaded up front with senior seven-footers Brad Daugherty and Warren Martin and juniors Joe Wolf and Dave Popson. But Ferry, who thought of himself as having an inside-outside game, still worried that he would wind up as the 5 man one day.

So when Coach K showed up for his official visit at the Ferry home, he brought a projector and some film of his 1985 team. The film flickered through Duke's offense and demonstrated not only who the Blue Devils had coming back for the 1986 season, but also who they were losing—namely, Meagher. "See where Meagher is?" Krzyzewski said. "That's how you will play." While it was not a promise of a starting position for Ferry, the implication was plain enough that he would be a mobile forward at Duke, that Carolina does not have a spot for you, but we do.

Duke was so adamant about Ferry not playing center and keeping that promise that while he played at Duke the Blue Devils would always introduce the starting lineups as three forwards and two guards, even going as far as to cross out the "C" on the box score forms from the NCAA and change it to an "F," showing that Ferry was a forward not a center.

Ferry called Duke "hungrier" than Carolina in his recruiting and heard from Krzyzewski and his assistants more frequently than from Smith and his staff, which was more Carolina's recruiting style in those days. Ferry talked about how long he had known Smith but how much he enjoyed getting to know Coach K.

Krzyzewski told Ferry bluntly, "We want you more than they do" and after getting a commitment from Ferry acknowledged, "He is the first big name player we beat Carolina for."

Another thing that helped Duke's cause was Ferry's friendship with Billy King, who came to Duke a year earlier. "Billy is one of the biggest reasons I came to Duke," Ferry explained. "He was the person I knew the best on the team. We had played on teams in the summer since we were 15 years old and had similar values about the game and life."

The two would go on in life to continue their friendship, talking weekly as players and as general managers in the NBA.

When Ferry chose Duke, it was a sign that the Blue Devils were ready to not only go head to head with the Tar Heels but surpass them someday. And the confidence that permeated the program helped the Blue Devils snap a 18-year losing streak in Chapel Hill when they blew out UNC 93–77 in 1985, while Ferry, still a senior at DeMatha, watched on TV.

Sure enough, during Ferry's freshman season at Duke, Krzyzewski won his first ACC championship and earned the first of his 11 trips to the Final Four. Ferry did not start and averaged only six points a game, but Duke beating Carolina for a player they both wanted invigorated the program.

Yes, Dean Smith and the Tar Heels wanted Ferry, but they did not push as hard for him because of another high school star coming up the next year, 6'8" forward J.R. Reid from Virginia Beach. Recruited by every major school in the country, Reid wanted to go to UNC but was not particularly keen on following Ferry there. They had faced each other in high school and All-Star Games, and Reid was considered the more talented if not the more dependable player. "You talk about everything: who was before you, who was behind you," Williams said. "We got some pretty doggone good players, and they got Danny, but those battles were pretty good, too."

While both schools got their guys, Ferry had a far better basketball career moving forward. He was a two-time ACC Player of the Year, two-time ACC Athlete of the Year, and three-time All-ACC first teamer, leading the Blue Devils in scoring and rebounding each year. The National Player of the Year, first-team All-American, and MVP of the 1988 ACC Tournament, he also set Duke's single-game scoring record (58 points vs. Miami as a junior) and was the first player in ACC history to have 2,000 career points, 1,000 career rebounds, and 500 career assists. And he played in three Final Fours. Ferry, now the Atlanta Hawks' general manager, had a 14-year pro career and won one NBA championship.

Indeed, Duke "milked" Ferry even more than DeMatha did.

By comparison, Reid only started faster, winning ACC Rookie of the Year in 1987, but he only made first-team All-ACC once and won ACC Tournament MVP once. He stayed at UNC for three years, winning one ACC championship. He played parts of 11 seasons in the NBA and did not win a ring. Neither player made an NBA All-Star team, but Ferry's career earnings were $44 million compared to Reid's $18 million. They personified one of the most bitter periods of the Duke-Carolina rivalry, battling each other physically and verbally until their last game against each other, the intense 1989 ACC Championship in Atlanta, won by UNC.

The Duke-Carolina rivalry did not simmer on or off the court after Ferry graduated and Reid turned pro following his junior season. Duke had signed fiery point guard Bobby Hurley from New Jersey, using the same tactics that worked with Ferry. Hurley's choice through the 10th grade was Carolina, remembering fellow Jersey City product Mike O'Koren's career in Chapel Hill. But Hurley and his father, Bob Hurley, who coached his sons at St. Anthony's, were offended by Dean Smith's candid recruiting approach.

For years, Smith had prioritized the players he was recruiting at every position and told them where they stood. It worked during the 1970s and early '80s, when kids were willing to wait for a scholarship offer from UNC. But with the emergence of AAU teams and summer leagues that drew not only college coaches but recruiting writers, it became somewhat insulting to be considered No. 2 or No. 3 on Carolina's list. Smith asked the Hurleys to wait on a decision from New York City superstar Kenny Anderson, the second cousin of former Tar Heel Kenny Smith, who early on was considered a lock to play in Chapel Hill.

Krzyzewski swooped in and told the Hurleys he was not recruiting Anderson and that Bobby was his first choice among point guards across the country. And with Quin Snyder graduating, he came as close as he ever had to promising someone a starting position. "The ball will be in your hands on the first day of practice," Coach K said. "The position is yours to lose."

It became a double win for Duke when Hurley signed with the Blue Devils, and Anderson shocked the recruiting world by picking Georgia Tech, where he could be the key piece from Day One and where he went on to lead the Yellow Jackets to their first Final Four appearance as a freshman in 1990. Sure, the rest of the ACC had to play against the smooth lefty, but UNC did not get him. It forced Smith to reevaluate his recruiting approach because who he was after was no longer a well-kept secret. The recruiting publications made sure of that. So while acknowledging who else he was courting, he did not tell them where they stood on his list. On several occasions Smith offered scholarships to two players and said he would take the first to commit, much like Krzyzewski had done with Dawkins. At least that way he was less likely to lose all of his top targets.

Two years older than Hurley, UNC's King Rice did not care who else Carolina was recruiting. When the starting position fell to him after Jeff Lebo graduated in 1989, he went after freshman Hurley with a vengeance and in two victories over Duke in 1990 had Hurley on the verge of tears in both games. And Rice thought he was going out with the last laugh the following season, when after losing both regular season games, the Tar Heels blew out Duke in the 1991 ACC Championship Game that had the Blue Devils barking at the officials and at each other by the time it was over.

Although Hurley had a stunning career at Duke, winning two national championships, he was a favorite antagonist for Tar Heel fans who at first considered him overrated but wound up praying he did not lead the Blue Devils to a third straight national championship in 1993 (when the Tar Heels won it). Hurley had made what is considered the biggest shot in the history of Duke basketball. Down five to UNLV with barely two minutes left in the 1991 National Semifinal, he drilled a three-pointer off a fast break. Had that shot missed and the Rebels rebounded, Duke would not have won its first NCAA title and gone into the 1992 season with the supreme confidence to win another. It was one of many big, clutch shots Hurley made during his career.

Describing his back-to-back trio of stars, Krzyzewski said, "Christian Laettner, the toughest; Grant Hill, the most graceful; Hurley, the most daring."

Laettner had heard from Carolina relatively late in the recruiting process but agreed to visit Chapel Hill. When Laettner's mother asked about the rivalry with Duke, Smith downplayed its ferocity. Then they toured the players' floor at Granville Towers residence hall, and stepping off the elevator, they saw Reid's nameplate on the door to his room, and right below it, a sign read, "Fuck Dook!" Laettner went ahead and signed with Duke.

The UNC coaches did not believe a thin white kid from a small, private school outside of Buffalo, New York, could be a five-star recruit, but they underestimated Laettner's combination of talent and toughness. After Ferry graduated, Laettner became the new leader of the team as a sophomore. Laettner and classmate Brian Davis played in four consecutive Final Fours and three straight national championship games, winning the last two.

As a junior and senior, Laettner was undeniably the best player in college basketball, saving Duke's second NCAA title with the turn-around jumper that beat Kentucky in the 1992 East Regional final in Philadelphia. It was his 10th out of 10 field goal attempts in the game (he also made all 10 of his free throws), and by then the Blue Devils had not only taken the mantle of America's Team away from Carolina but were treated like rock stars wherever they went—with screaming girls banging on the team bus and mobbing the players in hotel lobbies.

Grant Hill, on the other hand, was long considered to be headed for UNC. "I was always a Carolina fan," Hill told biographer Bill Brill. "As far back as I can remember, I rooted for Carolina. When they won the national championship in 1982, that's when I discovered basket-ball." Hill lived in the Washington, D.C., suburb of Reston, Virginia, and did not play in many summer All-Star Games and camps. College coaches watched him at South Lakes High School, where his regular attire was a "Carolina hat, T-shirt, shorts, anything. They were the dominant team then."

Smith believed Hill to be the prototype Carolina player, highly skilled but extremely unselfish and reared by a great family. Calvin Hill was a former NFL and Yale football star, and Janet attended Wellesley College, where she was a suitemate of Hillary Rodham Clinton, and worked as a lobbyist on Capitol Hill. Figuring Hill would wear Carolina blue, Smith went after a star-studded freshman class to play with him.

Center Eric Montross was also recruited by Duke but did not go gaga over Cameron Indoor Stadium on his official visit. The Indianapolis high school star had played in the RCA Dome and Butler Field House, and when he visited UNC, he saw the massive Smith Center as a logical next step. A third-generation college basketball player (his father and grandfather had played for Michigan), Montross wasn't particularly titillated by all the hype at Duke. After his weekend in Durham ended and when Krzyzewski asked for a commitment and did not get it, the Montross family took another ride through Chapel

Hill. Montross made all five of his official visits and in the end he chose Carolina over Michigan, not Duke.

The power forward in the Tar Heel freshman class was Clifford Rozier, a big time talent from Florida who never bought into the Carolina system and transferred to Louisville after one season. The small forward Pat Sullivan from New Jersey became an oft-injured role player, and Duke wound up with a better small forward in Antonio Lang. Sullivan's younger brother, Ryan (who eventually spent two years at UNC), was such a big Tar Heel fan that he refused to come out of his room during Krzyzewski's home visit.

The point guard was lefty set-up man Derrick Phelps, a wiry, tough-as-nails defender from Queens, New York, whom Smith considered the perfect backcourt mate for the 6'7" Hill. That spot was eventually filled by Phelps' fellow New Yorker, Bronx swingman Brian Reese but not before a shocking October surprise.

Part of Smith's recruiting strategy was to make the last home visit and have a player come to campus after he had been to all the other schools he was considering. Krzyzewski knew that and invited Hill for his official visit the weekend before Hill was going to Chapel Hill and Smith was scheduled at the Hill home. It was also the weekend of the Blue-White scrimmage with Cameron packed and the crowd well aware of Hill's presence. Hill had grown to like and respect Krzyzewski, and Coach K's counter was to ask a player he really wanted for a commitment at the end of the weekend.

This was the fall of 1989—after Duke had been to three of the last four Final Fours but was a young powerhouse not nearly as established as Smith's program. The Dean Dome was still relatively new, and Michael Jordan had been gone only four years, having made an impact on Hill as an impressionable grade-schooler. While encouraging every recruit to finish all of his official campus visits, Smith figured he had the advantage by making the *last* impression. But he never got the chance with Hill.

When Krzyzewski extended his hand and asked him to come to Duke, Hill shook it like he meant it. "I came back from my recruiting trip and I just knew that was where I wanted to go," Hill told Brill. "It's not like I had a great time on my visit or anything. It was just that when I got on campus, it fit. Everything I wanted—type of school, campus, coaching staff, style of basketball, opportunity to play—was there. I think it shocked my parents, my teammates, my friends. To tell you the truth, I think I shocked Duke."

Hill called Krzyzewski and committed that week. Knowing it was still a month from the official fall signing period, Coach K said that after the media got wind of it, Hill would be better off cancelling his trip to Chapel Hill, along with Smith's home visit the following Wednesday night. The Hills, however, decided to tell Smith when he came up for dinner, thinking that they owed it to the coach whom the family had admired for so long.

Smith and assistant coach Phil Ford arrived at the Hill home, and after dinner they adjourned to the living room for the final recruiting pitch. Only Grant excused himself and went to his room to do his homework. That's when his parents thanked Smith for recruiting their son and told him he had committed to Duke and wasn't going to Chapel Hill the following Friday. In today's world of Internet message boards and social media, Smith would have found out already, but he was flabbergasted that the Hill family made him travel to Washington, when a phone call would have sufficed. Smith was upset and reacted sarcastically, as he often did when angry. "We wish Grant great success at Duke," Smith said, "but I could have been home having dinner with *my* family."

It still ranks as perhaps Krzyzewski's greatest recruiting coup and completely blindsided Smith, who offered Hill's scholarship to Reese that week.

Krzyzewski had a secret weapon in his recruiting process in the Northern Virginia area. Over an eight-year period, Krzyzewski recruited the base of what would make him the coveted "Coach K" and bring Duke basketball to a level of national dominance not ever enjoyed by the school. From 1983 through 1991, he signed Dawkins, Tommy Amaker, King, Ferry, and Hill from the D.C. or Northern Virginia area. Three of the five have their numbers hanging from the rafters of Cameron Indoor Stadium, and they all captured national player of the year awards in some form (Amaker and King as Defensive Players of the Year) and all played for national championships.

The secret weapon was Mickie Krzyzewski's father, Bill Marsh, who had a four-wheel drive Ford Bronco and could pick up Mike at the airport and make sure he never missed a game of any Northern Virginia recruit, no matter the weather. In those days of recruiting, a coach could basically see every game a kid played in high school. It was almost a prerequisite that at least a member of the coaching staff be there to show how much they cared for this player. Mr. Marsh made it so Mike or a member of his staff could be at every game, no matter how deep the snow.

Hill had a tough start as a freshman at Duke and much of it had to do with Laettner, who as a junior had become the team enforcer on and off the court. The eighth-ranked Blue Devils opened their 1991 ACC season with a 17-point loss at No. 18 Virginia, and Krzyzewski made the team practice upon arriving back in Durham. Hill supposedly broke his nose in that physical scrimmage, but a story circulated for years that Laettner had criticized the freshman on the bus ride home for playing soft in his first ACC game and wound up punching him in the face. Hill had taken only five shots, scored six points, and was generally ineffective in his 26 minutes on the court. Laettner had 27 and 10 rebounds.

Wearing a protective mask over his nose, Hill played two minutes in the next game against Wake Forest and did not score. Also witnessing the side of Krzyzewski that recruits never see—the coach who can treat freshmen like Army plebes to toughen them up—Hill admitted it took him much of the season to get his rhythm and figure out the college game and its intensity.

Of course, Hill grew into one of Duke's rising stars by the 1991 NCAA Tournament, when his one-handed alley-oop dunk off a Hurley pass was the signature play of the national championship victory over Roy Williams' Kansas team. And years later, as a first-round NBA draft choice, Hill showed his support and appreciation for Krzyzewski by contributing the first $1 million to the new Legacy Fund that endowed men's basketball scholarships and funded upgrades and additions to Cameron Indoor Stadium such as the adjacent Krzyzewski Center and practice facility.

Hill did not enter Duke with the highest-rated recruiting class, and it wound up showing what a great player he became by leading an unsung 1994 team to another Final Four, upsetting third-ranked Purdue and Glenn "Big Dog" Robinson in the regional final before losing to Arkansas in the closing seconds of the NCAA Championship Game at the old Charlotte Coliseum. The best player who came in with Hill was his namesake, Thomas Hill, who ironically had reneged on his commitment to Kansas after Roy Williams replaced Larry Brown. The other four-year players in that freshman class were forwards Marty Clark and Lang, who doubled his career scoring average as a senior and made third team All-ACC.

Behind Hill the Blue Devils had reached an astounding seventh Final Four in nine years but then came the crossroads of Krzyzewski's career and Smith's retirement in 1997. Even before Coach K's illness and absence for most of the 1995 season and speculation over his return, recruiting had dropped off at Duke because Krzyzewski was not spending as much time evaluating high school players. He went right from winning Duke's second consecutive NCAA championship in 1992 to assisting USA Basketball head coach Chuck Daly with the Dream Team. Three Blue Devil signees who did not get to spend enough time with Krzyzewski were big men Joey Beard, Eric Meek, and Greg Newton. The Washington, D.C. native Beard, who was also recruited by UNC, transferred to Boston University after one year, while Meek and Newton were in and out of the Duke doghouse for all four years and had only stretches of success.

Attracted by the pitch to become the first five-star prospect from North Carolina in more than 20 years to wear royal blue, Jerry Stackhouse had considered Duke. However, Stackhouse was an even more important recruit for UNC because he was an in-state kid from Kinston who was supposed to go to the state university. It actually came down to Carolina and N.C. State, but Stackhouse had been a Tar Heel fan all of his life and was actually a distant cousin of Phil Ford. He eventually signed with Carolina and joined Philadelphia superstar Rasheed Wallace in the recruiting class, following UNC's 1993 NCAA Championship. Together with four starters returning from the national champs, UNC had the top-ranked team for most of 1994 and in 1995 delivered a third Final Four of the decade to the 64-year-old and rejuvenated Dean Smith.

The next year Carolina signed Vince Carter away from Duke and primarily Florida State, who was also chasing the phenomenal athlete from Daytona Beach, Florida. Carter was the only recruit to visit

Krzyzewski while he was laid up at home after hip surgery during his 1994–95 hiatus. Sympathy aside, Smith won over Carter and his family with frankness; he recognized Vince's tremendous physical abilities but said he needed to become a better basketball player. He challenged Carter to be the best player and student he could, which lasted through a rough freshman season until Carter learned how to play with intensity and eventually grew into a first-round draft choice and NBA All-Star highlight reel with the nickname "Vincanity."

Carter and freshman classmate Antawn Jamison of Charlotte were part of what was perceived to be Smith's change in recruiting philosophy of the 1990s, when UNC more actively went after the best high school players in the country who Smith knew would likely not stay for all four years. Phil Ford said it wasn't Smith's changing as much as the urging of his assistant coaches who watched recruits such as Carter dominating high school games. "There was really no comparison when we were evaluating players like Stackhouse, Wallace, and Carter against kids we knew would be four-year players," Ford said. "So I guess you can put that one on me. I said having certain players two or three years was better than four years of others we were recruiting. The trend was moving that way, toward having the best players for as long as you could."

Stackhouse and Wallace were the first UNC signees of that ilk and the first Tar Heels to turn pro as sophomores, leaving Smith with a young team in 1996 that began the season 16–4 and rose to No. 8 in the country. But when the confused Carter and double-covered Jamison became the focus of opposing defenses and the team's outside shooting fell off, the Heels lost seven of their last 12 games and had dropped all the way to 25th in the polls by the time they lost to Texas Tech in the second round of the NCAA Tournament.

Duke finished 18–13 and barely made the NCAAs in Krzyzewski's first full season back on the bench after missing most of 1995. He, too, was caught short on talent when shooting star Trajan Langdon redshirted with a knee injury and the team's leading scorers were guards Chris Collins and Jeff Capel, the only player on that team actively recruited by UNC (younger brother Jason Capel signed with Carolina two years later). By all accounts Jeff Capel had a difficult career at Duke after his freshman year, when he joined Hill and center

Cherokee Parks on the All-South Regional team before advancing to the Final Four in Charlotte.

The next three seasons were tough on Jeff Capel, despite making third team All-ACC as a junior when he led the team in scoring. In December of 1996, Capel played poorly at home against Florida State and was booed by the Duke students with Jason in attendance. After another poor showing in a home loss to Michigan, Krzyzewski received an angry phone call from Jeff Capel Sr., then the coach at Old Dominion University. Coach Capel accused Coach K of making his son an "outcast" by not starting him as a senior and jeopardizing whatever pro career he had.

It was not the first unpleasant conversation between the two coaches, and the Capel family barely considered Duke when it came time for Jason to pick a college. In fact in the spring of 1997, Jeff drove Jason to Chapel Hill to tell Dean Smith personally that he was coming to UNC. (Smith retired six months later and never coached Jason Capel, while Krzyzewski long ago patched up his relationships with the Capel family, twice hiring Jeff to join his staff.)

Duke returned to the top of the ACC in 1997 after taking Krzyzewski's first transfer, Roshown McLeod, getting Langdon back from extensive knee surgery, and signing rugged 6'6" freshman Chris Carrawell, who eventually was ACC Player of the Year as a senior, even though junior Shane Battier was the team's leading scorer that season. Battier and Elton Brand had highlighted Duke's stellar 1998 freshman class, and Carolina wasn't a serious contender for either player.

Krzyzewski rebuilt his team much the way Smith recruited in the mid-1990s, taking five-star recruits that he knew might not stay four years. Between 1999 and 2004, Duke lost six players early who gave up 10 total seasons of eligibility (Brand, two; Will Avery, two; Corey Maggette, three; Carlos Boozer, one; Jason Williams, one; and Mike Dunleavy, one). Battier was the lone five-star recruit to stay all four years during that span.

Despite Duke leading all the way, Carolina had gone after Battier hard in Dean Smith's last offseason of recruiting. Battier agreed to visit Chapel Hill in the fall of 1996 when his mother called the UNC basketball office to say she had not received the itinerary for the weekend. Smith's administrative assistant Linda Woods asked him about it as he was coming out of his office. "You mean, they do that now?" Smith said of sending out official visit schedules.

Unlike when he had eagerly studied Vic Bubas' recruiting habits 35 years earlier, Smith was not watching what the competition was doing as closely anymore. He had his system and routines that had worked so well for decades.

Battier and his family had set down strict rules about when coaches could telephone Shane, and Kentucky's Rick Pitino killed his chances by calling outside those designated hours from George Steinbrenner's box during the 1996 World Series. It was an attempt to impress Battier but actually eliminated the Wildcats from his list.

Battier was a perfect fit for Duke, a scholar-athlete at Detroit Country Day (which also produced Chris Webber), and Smith was not above being frank with those recruits he sensed were leaning elsewhere. On his official visit to the Battier home in Michigan, Smith bluntly asked Shane to tell him whether he was coming because "if you're not, I need to go recruit another player at your position."

Battier called Smith's home one morning the next week and awoke the coach who had stayed up most of the night watching practice film of the 1996–97 Tar Heels, who would lose their first three ACC games and later rally to win 16 straight and reach his 11th and last Final Four. Battier told Smith he was going to Duke. Smith groggily said, "Have a great career" and hung up the phone.

Never playing against Smith, who retired after the 1997 season, Battier won eight of 11 games against the Tar Heels, concluding with a brilliant senior season: 2001 ACC Player of the Year, first-team All-American, National Player of the Year, and Most Outstanding Player of the 2001 Final Four on Duke's national championship team. Also the sixth player chosen in the NBA Draft, Battier remains the poster boy for making the right choice between Duke, Kansas, and UNC. His college career was nearly perfect.

Brand was an impact player faster than Battier. Like with fellow upstate New Yorker Christian Laettner 10 years earlier, Carolina had started too late with Brand and soon learned he was headed to Durham. After averaging 18 points and 10 rebounds as a sophomore, when Duke lost to UConn in the 1999 NCAA Championship Game, Brand was the No. 1 overall player chosen in the NBA draft by the Chicago Bulls.

Will Avery entered Duke with Battier and Brand but was never seriously recruited by the Tar Heels after their coaches saw his high school transcript. Avery had basically dropped out of school during his junior year in Georgia but agreed to attend Fork Union Military prep for summer school and his senior year, graduating with an improved transcript that Duke accepted. He lasted only two years after reneging on his promise to Krzyzewski that he would stay for his junior season of 1999–2000, when Coach K had no experienced guard on the roster.

Krzyzewski was furious with Avery for going back on his word and when Avery's mother, Terry Simonton, drove up to Durham, they had a contentious meeting. According to Curry Kirkpatrick's controversial story "The Blue Flew" in *ESPN The Magazine*, Coach K told Simonton, "Your son is going to fuck up my program."

Krzyzewski did not deny that he used such language, which is part of his vocabulary, especially when he is angry. "I talked to William like I always talked to William," he said in the article. "I told him what I felt was the truth. If you don't want to hear that, you're not going to like what I say. But that's what I owe William."

Corey Maggette, who had been recruited by Carolina, also left for the NBA after the 1999 season, which also had something to do with Krzyzewski apparently forgetting to put Maggette back into the 1999 National Championship loss to UConn when he was so zonked out from painkillers for the hip he would have replaced after the season. The 6'6" Maggette played only 11 minutes, most in the first half, against the Huskies after averaging 18 minutes during the season and playing at least 20 minutes in 15 games.

Fortunately for Duke, UNC blew it with Jason Williams, not offering the 6'2" guard from New Jersey a scholarship right away and eventually losing him to the Blue Devils.

Tar Heel head coach Bill Guthridge was not sold on Williams as a point guard and already had a commitment from Hampton, Virginia, football-basketball star Ronald Curry, who never reached his unrealistic expectations in either sport. At Duke, Williams made third team All-ACC as a freshman, first-team All-ACC as a sophomore, and unanimous All-ACC as a junior, losing out to Maryland's Juan Dixon by three votes for 2002 ACC Player of the Year. Williams quarterbacked teams that went 7–1 against Carolina and turned pro after his junior year and was selected second overall in the NBA draft by the Chicago Bulls.

Mike Dunleavy was the third overall pick in 2002 by Golden State, after emerging as a star his sophomore year and making first-team All-ACC as a junior when he had not earned any previous All-Conference honors. Dunleavy's father, Mike Sr., played for Frank McGuire at South Carolina and had known Dean Smith for years. The Dunleavys initially preferred Carolina over Duke but were unsure how long Guthridge would be the head coach and who would succeed him. Smith actively helped recruit the younger Dunleavy and, while sitting with him and his father during a visit, heard them both say that if he were still coaching it would be an easy choice. The next week Mike Jr. committed to Duke, who had recruited him aggressively and actually turned down the more highly rated Casey Jacobsen to concentrate on Dunleavy. Jacobsen signed with Stanford and later played in two victories over the Blue Devils.

• • •

Shavlik Randolph was one of the most highly recruited high school players in the history of North Carolina whose entire college career was hindered by a chronic hip injury he suffered the summer after his high school graduation. The 6′10″ star had size, tremendous skills for a big man, and the legacy of having parents who went to UNC and a famous grandfather, Ronnie Shavlik, who had starred in the early glory days of N.C. State.

UNC wanted him because it had out-recruited State and Duke for every top player in North Carolina since David Thompson signed with the Wolfpack in 1971. But the Tar Heels had a commitment from Sean May, who played the same position as Randolph, and were in the middle of the three turbulent seasons under coach Matt Doherty.

Doherty handled Randolph's recruitment personally, which he did with the top prospects (adopting Roy Williams' policy that Doherty learned when he was at Kansas). Almost every day, Doherty sent letters or newspaper clippings or photos, such as Michael Jordan sitting behind his desk when he was part owner of the Washington Wizards, wearing a T-shirt that said "Shav Country."

State needed Randolph the most after finally making it back to the NCAA Tournament in 2002 and wanting to keep it going by adding a player of his ability. Plus, it would be a huge embarrassment if the blood relative of State's all-time leading rebounder (Ronnie Shavlik, who averaged 19.5 rebounds as ACC Player of the Year as a senior and had 49 points and 35 rebounds in a single game) would not come and help the Pack win its first ACC Tournament since 1987. But coach Herb Sendek's style of ball-control offense did not suit the run-and-shoot skills of a player with Randolph's size.

Ronnie Shavlik's grandson starred at Raleigh Broughton High School, where Pete Maravich had attended when his father, Press, coached N.C. State in the mid-1960s. Randolph was an outstanding student at what had become a prestigious school with the children of many prominent, well-to-do Raleigh families. The Broughton team was almost all white, and the Caps' cheering section at games was generally not dotted with many African Americans. Duke was the compromise school where Randolph could make his own name and also seemed to fit him the best as an outstanding scholar and athlete.

However, bothered by the bad hip, Randolph never averaged more than 7.4 points in his three injury-plagued seasons at Duke before surprisingly turning pro after his junior year. He knew he would not be drafted by an NBA team but said he hoped to catch on as a free agent with a franchise that was best suited for him. That turned out to be the Philadelphia 76ers, whose general manager at the time was former Duke player Billy King.

Randolph has played seven seasons for five NBA teams with moderate success and three years in China. Seth Davis, a *Sports Illustrated* writer and Duke graduate, tabbed Randolph as the biggest recruiting bust of the decade.

The Blue Devils beat Carolina for guard Greg Paulus and forward Josh McRoberts in 2006, but a much closer battle came the next year over Brandan Wright, a lanky 6'9" southpaw from Nashville, Tennessee. Wright was ticketed by most recruiting experts for Duke, so much so that Carolina decided it needed a contingency plan at the power forward position. Roy Williams offered a conditional scholarship to 6'8" Thaddeus Young of Memphis. "We had offered one guy [Young], and I told him that Brandan was coming in for a visit and that if Brandan accepted the scholarship offer, it was going to be his," Williams explained. "Brandan attended the Duke-North Carolina game at Duke and he attended the Duke-Carolina game at North Carolina. So we did feel like it was going to be one of the two, but I felt pretty good about it.

"Brandan did not surprise me. He surprised everyone else," Williams said, admitting he was more confident about Wright than any of his staff. Wright was a surprise guest at Late Night with Roy in October of 2005 and the next week he called Williams to say he was coming. Williams in turn had to tell Young, who then signed with Georgia Tech. "I remember J.J. Redick telling me at the Final Four that year that 'You really surprised us,'" Williams said of Wright, who stayed at UNC one season before entering the NBA draft. "I sort of smirked a little bit because I thought we were doing pretty well with Brandan to start with."

UNC and Duke both recruited Philadelphia high school teammates Wayne Ellington and Gerald Henderson the same year with the Tar Heels landing Ellington and the Blue Devils getting Henderson. Both started and played three seasons before turning pro, but Ellington had the better career, reaching two Final Fours and winning the Most Outstanding Player in 2009, when Carolina stripped the nets in Detroit. For Tar Heel fans, Henderson was forever identified with the vicious elbow he dropped on Tyler Hansbrough's nose in the 2007 game in Chapel Hill. Despite becoming a double-figure scorer with the Charlotte Bobcats (now Hornets) and having a much better pro career than Ellington, Henderson never became a fan favorite in the UNC-dominated Tar Heel state.

Harrison Barnes' college decision was delivered by Skype, the first recruit known to use that computerized video communication tool. He asked coaches from Carolina, Duke, Iowa State, Kansas, Oklahoma, and UCLA—the six schools he was primarily considering—to connect with him via Skype the afternoon of November 13, 2009, which turned out to be icing on the Tar Heels' recent national championship after Duke had been considered the leader for Barnes for almost two years.

The scheduled announcement caused all but UCLA to interrupt their practices to see and hear Barnes' final decision, and the once-confident Duke coaches found themselves completely in the dark that morning over the silky smooth 6'8" forward from Ames, Iowa.

Apparently, the worm had turned after Barnes and his mother visited Duke and sat behind the home bench. Throughout the game they heard Krzyzewski's fuck-filled criticism of his team and certain players, and afterward Shirley Barnes supposedly told her son, "It's your choice, but I would never want my son to play for a coach who talks to his players like that."

Nevertheless, all six schools still connected with Barnes through Skype the next afternoon. Williams left practice and walked about 50 yards off the court to the press room at the Smith Center where video coordinator Eric Hoots and assistant coach Steve Robinson had booted up the laptop and made connection. "I didn't know what we were doing; they just set up a computer and told me to sit down in front of it," the low-tech Williams said later. "Then, all of a sudden they lost Harrison, and Hootsie and Coach Rob's blood pressure went up drastically before they got him back on."

When Williams heard Barnes say his name, he knew he had landed the best high school player in the nation of the last two years. "That's another one I probably felt better about than the general public did," he said.

Williams' own personal measuring stick on such things is how hard he works on a specific recruit. Using one of the three private planes at his disposal, he had made 11 trips to Ames, compared to three by Krzyzewski. In these sophisticated software days when computer programs can trace the destination of aircraft based on their registration numbers, Duke knew when Williams was in Iowa, and it was repeatedly. During one of his last visits, a Duke assistant coach called the Barnes home to confirm that Carolina had gone in after Krzyzewski's final trip.

The Duke coach said to Shirley Barnes they did not know that Williams was following them. "You never asked me if he was," she said.

After losing Jon Scheyer (and two other starters) off the 2010 National Championship team, Krzyzewski thought Barnes was the missing piece to join returning stars Nolan Smith and Kyle Singler that would make the 2011 Blue Devils serious candidates to repeat. And, sure enough, Barnes was the run-away winner for ACC Rookie of the Year at UNC. However, Duke did land five-star point guard Kyrie Irving, a high school teammate of UNC's Dexter Strickland at St.

Patrick's in New Jersey who was rumored to be going to school with Barnes. By the time Barnes picked Carolina, Irving had committed to Duke, and the Tar Heels had landed another point guard in Kendall Marshall along with Reggie Bullock.

During those players' senior years in high school, Duke won the 2010 NCAA title with only one player that had seriously considered the lighter shade of blue. Forward Ryan Kelly played for one-time Duke guard Kevin Billerman at Raleigh's Ravenscroft High School, which he said was littered with UNC fans, but would not let on where he was going until the day he announced for the Blue Devils. Kelly turned out a far better player than Randolph, the last in-state recruit Krzyzewski took away from UNC. He stayed four years and was drafted by the Lakers, for whom he started as a rookie. Although Kelly was only a freshman that season, the key to Krzyzewski's fourth NCAA title in 2010 was keeping a veteran team together of three seniors and two juniors in the starting lineup. Kelly followed the same four-year path and as a senior missed the Final Four by one game. Later, Coach K admitted he should have redshirted Kelly as a freshman, so he could have returned as a senior in 2014, when the Blue Devils lacked leadership.

After Duke defeated Carolina to win the 2011 ACC Tournament championship, Irving returned from a toe injury that had kept him out for most of his freshman season and the top-seeded Blue Devils lost to No. 5 seed Arizona in the West regional. Irving turned pro, and the following season top recruit Austin Rivers picked Duke over Carolina after de-committing from Florida. Rivers made the long buzzer-beater to stun the Tar Heels in Chapel Hill but left Duke after the Blue Devils played without Kelly in their embarrassing loss to 15 seed Lehigh in the 2012 NCAA Tournament.

So Irving and Rivers made it 15 players and four one-and-dones who had left Duke early over a 13-year period for a program that had long prided itself on keeping players all four years. Clearly, Duke's recruiting philosophy had changed by necessity just as UNC's had in the mid-1990s and into the next decade when the Tar Heels lost four players early off their 2005 National Championship team and two from their 2009 NCAA titlists. And there were more to come for both schools.

Krzyzewski got an early jump on the next physically dominant high school player, Jabari Parker from Simeon Career Academy in Coach K's native Chicago. Parker was recruited by every school that could make inroads, but Duke remained the odds-on favorite from the time the inner-city coach and player's family first bonded. In the fall of 2012, Roy Williams was scheduled to make his in-home visit to Parker, but doctors would not let Williams travel after undergoing surgery on his kidney that was first thought to remove a cancerous tumor.

Parker made it official by signing with Duke a week later. And it was clear how much Parker was needed after Duke advanced to the 2013 Midwest Regional final against top-seeded Louisville, which dominated the Blue Devils inside and held them to 37 percent shooting. Mason Plumlee had decided to return to Duke for his senior year, following an off-season controversy in which his Christ School coach David Gaines (a longtime Carolina fan) criticized Krzyzewski for underutilizing the second and most talented of the three Plumlee brothers.

Duke was losing Kelly and Plumlee, who developed into a first-round draft choice, and would have to rely on the 6'8" Parker and 6'8" Rodney Hood, a Mississippi State transfer, for points in and around the paint in 2014. The Blue Devils climbed as high as No. 4 in the polls but were knocked out of the NCAA Tournament by a double-digit seed (Mercer) for the second time in three years.

Meanwhile, the Tar Heels missed on the No. 1 prospect from the high school class of 2013, Andrew Wiggins, and fell back on the more conventional route of developing players over the course of their college careers. They had received commitments from talented but unpolished 6'9" Kennedy Meeks from Charlotte and 6'8" Isaiah Hicks, the North Carolina prep player of the year from 3A state champion Oxford Webb, but were not expecting to lose leading scorers Reggie Bullock, who entered the NBA draft as a junior, and P.J. Hairston, who was suspended for NCAA violations over the summer and never reinstated to the team.

After a slow start (1–4 in the ACC) and a surprising 12-game winning streak over late January and February, Carolina made it back to the NCAA Tournament as a No. 6 seed before losing in the round of 32. The Tar Heels looked ahead to their freshman class of 2015, which had three top 20 players in 6′0″ Joel Berry, 6′7″ Justin Jackson, and 6′6″ Theo Pinson, another native North Carolinian they took away from Duke and N.C. State.

Krzyzewski, who turned 67 in February, was expected to retire around his third stint as USA men's basketball coach at the 2016 Olympics in Rio. Hoping to hang his fifth national championship banner in Cameron Indoor Stadium before he left the bench, Coach K signed the nation's top recruiting class led by 6′10″ Jahlil Okafor, 6′1″ Tyus Jones, and 6′5″ Justise Winslow. Okafor was already listed as the top pick on most 2015 mock draft boards while still a senior in high school. "We're ecstatic about the young men that are coming to Duke," Krzyzewski said. "We consider Jahlil Okafor as good a big man as there is in the country but not just a big man. We think he's a great basketball player. He's had an amazing amount of experience playing for the United States and for a great high school program. In Tyus Jones, I think we have the best point guard in the country, someone who has won state championships, USA championships and is the consummate leader on the court. Justise Winslow is a great wing player. He is a guy that can guard every position and is an amazing rebounder and scorer. The great thing about all of the kids is that they want to share a spotlight, and they want to be on a great team. They're team-first guys, even though they have this excellent amount of individual talent."

Duke's continued recruiting success in the twilight of Krzyzewski's career was clearly tied to his 12 years as head coach for USA Basketball, which not only included the Olympics but also international development teams each summer made up of college and prep players who hoped to someday represent their country on the biggest stage. While Krzyzewski had done a remarkable job restoring the pride and importance of playing on USA teams to dozens of young basketball stars, the advantage of holding the position for three Olympiads was not lost on his rival college coaches. Without ever mentioning USA Basketball, Coach K recruiting top high school prospects carried a tacit reminder that they would have the potential advantage of playing for their country during the summer and perhaps someday winning a gold medal if they chose Duke.

And NBA stars he coached on the Olympic Team from Kobe Bryant to LeBron James, who did not attend college and thus were not considered representatives of Duke University, could gladly call recruits on occasion and recommend playing for Krzyzewski. Many NCAA Division I coaches thought of this 12-year run as a wholly unfair advantage, bordering on the absurd. Though never quoted in public about it, Roy Williams was one of those coaches.

From left to right: UNC's Dean Smith, Duke's Vic Bubas, and N.C. State's Everett Case (Bubas' mentor) were three of the forefathers of the great Tobacco Road rivalries. (Courtesy of the ACC)

Though UNC's Larry Brown (left) and Duke's Art Heyman (right) were both Jewish playmaking guards from Long Island, New York, they became antagonists, inflaming the Duke-Carolina rivalry. (AP Images)

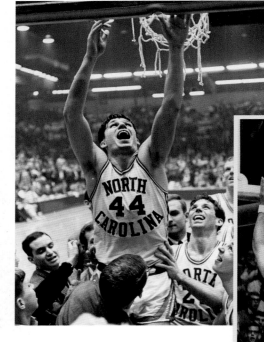

ACC Tournament MVP Larry Miller, who scored 32 points on 13-of-14 shooting, cuts down the nets in 1967 after leading Dean Smith's Tar Heels to the first of three straight ACC championships.

Duke All-American Mike Lewis blocks a shot from UNC All-American Larry Miller during Carolina's 75–72 home victory in 1968. Duke would win the rematch in Durham in triple overtime.

During Duke's 87–81 victory in Durham in 1969— Vic Bubas' final home game—Dean Smith marches onto the court after a near scuffle breaks out between players.

The Cameron Indoor crowd acknowledges one of its favorites, Jim Spanarkel, on Senior Day in 1979, following the famous stall game, which featured a 7–0 halftime score. (Duke University Archives)

Coach Bill Foster talks to Chip Engelland, who would become an assistant coach with the San Antonio Spurs. (Duke University Archives)

Kenny Dennard poses next to "The Speedo Guy," a Cameron Crazy who gained fame, in Durham in 2008.

Though Coach K surpassed Dean Smith in total wins and national championships, he was only 14–24 in head-to-head competition and credits the battles against Smith for making him a better coach.

Wearing a protective cast on his broken left wrist, Kenny Smith drives on Tommy Amaker during the climactic 1984 regular season finale, which Carolina won in double overtime. A week later the Blue Devils would upset the Tar Heels in the semifinals of the ACC Tournament, a game that represented Duke's ascent to ACC power.

The two blue-chip recruits for their respective schools, Duke's Danny Ferry and Carolina's J.R. Reid, battled in the paint from 1987 to 1989. (Courtesy of Bob Donnan)

After losing twice to Duke in the regular season, King Rice, who held Bobby Hurley to two points, celebrates the 1991 ACC Championship victory. Both teams would advance to the same Final Four for the first and only time, but Duke would win the title.

After winning their first national championship in 1991, the confident Blue Devils took on a rock star-like profile.

Duke's Christian Laettner covers UNC big man Eric Montross, who may have been bloodied but still led UNC to the 75–73 upset of top-ranked Duke in 1992.

After defeating Michigan 71–51, Duke, which lost just two games during its dominating 1992 campaign, celebrates its second consecutive national championship.
(AP Images)

Al McGuire, who coined the term "Cameron Crazies," ventures into the Duke crowd with a pith helmet and a whip to tame the Duke fans.

Through creative antics and their passion, the Cameron Crazies give Duke one of the best and most famous home-court advantages in basketball.

Mike Gminski, the big man who helped resuscitate the Duke program in the late 1970s and now works as an announcer, interviews Roy Williams.

Dean Smith stands next to Charlie Scott, the first African American basketball player in the UNC program.

Chapter 4

Gaining Respect

*O*ne of the craziest games I ever covered began with one team failing *to score in the first half and ended with both teams and coaches yelling at each other in the middle of the playing floor.*

I was walking out of Cameron Indoor Stadium to my car, heading back to the newspaper office to write my game story when a tall, angry man yelled at me. Turning around, I immediately knew who it was—Joe Gminski, the father of Duke's star center who had been given a fla-grant foul in the last 30 seconds and ejected from the game. "Hey!" Joe Gminski was yelling. "Your fucking coach is an asshole, and tell him to never talk to my boy again, you hear me?"

I kept walking, and big Joe kept yelling. Finally, I stopped and turned around.

"Joe, he's not my coach and he's still in Cameron, so you can go back in there and tell him yourself."

I shrugged and continued on to my car. Just another Duke-Carolina game, I thought to myself.

—AC

Duke rebuilt its basketball program from 1976–80 with an unlikely cast of characters, to say the least. The foundation turned out to be a player no one else wanted—"not very fast or quick, can't jump, and not a very good shooter," said his own high school coach.

The All-American man in the middle was a player UNC didn't want—rejected for being slow afoot and a "non-aggressor" by usually astute judges of high school talent. The superstar was a player everyone wanted but, thanks to his confidence and ego, turned down the power programs for the doormat of the ACC at the time. The unsung forward always wanted to wear Carolina blue but never got an offer and spent four years playing for Duke and partying in Chapel Hill.

And the two point guards were transfers from schools that didn't work out for them and wound up fighting over the position Duke needed to run the show. This distinctly different group led the Blue Devils from the abyss of last place in the ACC to the top of the college game in a short—but critical—three-year span that basically pulled the once-storied program off life support.

Once the new team had been constructed by coach Bill Foster through obsessive effort and a little luck, Duke and North Carolina played 11 pretty incredible games over three seasons; the Blue Devils won five of them, and the Tar Heels won six of them. Before this stretch perennial national power UNC had won 16 of the last 17 meetings.

All 11 games had their own stories, from redemption to resiliency to heroism to histrionics, and each of them has a back story worth telling. But the one game most remembered for its rarity and ramifications occurred on February 24, 1979, when one team failed to score in a first half that unwittingly invented an everlasting chant in gyms across the country and ended with an on-court controversy that signaled the official return of the Duke-Carolina rivalry.

But the infamous "7–0 Game" did not just happen. It was a matter of one program painstakingly piecing together a nationally ranked team that became the equal of its archrival that had left it in the dust over the last decade, and that rival recognizing it had been caught from behind and needed to resort to strategy to stay ahead of the neighbor eight miles down the road, yet eons apart in so many other ways.

The seeds had begun to be planted several years earlier when Duke hired a new coach who turned out to be the savior of the program and the critical bridge to a rivalry that today has no comparison. Had Foster not come clear across the country to take the Duke job in 1974 and figured out a way to compete with his coaching peer in age, if not accomplishment, the competition with North Carolina would have been so one-sided for so long and the program in such dire straits—who knows if it could have ever been revived by Mike Krzyzewski in the 1980s.

Foster arrived from the University of Utah in the spring of 1974, right after his Runnin' Utes had lost to Purdue in the championship game of the National Invitational Tournament (NIT) when it was still a big deal. (In those days the NCAA Tournament began with only 25 teams, nearly one-third of today's 68-team field.) Salt Lake City was a great place to live and enjoy the outdoors, and Foster's predecessor Jack Gardner was a legend in his own right after 18 iconic seasons and two Final Four appearances at Utah. But except for UCLA's dominance under John Wooden, the West was still an outpost for college basketball. So making it all the way to the NIT championship game at Madison Square Garden was not to be ignored by Duke athletic director Carl James, who was looking for a new coach following five disastrous seasons since the retirement of Vic Bubas in 1969.

After a year of flying around the country, watching numerous basketball games and talking with dozens of people about who would be the right man for the job, James had Foster at the top of his list. "I was a little shocked when they offered me the job, but it seemed like a great place," said Foster, whose three-year record at Utah was only 43–39 (18–24 in Western Athletic Conference play). Undaunted at first, he was taking over a team coming off four consecutive seasons of double-digit losses and a 1–4 record in the ACC Tournament. However, he was well known in the profession as a rebuilder of programs.

Before his three years at Utah, Foster spent eight at Rutgers, where he posted a 120–75 record and coached a precocious kid named Jim Valvano. In Valvano's senior season in 1967, he teamed with All-American guard Bob Lloyd to lead Rutgers to a 22–7 record and a spot in the NIT, the first time the school had played in a postseason tournament.

Having begun his head coaching career with three stunning seasons (45–11) at Bloomsburg State in New Jersey, Foster truly returned to his roots and his comfort zone at Rutgers after growing up in New Jersey and graduating from Elizabethtown College before entering teaching and coaching.

He knew about UNC coach Dean Smith, who was his same age, and had met the man who had rebuilt the Carolina program after Frank McGuire left it on NCAA probation. Foster knew of Smith's four ACC championships and trips to the Final Four in six years but was also concerned with the other school in what he learned was called the Triangle Area—N.C. State, which had ousted seven-time champion UCLA and won the 1974 NCAA title behind All-American David Thompson and a star-studded supporting cast.

Bob Boyd, the coach at Southern Cal, talked to James several times about the Duke job but ended up staying put. Boyd knew that John Wooden was nearing retirement at UCLA and feared that Smith and N.C. State coach Norman Sloan might be like tangling with a two-headed Wooden. So it was Foster who arrived in Durham with his assistant coaches, Lou Goetz and Bob Wenzel. All three were New Jersey-Pennsylvania guys, and that's where Duke would go to begin constructing an ACC contender.

Foster watched endless film of the roster he inherited, especially the last two games against UNC that Duke should have won before blowing both of them in the final minute. There were some talented holdovers, including three returning senior starters who had been in the last class of college basketball to play on freshman teams: Bob Fleischer, a 6′8″ forward with a varsity career scoring average of 13 points; lefty sharpshooter Pete Kramer; and cocky point guard Kevin Billerman, who played and acted tougher than he really was, though it seemed to work for him. Also there was 6′9″ junior Willie Hodge and a blond sophomore from Houston named Tate Armstrong, who looked like a surfer dude but as it turned out could shoot it like a young Jerry West.

Because Foster quickly ascertained that grit was a missing ingredient in these Blue Devils, he immediately signed a 24-year-old junior college forward from New York City named George Moses and went back to his familiar stomping grounds in New Jersey, looking for the biggest motherfucker he could find to recruit. Foster had serious connections in that part of the country from his summer camp in the Pocono Mountains that he owned and ran with legendary Temple coach Harry Litwack, who had just retired after leading the Owls for 21 seasons, all but one with winning records. Litwack, an ad hoc scout for the Blue Devils, would become far more than a business partner to Foster.

Foster quickly learned that Duke had lost its luster from the days Bubas owned Pennsylvania and New Jersey recruiting, signing up the likes of Dick DeVenzio, Bob Verga, Jack Marin, and Steve Vacendak, plus Jeff Mullins from nearby Lexington, Kentucky. UNC's Smith now had the stranglehold on that region, having landed Larry Miller, George Karl, Dennis Wuycik, and Steve Previs, plus native New Yorkers Charlie Scott and Bill Chamberlain. Those kids were gone, but their legacy and how Smith was beginning to dominate in-state recruiting had the Tar Heels on their way to becoming the new America's Team. Many of their games were televised into that region, giving Smith an electronic entry.

Symbolic of Foster's challenge was that his first season at Duke coincided with the freshman year of Phil Ford, a Rocky Mount, North Carolina, native. UNC, Clemson, Maryland, N.C. State (and even Duke) recruited the 6'1" high school All-American who could do just about everything with a basketball but dunk it. The April night Smith and assistant coaches Bill Guthridge and Eddie Fogler got into Smith's Cadillac in front of Carmichael Auditorium for the trip to Rocky Mount, Smith said without being boastful, "Isn't this fun? We're going to sign the best point guard in America."

Having been almost 3,000 miles away, Foster had not realized what became of the two iconic college basketball names, Duke and North Carolina. For the first five years of the decade, the Duke-Carolina rivalry was basically non-existent. The Tar Heels spent most of those seasons with a single digit in front of their name, while the Blue Devils hoped to keep their overall loss total from reaching double-digits in any given season. Carolina had developed more important rivals, such as N.C. State and Maryland.

Things got so bad that in 1974 Duke was operating with interim coach Neill McGeachy, a skeleton staff, and had a 10–16 record. Foster flickered through film of past losses to Carolina, the last when Smith's team rallied from eight points down with 17 seconds left to force overtime and eventually win to author the most famous comeback in college basketball history. Now, Ford was enrolling at UNC to make the perennially powerful Tar Heels even better—and Duke even less of a threat.

Foster also learned that his new program came apart after former athletic director Eddie Cameron had hired Bucky Waters to succeed Bubas, and Waters ran off many of the quality players he had signed based on Duke's prior reputation. Cameron's successor was already looking for a new coach when Waters quit suddenly in September of 1973, leaving James no choice but to try to hire the retired Adolph Rupp and eventually give the job to McGeachy for one year while he searched for a new permanent coach.

Foster was a multi-tasker with boundless energy, often banging out notes, plans, and to-do lists on a portable typewriter while sitting in the bleachers before practice, as his players shot around. Besides Duke being mired in the shadow of UNC and N.C. State, he soon recognized that the university was in a debate over just how much athletics added to its growing academic reputation. Cameron Indoor Stadium, which had yet to become the Mecca of college basketball because it often hosted half-empty home games, was in serious need of upgrades or even total demolition. Foster, the marketer, got busy promoting his new program and selling tickets. While leaving his wife and three daughters home during long road trips, he went looking for players who could change all this. He always carried a notepad so he could write down thoughts as they popped into his head about building Duke basketball.

In Foster's first season, his enthusiasm seemed to rub off on the players, as the four seniors got pep talks from their fourth coach in four years. As freshmen they had Hubie Brown, as sophomores they had Waters, as juniors they had McGeachy, and now they had Foster. Brown left after their freshman season in 1972 and began a long career coaching pro basketball.

Billerman, Armstrong, Kramer, Fleischer, and Hodge were not a bad starting lineup—just one that had become accustomed to losing. Foster emphasized the running game, and Duke ran off to a 5–1 start, beating Princeton and Pittsburgh while losing only to LSU, going into the Big Four Tournament, a December event that paired Duke, UNC, N.C. State, and Wake Forest on a rotating basis and often resulted in three Duke-Carolina games during the regular season until the Big Four ended a 10-year run in 1980.

In Foster's first Big Four, Duke's opponent on opening night was UNC, which was also 5–1 with freshman Ford at point guard. Ironically, Carolina's fifth victory was over Foster's old Utah team. The Tar Heels were ranked eighth but more on reputation than anything else.

Indeed Foster seemed like a savior in his first game against Carolina, breaking the Blue Devils' eight-straight losing streak to UNC with a 99–96 overtime victory at the stunned Greensboro Coliseum. After the game he joked to his staff, "What was so hard about that?"

Unfortunately, that would be the single highlight of the season as the Blue Devils lost their home-and-home series to the Tar Heels and finished tied with Wake Forest for last in the ACC (2–10) and 13–13 overall, dropping their first game in the ACC Tournament, one of seven losses by fewer than 10 points, to Clemson.

By the time Carolina beat defending national champion State to win the 1975 ACC Tournament, where Ford was the first freshman named MVP, Foster was long gone on the recruiting trail, following up the occasional visits, frequent phone calls, and endless notes and letters he sent to recruits and their coaches. Convinced by his team's failure to finish off games, he was looking for the toughest, best basketball players he could find.

The first who would seriously consider Duke was a street-wise, pigeon-toed kid from Jersey City named Jim Spanarkel, a 6'5" guard-forward who played for Hudson Catholic coach Rocky Pope, who candidly told Foster's assistant Bob Wenzel: "About the only thing he will do for you is win. He's not very fast or quick, can't jump, and is not a very good shooter. But when the other team presses, we give him the ball. When we need a basket, we give him the ball. If we're having trouble stopping a big man, we put him on the guy. If we're having trouble with a guard, we put him on that guy."

Although he had hoped to land a recruiting class that fit his needs, Foster wound up doing it one player at a time. He signed four other freshmen with questionable major college ability, but Foster admitted he couldn't tell how good Spanarkel might become, though he knew he had his first motherfucker. "We signed this Spanarkel kid out of New

Jersey," he said with a sly grin about his first recruiting class at Duke. "I know he isn't all that highly touted, but I think people are going to like him. I think they will appreciate the way he plays the game. One of the reasons we wanted him was because he was tough. We wanted a tough kid because we knew he was coming into a tough situation."

Well aware of what was expected of him, Spanarkel knew he had to get into great physical shape. As a freshman he felt so chubby that he ate Kellogg's Corn Flakes for five weeks in order to lose 20 pounds. It helped that his father was a regional salesman for Kellogg's.

Spanarks, as he became known, was a hard-nosed defensive player who turned into one of the ACC's best rebounding guards, averaging more than four a game, and would drive hard to the hole before settling for a jumper. A sophomore who led the nation in free throws attempted and made, he was also a deceptively good athlete with quick hands and a lot of what they call "basketball savvy."

Compared to the streets of Jersey City, Spanarkel found Duke more like a paradise with pretty girls galore and plenty of parties. But he also worked diligently at his craft. Between classes he went to Cameron to shoot free throws alone, putting a bounce-back net under the goal, so the ball came right back to him after every shot. He often did not change from his school clothes, using every possible minute to improve. Not surprisingly, he went on to make 81 percent of his career free throws, once knocking down 52 in a row.

As a freshman in 1976, Spanarkel teamed with junior Armstrong in a backcourt that was hot from the first game and led the team to a 6–1 start before losing to State and UNC in the Big Four Tournament. Once again, conference play did in the Blue Devils as they went 3–9 to finish dead last in the league standings, losing 13 of their last 20 games to go 13–14 overall. For the second straight season, they were ousted from the ACC Tournament in their first game by two points, this time to ninth-ranked Maryland.

A slimmer Spanarkel averaged better than 13 points and four rebounds and won ACC Rookie of the Year in a landslide. Golden boy Armstrong averaged 24 points a game—good for second in the ACC—and shot 52 percent from the field. The fact that he joined four stars from the top three teams in the conference on the All-ACC first team proved what an outstanding and respected player he had become.

That summer Armstrong made the U.S. Olympic Team coached by Carolina's Smith, though he did not get many minutes in Montreal because Smith found out that playing so much zone at Duke left him lacking in man-to-man defensive skills. Nevertheless, Armstrong stood proudly on the podium after the U.S. defeated Yugoslavia in the gold medal game.

Foster was proud of Armstrong but miffed that Smith chose four of his own players as Olympians, including one—Tom LaGarde—who didn't make any All-ACC teams. "Having one player [on the Olympic team] is good," Foster deadpanned. "Having four is better."

Buoyed by his decorated backcourt returning the next season, Foster remained frustrated over the close losses, particularly a two-point defeat to Carolina in Cameron after Duke led for most of the second half. Back on the recruiting trail, he sought a difference-maker in the middle and the next building block. He found one, thanks to what turned out to be an evaluation blunder by UNC.

Growing up in Monroe, Connecticut, Mike Gminski had always been big and a good athlete for a kid his size. At age 11 he was 6'1" and won the national punt, pass, and kick competition. Gminski was used to performing in big time venues, traveling to a New York Jets game at Shea Stadium and the PP&K Finals at the Pro Bowl in Los Angeles.

Gminski was a different youngster from most high school recruits. Very intelligent and in control of his life, the now 6'8" gentle giant had a plan. The summer before his sophomore year, he decided he would graduate in three years and took 14 classes between September and June. That summer he began visiting colleges, hoping to find one where he could continue his education and also play basketball.

He and his parents drove down to William & Mary, Davidson, North Carolina, South Carolina, and then flew to Notre Dame.

It was later that summer, while Gminski was attending basketball camp in Maryland, that Duke would enter the picture—quite by accident. While at camp he told one of his counselors, Duke basketball player Terry Chili—who happened to be working there—that he would be graduating early. On his return to Durham, Chili told Foster, and Duke turned up the recruiting process for the big man.

Monroe High School coach Bob Baroni was very protective of Gminski, whom both Baroni and the 16-year-old's parents knew could be a valuable asset to the right college program. Because Gminski was also an honor student, they figured a long list of schools would be after the kid who was still growing.

The first school Baroni invited to visit Gminski was the University of North Carolina. Smith sent his trusted associate and big man coach Bill Guthridge to Monroe. After watching practice Guthridge went back to Chapel Hill and reported to Smith that Gminski wasn't a good fit for Carolina because he was too slow afoot and a "non-aggressor" who would never be a dominant center. That was an assessment the Tar Heels lived to regret.

Gminski's first campus visit was to Duke, and that's all he needed to see. He was in Durham on a gorgeous October weekend with the fall foliage in its colorful glory and the soaring Gothic buildings almost calling his name. Gminski returned to Monroe, graduated early, and arrived at Duke as a peach-faced jolly giant in late August of 1976 with his blond, bushy hair making him seem even taller than 6'11". "The big kid is here," Foster said whimsically, "the big kid is here."

The second pillar was in place. In his rookie 1977 season at Duke—as just a 17-year old—Gminski averaged 15.3 points (eighth in the ACC) and 10.7 rebounds (second in the ACC) and was named the Blue Devils' second straight ACC Rookie of the Year, somehow tying with N.C. State's Hawkeye Whitney, who wasn't among the top 10 in either category for the now-middling Wolfpack. Sparnarkel finished third in scoring with a 19-point average, which was ahead of Ford, but he made only second team All-ACC because of another last-place finish in the league for Duke.

Just as demonstrative on the court as Spanarkel, Gminski grew into an early leader by exhorting his teammates to play with emotion and celebrate big baskets by high-fiving and hugging—much like Carolina had been doing for years. And the handsome Armstrong was turning into a matinee idol. Foster loved flash. Flash and good looks could put people in the seats for games, and Cameron was full again after a

10-game winning streak that included a road upset of No. 15-ranked Tennessee and its All-Americans, Bernard King and Ernie Grunfeld.

After a 10–1 start, however, the Blue Devils collapsed when Armstrong went down for the season with a broken wrist sustained while scoring 33 points in a win at Virginia. While limping to Foster's first overall winning record at Duke (14–13), the Blue Devils won only three of their last 13 games, finished with five consecutive defeats, and the ACC doormat suffered its third straight Thursday ouster from the ACC Tournament.

Meanwhile, the program they were trying to emulate and eventually catch finished first in the ACC, won the 1977 ACC Tournament, and went all the way to the Final Four in Atlanta before losing a heartbreaker to Marquette. The Tar Heels suffered a string of injuries over the last six weeks of the season, causing Smith to employ more of his Four Corners delay when they led late in games. It was a strategy Foster abhorred and literally could not watch.

He and his assistants were recruiting in Washington, D.C., and decided to take in the NCAA East regional championship game in College Park, Maryland, where UNC was picked to lose because Ford had been injured late in the Sweet 16 win against Notre Dame and could not go against 13th-ranked Kentucky (the team Duke would face for the national championship one year later). Holding a small lead early in the second half, Smith called for the Four Corners with senior John Kuester in the middle in place of Ford. A running game had turned into cat-and-mouse contest, so Foster and his aides got up and left Cole Field House. The Tar Heels hung on to beat the Wildcats of coach Joe B. Hall 79–72 with Kuester winning MVP of the regional.

The following weekend at the Final Four, where the college coaches held their annual convention, Carolina upset fourth-ranked UNLV by again using Four Corners for most of the second half. UNC freshman Mike O'Koren, a high school teammate of Spanarkel who had picked the Tar Heels over Duke and Notre Dame, scored 31 points mostly on backdoor passes from Ford, who was playing with a sore right elbow that inhibited his shooting. When Carolina pulled the ball out midway through the second half of the national championship game against Marquette, Foster again left the arena and missed the Tar Heels losing to the Warriors when Smith's ploy finally backfired.

Although he never expected to play for the NCAA title so soon, Foster's confidence was growing with his continued recruiting success. Bob Bender, a former Mr. Basketball in Indiana, had sat on the bench for the Hoosiers' undefeated 1976 National Champions and transferred to Duke in the middle of the 1977 season. John Harrell, another talented guard from North Carolina Central in Durham, had also transferred to Duke. Foster would have both of them for the 1978 ACC season and set his sights on two forwards who would complete what amounted to a dream lineup for the Blue Devils.

• • •

With his leader in Spanarkel, his big man in Gminski, and two point guards in hand, Foster knew his next signings had to be special to truly challenge North Carolina, State, and Maryland in the ACC. If the Blue Devils could do that, they would automatically be national contenders. It was essentially a plan to go from worst to first that nearly worked.

With the help of his camp partner Litwack, Foster had an in with the best prep player from Philadelphia since Wilt Chamberlain. Gene Banks, a 6'8" man-child, not only had game but enough bravado to put the love of an entire city, not to mention a college basketball program, on his broad shoulders. His coach at West Philadelphia High School, Joey Goldenberg, said he would "take Banks over any high school player I've ever seen except Chamberlain, and that would be a toss-up."

Better known as "Tinkerbell" for how he seemingly floated above the court when taking off for one of his slam dunks, Banks was courted by most major schools in the country—from the Carolinas to UCLA—and enjoyed every minute of the attention. More than 200 schools wanted Banks, who had the charm to make them all think they were in it with Tinkerbell.

Using Goldenberg, who had played for Litwack at Temple, Foster worked tirelessly to land a recruit to match any signed by Bubas in the 1960s. On the surface, though, it seemed improbable that such a sought-after star who averaged 20 points and 20 rebounds for his inner-city high school would consider a school that was academically rigorous, socially conservative, and overwhelmingly white. Fortunately for Foster, Banks liked challenges.

With official visits limited by the NCAA, Foster was one of the best at talking with players on the phone. He used those conversations in many different ways. On one of his early trips to see Banks play, he ended up walking right past "Tink" at the end of the game and not saying a word. Banks was offended, telling his mother later that evening that despite playing a great game the coach from Duke "must not like me" because he didn't say a word.

Foster called that night and coyly told Banks he wasn't sure his game was good enough to play at Duke. He was gambling that Banks wanted to be the final piece of the puzzle that would transform the Blue Devils from losers to winners, and sure enough, the confident player now wanted to show Foster he could be that agent of change. In later years the two laughed about the conversation, but it did exactly what Foster had intended and put Duke squarely on the mind of the kid from West Philly.

Typical of Banks' penchant for showmanship, he did not wait until the April 7 date to publicize he was signing with Duke; he wrote a letter to the Philadelphia newspaper *The Evening Bulletin* to announce his intentions in his own words. He said he had met many people at Duke "with realness," and that's what made him want to be a part of the Blue Devils. "If things go well and I have God's grace," Banks said, "I think I can finish up as the most versatile, complete, exciting, flamboyant, hustling player that Duke has ever had," he said. "I really felt that once the smoke cleared, I could make them a national power,"

Going public also placed the Duke admissions office in a dilemma. Although Banks was a good student, his SATs were far below the university's standards. But how could it reject a kid who publicly committed and could complete Foster's rebuilding program? With Foster making it clear that denying Banks admission would be about his last straw at Duke, the university made an exception that turned out to be a brilliant move because Banks not only graduated on time but was a commencement speaker his senior year.

Indeed, Duke had never had a player quite like Gene Banks. He was a legend in high school basketball, having played and won one of the most talked about games in history, when his nationally No.

1-ranked West Philly Speedboys took on third-ranked Brasher out of Pittsburgh with future Pitt Panther and NFL great Sam Clancy at center. Banks scored 32 points and pulled down 19 rebounds, completely outplaying Clancy in the 69–65 victory.

In front of 7,500 fans at The Palestra in his final high school game after he had already won the tournament MVP and his team won the city championship for the third straight year, Banks exited the playing floor to a roaring ovation and tossed roses to the crowd to show his appreciation—something Duke fans would become familiar with four years later.

But even with all his candor and confidence, Banks was a team player. He could be just as effective dishing out assists and pulling down rebounds as he was scoring. During his college career, both Foster and his coach for one season, Krzyzewski, would implore Banks to be less unselfish and shoot the ball more.

Banks became the third pillar and the addition of players like Kenny Dennard, Bender, and Harrell completed the transformation. Dennard, a 6'7" forward from King, North Carolina, was the diamond in this rough recruiting class Foster coveted. Like so many other kids growing up in North Carolina, Dennard had wanted to attend UNC but was not offered a scholarship by Smith because Carolina already had O'Koren, who played the same position.

Dennard added another level of cockiness to the Blue Devils. He played hard and partied hard, often doing the latter on Franklin Street in Chapel Hill because Durham did not have a main drag where students hung out at that time.

The changes Duke was making were duly noticed by UNC. "Duke getting Banks instead of Carolina was a breakthrough," Smith said, "like in 1964 when we out-recruited them for Larry Miller."

Now all the Blue Devils had to do was win. They had the attention of the ACC but had to prove they could put these pieces together and play as a team. They opened the 1977–78 season 14–2 but were still unranked before the January 14 visit from the No. 2 Tar Heels and Ford, a senior All-American and National Player of the Year candidate.

Duke had already lost to Carolina in the Big Four Tournament, but that was before Bender was eligible and the team had meshed on the court. Off the court they were loose and easy as if they knew something special was about to happen.

Banks and Dennard loved to walk around the locker room naked before games, posing in front of the mirror, while Banks picked the music that blared over the speakers. Spanarkel often sat by himself, planning to combine his knowledge of the opponent with his craftiness on the court. There was a clear dichotomy between the stars and the role players who knew they would not get a lot of minutes.

When they left the locker room before each game, the different makeup of individuals evaporated into thin air. Away from the locker room, away from the coaches, just feet from the court they were about to perform on, they huddled together and listened to the one voice of their leader Spanarkel and came together as a team.

Three years into college basketball, he still did not look like a typical all-around athlete, but he was. He was so pigeon-toed that Banks swore he could hear his knees clicking together on fast breaks. One of the reasons Spanarkel went to Duke was because Foster promised him he could play baseball. In his freshman season, he pitched a one-hitter against Clemson but soon decided he had a better chance of making the NBA than the major leagues.

While he was an outstanding basketball player, Spanarkel also brought a hard-earned swagger to this team. Call it toughness, confidence, or cockiness, Spanarks had it. And he had it both on and off the court. He drove a beat-up Volkswagen that he picked up after getting rid of his Nissan 280Z because the payments were too high. He worked one summer as a stagehand in New York on the soap opera *Ryan's Hope* and, even though he wound end up marrying his high school sweetheart, he had the attention of many a Duke coed throughout his career.

He never joined a fraternity at Duke because Spanarkel was a one-man fraternity. Wherever he showed up, it made that gathering an *event*.

At the annual *Playboy* All-American party and photo shoot at Lake Tahoe before his senior year, Spanarkel and Michigan State's Earvin "Magic" Johnson took to heart the offering of complimentary room service if any of the athletes needed something. They ordered cases of beer, a dozen jumbo sandwiches, and invited everyone to a party for which Duke and Michigan State wound up splitting the bill later that year.

As Duke was ready to conquer the world, this was exactly what Foster had been looking for. He had his front man, a tough, I-can't-believe-he-just-did-that kind of player who was everyman's beer-drinking-down-to-earth buddy and loved by the fans, media, and the students. Sparnarkel was your older brother, younger brother, the son you wish you had, a guy you couldn't help but pull for. Except if you cheered for the Tar Heels.

Early in one Duke-Carolina game, the nasty side of Spanarkel came out when he fouled his old buddy O'Koren on a fast break and ran into a male UNC cheerleader, who shoved Spanarkel out of the way following the contact. Before returning to the court, Spanarkel turned and said to the cheerleader: "If you touch me one more time, I will shove your ass into your megaphone."

It occurred near the Duke bench, and Foster grinned with his hand over his mouth. That toughness was exactly what he needed to win in this conference. There stood his captain of the ship that would lead Duke basketball back to national prominence.

Foster was right. Spanarkel's two-year reign as captain saw Duke return to the top 20 in the national rankings, play for an NCAA title, and become one of the most beloved teams in the nation, essentially telling the Tar Heels to move over.

Carolina had just played for the 1977 National Championship. Duke lost that first meeting to Ford and the Tar Heels the next season but came back on January 14, 1978, to break the eight-game losing streak in Cameron Indoor Stadium with a resounding 92–84 victory. It was a touché moment for Foster, whose team got the lead in the second half and refused to stall the game away by breaking the UNC press and going all the way to the basket for layups and dunks.

Though Ford's spectacular performance in his final home game, rallying the Tar Heels with 34 points, allowed the Tar Heels to defend their ACC regular season championship, Duke came back to win its first ACC Tournament in 12 years and advance all the way to the Final Four in St. Louis before losing to Kentucky 94–88 in Monday night's championship game, when Banks had 22 points and eight rebounds, Spanarkel had 21 points, Gminski had 20 and 12 rebounds, and

Dennard had 10 and eight. Led by Jack "Goose" Givens' 41 points and Rick Robey's 20, who combined for 26-for-38 from the floor, the Wildcats shot 57 percent.

Yet, for Duke, one great season does not a program make.

When the Blue Devils returned from St. Louis, Foster went to his office and picked up a copy of the *Durham Morning Herald* and flipped it across the room in anger. Just two days after Duke had played for the national championship, the lead headline was about North Carolina recruiting and not a follow-up story on the Blue Devils. That was at the bottom of the sports page.

The national respect had resurfaced for the Blue Devils, but they still stood in the shadow of a Carolina basketball program they had beaten just twice in the last 19 meetings. It was time to earn respect from the Tar Heels who had not considered them their archrival for years.

• • •

Duke had everyone back for the 1978–79 season and added freshman Vince Taylor from Lexington, Kentucky, a 6'5" scorer with size and blazing speed. Taylor had grown up wanting to go to Kentucky, but the Wildcats were limited to one scholarship due to recruiting violations under coach Eddie Sutton, and Taylor did not get it. So he signed with Duke.

The Blue Devils made the cover of *Sports Illustrated* as the magazine's pick to win the national championship. Obviously, with Ford having graduated, Duke was also the overwhelming pick to win the ACC regular season race for the first time since 1966.

After beating the Tar Heels by 10 points in the Big Four Tournament and running off to a 4–0 start, No. 1-ranked Duke faced the first of what would become commonplace during the new season. Teams began to stall to pull the Blue Devils out of their beefy zone defense and make them play man-to-man.

LaSalle, whose coach Paul Westhead was known for his fast-paced offense, opened the December 5 game at Cameron by sitting on the ball. With Duke refusing to budge from under the basket, the Explorers led 4–0 with six minutes to play in the first half before the Blue Devils finally scored. They came out of the zone late in the first half and trailed 12–6.

Matching LaSalle's tenacity in the second half, Duke won 62–42 behind 32 points by Banks. He wasn't about to lose to his old home-town team, one of Philadelphia's so-called Big Five, but nevertheless how LaSalle played became a blueprint for future opponents game-planning against the nation's top-ranked team. That was never more evident than when they traveled to Clemson, the ACC's fifth-place team, on February 21.

In an earlier meeting in Durham, Duke had easily handled the Tigers 73–54, crushing them on the backboards 43–26 and hold-ing them to 37 percent shooting behind that intimidating 2-3 zone. Clemson's coach was also named Bill Foster (Duke had kiddingly asked that all mail to its coach be addressed to "the Real Bill Foster"), and Clemson's Foster wasn't about to let another blowout happen in Littlejohn Coliseum. "Before the game in Durham earlier this year, we had a gameplan as big as the Bible," the Clemson coach said. "We knew their favorite foods, who their girlfriends were. This time our game plan was two words: play smart."

The Tigers played keep-away, bringing the Blue Devils out of their zone defense and frustrating them early. The pressure of the season looked to be taking its toll on Duke's head coach and the team captain. "The Real Bill Foster" was coaching with a heavy heart, having lost his mother and was scheduled travel to her funeral the next day in Pennsylvania. Understandably, he wasn't at the top of his game. Neither was Spanarkel.

With 6:34 remaining in the first half, Spanarkel was called for a charge on Clemson's Billy Williams. Foster came flying off the bench with his hands around his neck to signify that official Dan Woolridge had "choked" on the call. He was slapped with a technical, and sud-denly the Blue Devils were down 18–10.

Twenty-seven seconds later, Spanarkel was called for a foul by offi-cial Joe Farris while Williams was shooting. As he lay sprawled out on the court, Spanarkel slammed both hands on the floor in frustra-tion. Bam! Another technical and now the Tigers had a 25–10 lead. The shaken Blue Devils would go on to lose 70–49 with a season low offensive output.

The loss gave Duke an 8–3 ACC record compared to 9–2 for Carolina, which had improved dramatically as the season progressed and was on a six-game winning streak. The Blue Devils would now have to beat the Tar Heels on Spanarkel's Senior Night to tie them for first place in the ACC standings and force a draw for the top seed and first-round bye in the ACC Tournament the following week.

The small locker room at Littlejohn looked like a morgue with players lying on the floor and holding their head in their hands, not sure exactly how such a blowout had happened for a team that began the season confident of winning every game on the schedule. Despair turned into anger, as a couple of players ripped down stall doors in the restroom area.

The inconsistency of this team was a worry for Foster, as he headed for his mother's funeral. He felt guilty about having to return so quickly to get ready for Carolina on Saturday night, but his captain was holding things together back in Durham. The surprising Tar Heels had won the earlier game in Chapel Hill, which might have contributed to Duke looking ahead and a poor performance at Clemson. "This game's been building up like a snowball, and everybody will be geared up for it," Spanarkel said. "We'll be ready for Saturday."

• • •

February 24, 1979, was Senior Night at Duke as the Blue Devils readied to face North Carolina. It was much more than just a special day. It was the final game in Cameron Indoor Stadium for Spanarkel, the player who best personified the resurgence of Duke basketball in the 1970s, the motherfucker Foster needed to begin it all.

On February 20, prior to that Senior Night, Duke president Terry Sanford sent a letter to the entire student body to try and get them to calm down their antics in Cameron. The "Cameron Crazies" were in their infancy at this point but were a very rowdy and supportive group. They, however, used the word "bullshit" maybe a little too much, their signs could sometimes be off-color, and they were fueled by plenty of alcohol. "Since the middle of December I have received literally hundreds of letters from friends of Duke University who are extremely distressed by 'the language and conduct of students at basketball game,'" wrote Sanford. "I am distressed that this criticism is justified." He continued in the letter to remind the students that "drinking whiskey in the stadium is illegal."

Duke University
Durham
North Carolina 27706

Office of the President

February 20, 1979

To Undergraduate Students at Duke University:

Since the middle of December I have received literally hundreds of letters from friends of Duke University who are extremely distressed by "the language and conduct of students at basketball games." I am distressed that this criticism is justified.

This reaction, represented by this many letters, more than I have received on any other issue since I have been at Duke, obviously represents a far larger group of people who share the same opinion. There is no doubt in my mind that this conduct has severely damaged Duke University in its community relationships, its Alumni relationships, and its ability to raise money.

More important, beyond the external reactions, we simply should not be doing these things, just because decent people, in my own personal opinion, do not engage in obscenities or even acts of bad taste in public. Surely there is both a sense of pride and a sense of personal honor to be observed by people in an institution dedicated to promoting the civilizing influences of society. In my final opinion, it is not what others think of us that is significant, it is what we think of ourselves.

I had hoped that I would not have to write this letter, although perhaps I should have attempted to do something in December. Jim Spanarkel and Coach Foster, who mean so much to Duke, spoke to you, but apparently their words had only a very temporary effect.

I now add the official concern, and ask you, as Duke students, to change your behavior on your own. Drinking whiskey in the stadium is illegal, and a word of warning ought to be sufficient on that. That is not what people are complaining about. They are complaining about what they consider obscenities, statements that are in bad taste, and unnecessary crudeness. It has been contended by some students that vulgarities, obscenities, and crudeness by students is necessary to help win games. That, if you stop to think about it, is an insult to our team.

We can have plenty of fun, kid others to whatever degree we want to, but there is a line that decent people simply have to draw. I contend that a Duke student has enough sense to know where to draw the line. I am counting on you to draw it.

We have only one home game left, but we hope to have many post season games, so now is the time to start.

I thank you.

Sincerely,

Terry Sanford

On this cold, rainy evening, Cameron was warm and very much alive, jammed to the rafters. Although they cheered loudly for the four other seniors—Steve Gray, Scott Goetsch, Harold Morrison, and Rob Hardy—the roar for No. 34 was deafening. The fans not only knew Spanarkel's records and accomplishments, but they also loved him for placing heart and soul into this program to turn it around.

UNC's Smith knew this might happen and decided to take that emotion and enthusiasm out of the building. He always regarded winning on an opponent's Senior Night against a good team (and especially with an outstanding senior or two) as one of the hardest tasks in coaching. The year before, his banged-up team rode senior Phil Ford's 34 points to an upset of the Blue Devils, who would go on to win the ACC Tournament and advance to the NCAA Championship Game.

Smith and his staff worried about the normally raucous Cameron crowd but more so about Duke's imposing 2-3 zone anchored by Gminski, the leading candidate for ACC Player of the Year and the extra emotion because Spanarkel—the self-made star—was playing his last home game in a Duke uniform. They decided to copy Clemson, and Smith told his team just before boarding the bus for Durham that they would play Four Corners on their first possession and see if the Blue Devils came out to chase.

Not everyone loved the idea. These were competitive basketball players who had already defeated Duke in Chapel Hill and wanted to silence the Cameron crowd by outscoring their team, not stall the game away. But Smith was the boss, and as the Tar Heels huddled around him before the opening tip, he said simply, "Okay, you know what to do."

After Vince Taylor scored on a follow under the basket to give Duke a 2–0 lead, Carolina crossed the time line and point guard Dave Colescott held the ball as his teammates went to the four corners of the front court. The only passes Colescott made were to Dudley Bradley and Al Wood out near the center line. The crowd hooted, but after what happened at Littlejohn, Duke was having none of it and sat back in its customary defense. The Tar Heels played keep-away for 11 minutes before attempting a shot.

Finally, Carolina moved the ball close enough for junior center Rich Yonakor to shoot from the left baseline, and he missed the rim by at least a foot. The Duke students immediately launched into an impromptu cheer, which would become famous, chanting "Air ball! Air ball!"

On the Duke bench, Foster wasn't about to give in to Smith. He had seen enough of this stall tactic at Clemson and against earlier opponents. He was going to stay in the zone, especially with the lead. "A 2–0 win is as good as winning, scoring 90 points," he said after the game.

"We didn't want to play against their zone," Smith countered. Of the rash of criticism that followed, he said only, "What I did was so sound."

Smith sat on the bench, legs crossed, hoping Duke would come out and chase. Foster's assistants kept asking him what to do, but after losing by 21 at Clemson, he knew exactly what to do: nothing and make Smith play against his defense. "We thought the frustration of the Clemson game would make them chase us," Smith explained. "But they didn't choose to chase. The 2-3 zone is the strength of their defense, and we wanted them to play man-to-man."

"This was before the students were called the Cameron Crazies, but they were jumping and doing crazy things," Dennard recalled later. "We did jumping jacks, anything to stay active while Carolina held the ball. They had to advance the ball forward every few seconds to retain possession, so we had to stay ready. It was the weirdest half of basketball I have ever played."

What really ruined Smith's plan was Duke scoring first, meaning the Blue Devils did not have to come out of its zone, according to the rules in those days before the shot clock.

After Carolina had stalled away 11 minutes, Yonakor's air ball was converted into a three-point play by Gminski, and the Tar Heels, now trailing 5–0, sat on the ball until they turned it over with three minutes left in the half. This time Duke held the ball against a confused UNC team until Spanarkel hit a bank shot with three seconds left. Colescott's desperation heave missed everything, and the first half ended with the football score of 7–0. 7–0.

Carolina was 0–2 from the field with no rebounds. "It should have been 2–0 at the end of the first half or something like that," said Smith, who was roundly booed leaving the court. His team had gone an entire half without hitting the rim while Duke shot 3-for-3, and Yonakor's errant shot led to the creation of the now-iconic "air ball" cheer that is heard in every basketball gym.

"It didn't get weird until the last five minutes of the first half," Banks said after the game. "We didn't think they were afraid of us early on, but then we realized they were afraid of going against us the way we wanted to play them, and I felt a lot of pride. We suddenly knew we had a chance of shutting them out for a half and we had gained their respect. It was quiet in the locker room at halftime. It was hard to figure out what was going on; we were concerned with going through it for another half, so we prepared for Carolina to keep holding the ball. We knew what to do if they came out and wanted to play."

Devil's Head and Other Pranks

The student bodies at Duke and Carolina are both a major part of the rivalry. The Cameron Crazies are well known for their antics during games. Their creative enthusiasm and support during games has become legendary. There is a reason the Duke student body receives all the accolades—they cheer for one of the only four big time basketball programs where the TV cameras are located behind the benches shooting directly at the student section.

That camera angle at Duke has to do with where 75-year-old Cameron was built—against a massive hill of dirt and where TV trucks can get on only one side of the building to drop cables in and broadcast the game. So the Duke blue students, dressed in crazy attire, painted up with blue faces and bodies, get all the publicity, while down the road in Chapel Hill the Dean Dome is known to have a "wine and cheese crowd."

In 1991 Florida State guard Sam Cassell dubbed the Carolina crowd with this honor. "It's not a Duke kind of crowd. It's more like a cheese-and-wine-crowd, kind of laid back," Cassell said.

When Duke plays at Carolina, the Blue Devils never see or hear from the wine and cheese. Whether in the old Carmichael Auditorium or the Dean Smith Center, the place is always rocking when the Dukies come to town.

In 1978 when Phil Ford for Carolina hit a long-range shot at the end of the first half, the roar was so loud and raucous that the plastic covers for the lights on the catwalk press box fell on the writers.

Even before the Cameron Crazies became a national phenomenon, the student bodies have always pulled pranks on each other. One of the best took place prior to the February 13, 2013 game.

The head of Duke's Blue Devil mascot was stolen and placed on a pole—*Game of Thrones* style—above a University of North Carolina campus store prior to the showdown in Durham.

A few days earlier, the Blue Devil and Carolina Ram mascot had been in Durham to shoot a video promo for ESPN. Following the shoot, the Blue Devil mascot, showing professional courtesy, took the Ram mascot down to his secret room in the basement of Card Gymnasium to change clothes. This is where the Blue Devil stores his uniform and alternate head, which not coincidentally was stolen in the next two days.

In 2012 Duke students dressed Chapel Hill's famous "Silent Sam" statue of a Confederate soldier in Blue Devil gear the week before the game. Tar Heel fans have pulled some pretty good pranks themselves. In 1992, following the Blue Devils' national championship and several months prior to the Duke-Carolina game in Chapel Hill, a ball and net from the 1991 Final Four went missing out of the trophy case in Cameron Indoor Stadium. The day after Carolina's 75–73 victory, the ball and net showed up very neatly displayed at the Old Well on the UNC campus.

Duke fans believe that the greatest prank ever pulled off in this rivalry was in 1998 when four students stole Michael Jordan's retired jersey from the rafters of the Dean Dome and hung it inside of Cameron Indoor Stadium. How they got in there—and up there—has remained a secret of the rivalry.

A group of Carolina students in the Robertson Scholarship program pulled off the most prolonged prank in the rivalry in 2006. Robertson Scholars are accepted to either Duke or UNC but take classes on the other campus throughout the year. This time 18 scholarly Tar Heel brainiacs infiltrated tents in the famous Krzyzewskiville village before the game in Cameron. They camped out among "fellow Dukies" for weeks, pretending to be with them.

When game night arrived and all the tent dwellers lined up to get the best seats in the best camera angle for national TV, the Robertson traitors instead ran to the opposite side of the court, took seats directly behind the visitors' bench, and pulled off their Duke shirts to reveal bodies painted in light blue. Duke complained to the Robertson Scholarship office and pledged tighter security at Krzyzewskiville in years to come.

The Tar Heels abandoned their stall strategy in the second half, which was played at a normal pace. And it was an even 40–40 over the last 20 minutes. Duke's seven first half points made the difference and enabled Spanarkel and his classmates to go home happy on Senior Night with the 47–40 victory.

Spanarkel scored 17 points, 15 in the second half as he hit on 8-of-9 shots from the field. The students hoisted him on their shoulders, setting him down so he could run off the court with his index finger extended above his head.

While most people have a recollection of the 7–0 halftime lead and that Spanarkel did not lose his senior game, the incident that further inflamed the Duke-Carolina rivalry happened with 30 seconds left when Gminski was fouled on a rebound by the Tar Heels' Wood.

Trying to get Wood off his back, Gminski swung his elbows and caught the Tar Heel sophomore on the side of the face. Wood went down, and players from both teams began shoving each other and squaring off. O'Koren, who was an offseason friend of Gminski's, headed right for the Duke big man. With his arms spread, O'Koren basically pleaded, *Why Mike? Why Mike?* Gminski stood there like a statue with the ball still clutched in his hands, holding his ground.

Smith headed out to check on his fallen player, who was actually unharmed and wanted to get up. Smith was pointing at Gminski while— out of the side of his mouth—telling Wood to "stay down, stay down." "You knew what we were trying to do!" Smith said, looking up at Gminski. "We were trying to stop the clock. There is no need to play like that."

Gminski said back to the Carolina coach, "They weren't calling any fouls. I was just trying to protect myself."

Spanarkel went over to O'Koren and reminded him that Gminski wouldn't have done it on purpose. He wasn't that kind of player. A non-aggressor, UNC's Bill Guthridge had called Gminski during recruiting.

In fact, Gminski never fouled out of a college game but was ejected from this one by referee Gerald Donaghy, who slapped him with a flagrant foul. The Cameron crowd hooted until the final seconds ran off the clock and booed the Tar Heels as they left the court, especially Smith.

After the game Foster said, "Well, you've gotta come down with the rebound. They said the elbow was flagrant. We had a freaky thing like that happen with Dave Colescott over at Carolina this year."

In the earlier game in Chapel Hill, Colescott ran into Gminski's elbow with his eye, causing Colescott to wear goggles for the next few weeks.

Now the so-called non-aggressor had just knocked a Tar Heel on his ass, led his Duke squad to another victory over Carolina, and brought the rivalry right back where it belonged. Whereas both factions respected each other, now there were stronger emotions involved. The familiar words of Foster rang true, "If we weren't bothering them, they wouldn't hate us."

But it was Foster who seemed bothered on his radio show Monday evening, when he said of the first-half tactics employed by Smith: "If this is what's happened to the game, maybe it's time for me to do something else."

Earlier that day, Smith had called O'Koren into his office over remarks his star forward had made to reporters after the game, saying that he didn't know why they stalled and he would have preferred to play. Smith still smoked at the time, and years later O'Koren joked about it being like God speaking to him from behind a cloud. "I'll coach; you play," Smith said to O'Koren.

They would all have another chance to do it again, the following Saturday night in the championship game of the 1979 ACC Tournament.

Chapter 5

Black and Blue Sunday

On Sunday morning, March 11, Duke Sports Information Director Tom Mickle and his assistant (me) arrived early in Raleigh for a shoot-around with the team prior to the NCAA Tournament double-header between North Carolina and Pennsylvania in the first game and Duke and St. John's in the second game.

Upon entering Reynolds Coliseum, we ran into Dick Herbert, the retired sports editor of The Raleigh News and Observer and a Duke graduate. Herbert told us, "Your big aircraft carrier is sick."

I didn't believe him. I had been with Mike Gminski and the team for dinner the night before and hung around with them at the hotel. I left to go back to Durham and spend the night at home as they left to get some pizza before they went to bed.

Mickle and I quickly headed down the steps to the coliseum basement and found the designated Duke locker room. We walked in and saw Gminski in the bathroom throwing up into the toilet."What happened?" I asked.

"Must have been something I ate last night," he explained very weakly.

"What did you eat last night?" I said.

"Just a pizza at Brother's," he said.

Jim Spanarkel, in his New Jersey way, quickly added, "I think he ate a whole Sicilian pizza."

—JM

March 11, 1979, will live in infamy for North Carolina, Duke, and ACC basketball. It was the day the unthinkable happened.

Both ranked among the top six teams in the nation and with a good chance to win a national title, the Blue Devils and Tar Heels lost in back-to-back games on the same afternoon in the familiar if usually hostile confines of Reynolds Coliseum on the campus of North Carolina State University. It was a day that began with such nervous energy. Two rival fan bases had converged on an arena where they hadn't been together since the last ACC Tournament there in 1966, hoping for a victory for their team and a defeat for the other but knowing the probability that both would advance to the Greensboro Coliseum and a possible fifth meeting in a season that was already filled with controversy and close games.

The rivalry was again fully ablaze after Duke had broken an eight-game losing streak to UNC the previous season and advanced to the 1978 National Championship Game while the Tar Heels were long gone from the NCAA Tournament, and the blue bloods had split their last six meetings. And what games they were.

The Blue Devils had proclaimed their return and snapped a five-game drought at the hands of Carolina in Cameron Indoor Stadium with a resounding 92–84 victory after which delirious Duke students had actually cut down the nets.

The Tar Heels were reeling and beaten up for the rematch in Chapel Hill, but the magic of Phil Ford's last home game resulted in a UNC victory when Duke was clearly favored and had become the better team. Crying during 1978 Senior Day ceremonies and with his mother, Mabel, watching in person for one of the few times in his college career, Ford had somehow managed to score 34 points with a sprained left wrist that had kept him out of the game at N.C. State two days before. He hit 13-of-19 from the floor as the Tar Heels won 87–83. "He proved why he's the greatest guard in America," said teammate Mike O'Koren.

The teams missed a chance to meet in the 1978 ACC Tournament when Carolina lost to Wake Forest, and Duke downed the Demon Deacons to win the school's first ACC championship in 12 years.

All of those Blue Devils were in grade school when Duke last played in the 1966 NCAA Tournament, and they barely survived a last-second shot by Rhode Island during the 1978 NCAA Tournament's second-round game at the old Charlotte Coliseum. But with confidence buoyed by cocky freshmen Gene Banks and Kenny Dennard and gentle giant Mike Gminski in the middle, they rolled through the East regional against Penn and Villanova in which the daring Dennard punctuated Duke's first trip back to the Final Four in 12 years with a reverse dunk on national television that became one of the iconic photos in Duke history.

Meanwhile, the Tar Heels, who had been to two Final Fours in the 1970s and won three ACC championships, went home, licking their wounds after getting bounced by Bill Cartwright and San Francisco in the West regional. With Ford graduating and Duke slated to have everyone back, it gave Bill Foster's program so much faith in the future that not even a heartbreaking loss to Kentucky in the 1978 National Championship in St. Louis could shake the Blue Devils' newfound conviction.

Smith nearly gave Duke even more reason for euphoria. In October he was at the World Series and watched the opening game at Yankee Stadium from George Steinbrenner's box. The next morning Smith met with Sonny Werblin, who had taken over as president of Madison Square Garden and the New York Knicks. Werblin wanted to fire Knicks coach Willis Reed and was ready to make Smith an offer he (almost) couldn't refuse, much like how he had signed rookie Joe Namath out of Alabama when he owned the New York Jets in the 1960s. Werblin told Smith he could name his price to leave Chapel Hill and coach the Knicks in a city Smith had come to know well from recruiting there for almost 20 years.

Smith considered Werblin's proposal and decided to stay at UNC. It was the second serious offer he had received in less than two years after UCLA athletic director J.D. Morgan asked him to coach the Bruins in 1977. Along with his longtime chief assistant Bill Guthridge, who had turned down the Penn State, Auburn, and LSU head coaching jobs, Smith made up his mind that Carolina would be where he worked and lived for the long run. With Ford gone he had a major retooling job with his team and serious competition from eight miles away that the Tar Heels hadn't had in more than 10 years.

After all, Duke began the new season still floating on cloud nine from the incredible 1978 run, losing to a Superman outing by Kentucky's Jack "Goose" Givens who made the cover of *Sports Illustrated* that called him the "Golden Goose." Duke's wonderful ride from worst in the ACC to almost first in the nation was captured in alumnus John Feinstein's book *Forever's Team*.

With all five starters returning, the Blue Devils were the unanimous choice in both preseason polls as the No. 1 team in the country.

Heading into the 1979 season, which could end in Salt Lake City on the same court where Foster had coached Utah before bolting for Duke, the carryover momentum made it seem like Duke at long last had found the magic bullet. When asked about the possibility of going back to Utah to again play for the NCAA title, longtime Foster assistant coach Bob Wenzel said smugly, almost as if it were a given, "We'll be there. We'll be there."

And who doubted him when the Blue Devils handled sixth-ranked N.C. State and a rebuilding No. 14 Carolina team in the Big Four Tournament in Greensboro? The still Cinderella Blue Devils seemed like they would be around forever.

But the ride suddenly got a lot bumpier. Almost inexplicably, Duke blew large second-half leads to both unranked Ohio State and St. John's in the Garden, lost its No. 1 ranking, and found out the following Monday that a *Sports Illustrated* story on Sparnarkel, Gminski, and Banks as the three best players in the country at their positions had been scrapped after the Blue Devils fell from the unbeatens in the Big Apple embarrassment.

They also found themselves four spots below surging and third-ranked UNC for the first home-and-home game in Chapel Hill on January 13. The Tar Heels, now seemingly a starless team without Ford, had found their way behind sophomore Al Wood, junior Mike O'Koren, and senior Dudley Bradley, who had been dubbed the "Secretary of Defense" for his stellar play on that end of the court. They defeated a be-Deviled Duke team 74–68 to claim first place in the ACC, which they would hold until the last weekend of the regular season.

The game was supposed to clear up a number of questions about which team would take charge of the ACC. *Durham Morning Herald* columnist Keith Drum had some other answers: "One, Duke won't go undefeated in the Atlantic Coast Conference because, two, the Blue Devils can't win in Carmichael Auditorium where they have lost 13 straight and, three, the Tar Heels aren't about to give up their regular season championship without a fight."

Duke turned the ball over 21 times, compared to 14 for Carolina, and left Chapel Hill lamenting their own errors and bitching about the officiating.

Duke and Carolina weren't just talented teams. They had players who knew how to get the calls and manipulate the game to their advantage. "This league could go Hollywood pretty easy," said Dennard, who claimed his reputation as an aggressive defender hurt him with the referees.

Dennard was called twice for fouls on attempted steals against UNC's Wood, who was casually dribbling the ball in the four corners set to milk the clock and hold the late lead. "The first one was a foul, but the second one—and another foul just like it in the first half— were clean," Dennard said. "Everybody's a pretty good faker in this league, and the refs go for a lot of them. The refs hate me. I know that. They won't even let me talk to them on the court. They tell me to hush because I'm known as an aggressive player."

Dennard did admit that Carolina's defense and his own team's inconsistent offense were the key factors in the game, not the officiating. "They got the shaft as much as we did," he said. "It's just hard to play above it most of the time. The refs have so much control. I blocked Al Wood when they called a charge on him. I admit it. I was moving along with him, but in a game like this, I figured it was worth a try. They missed so many other calls. I thought they might miss that one, too."

"When a game is as loosely called as this one was, I just try to go the boards like a maniac," said Carolina's O'Koren. "Nine out of 10 times, you're going to get a piece of the ball or get in a good fight. You don't worry a lot about fouls."

While the game itself may not have been an artistic masterpiece, it was a tense and fiercely fought contest between what would be the two best teams in the ACC.

Carolina led by nine points twice in the second half and was still ahead by eight with 90 seconds to go in the game. A four-point play by Bob Bender gave Duke another chance. After Duke cut the deficit to three at 69–66, UNC freshman Jimmy Black, seeing significant time in his first Duke-Carolina game, hit two free throws with 38 seconds left and then added another to seal the six-point victory.

The loss was tough for the Blue Devils, who had dreams of breaking the long losing streak in Carmichael that dated back to 1966. "It's really disappointing to lose here," senior Jim Spanarkel said. "Not just because I've never won here, but because we wanted it so badly for our season."

Wins over No. 14 N.C. State in Raleigh on Super Bowl Sunday and No. 13 Marquette on national television—the day NBC's Al McGuire first called Gminski the "Aircraft Carrier"—put Duke back on a seven-game winning streak, but clearly the *joie de vivre* that had characterized this team was missing. Dennard personified the difference, partying through the summer (much of it in Chapel Hill) and never getting into the same shape he was as a precocious freshman. His stats, which dropped drastically in every category from scoring and rebounding averages to field goal and foul shooting percentages, reflected it. Whatever he was doing off the court, he was having less fun on it. But—consistent with his mischievous personality—the overweight, less-conditioned Dennard managed to set the Duke single-game steals record of 11 against Maryland that still stands.

Smith knew his program was no longer superior and needed something special to beat the Blue Devils in their own house on Spanarkel's Senior Night: the stall-inflicted scoreless first half that backfired into a 47–40 loss in the last game of the regular season and a tie for first with Duke, heading into the 1979 ACC Tournament in Greensboro.

The ACC had not replaced South Carolina and remained a seven-school league (very strange in today's expansion to 15 and counting), so the regular season champion drew a first-round bye in the tournament. The Duke-Carolina deadlock would be broken by a draw at the ACC offices in Greensboro, and WCHL radio of Chapel Hill actually covered it live by peeking in the window and watching assistant commissioner Marvin "Skeeter" Francis pull a slip of paper out of a bowl to decide which team would automatically advance to the ACC semi-finals that weekend in the Coliseum only a few miles away.

After Francis announced the results of the most famous draw in ACC history, the Chapel Hill radio audience heard one Tar Heel fan scream into the microphone, "We got the bye!" as he ran back to his car. Foster, already so flummoxed by Smith's strategy that almost ruined the senior night for his self-made star Spanarkel, could only say of having one more game in the tournament than the Tar Heels, "Our guys like to play. It makes no difference to us."

Among the ACC's funniest and most accessible coaches when his Blue Devils were lovable losers his first three years in Durham, Foster now found himself feeling the pressure of being ranked and called the equal of Carolina. His quips and one-liners were fewer, and he was secretly considering taking another job in an easier and less competitive climate. Looking at Foster's history, he had never stayed in one place more than eight years—usually less.

Foster was so emotional that his assistant coaches and support staff had to find the happy medium between watching out for him and staying out of his way. Several times when Foster's favorite band, The Oak Ridge Boys, were playing anywhere within driving distance, the coaches would take Foster to the concert to get his mind off basketball for a few hours.

After tough losses Foster had kicked the locker room door open and began disrobing immediately—coat off, tie undone, and often into the shower before facing the press. In the days before both coaches went to a common media room, Foster kept reporters waiting so long outside the Duke locker room that the ACC instituted a "15-minute rule" for how long they could stay with their teams before coming out to take questions from the press.

The season's fourth meeting, which came in the 1979 ACC Championship Game, followed a week of back-and-forth sniping along the eight-mile Chapel Hill-Durham Boulevard that separated the two campuses. Smith had grown so defensive over the critical storm caused by his holding the ball at Cameron that he had no intention of doing it again in Greensboro. He would play against Duke, whatever defense the Blue Devils decided to put up. And forever the psychologist as well as the tactical mathematician, Smith knew that his team was sick of the "football score" first-half references coming from the other side and would be frothing for another shot at the Blue Devils.

In less than two years, the rivalry had suddenly become venomous among fans and basketball programs—much worse than the almost gentlemanly competition between Vic Bubas and Smith and far more comparable to the fractious Frank McGuire's hatred of Eddie Cameron and Duke in the 1950s. The atmosphere in the Greensboro Coliseum on the Saturday evening of March 3, 1979, was bitterly contentious.

Duke was already shaken from barely escaping a Wake Forest rally in its extra game and surviving a great performance by N.C. State in the Friday semifinals. Carolina enjoyed its bye/day off and absolutely demolished Buck Williams and a pretty good Maryland team in the other semifinal 102–79 with Smith playing no starter more than 28 minutes. But the real buzz at the Coliseum was the rumor that Blue Devils starting point guard Bob Bender had been rushed back to Duke Hospital early Saturday for an emergency appendectomy.

When Duke took the court, Bender was watching from his hospital room and hoping the player he had unseated from the starting lineup, junior John Harrell, could regain his old confidence and get the job done. After transferring from North Carolina Central, also in Durham, Harrell had started 25 games and played in all 34 of Duke's dream season. But when Bender, a transfer from Indiana, became eligible at the semester break, he quickly joined the starting lineup and ate up most of Harrell's minutes. Harrell had sulked through the 1979 season, averaging only 13 minutes a game and, like Dennard, never getting into top shape.

Duke had to play for the third time in three days, suddenly without Bender, who was on his way to an All-Tournament berth after going for 34 minutes in each of the first two games, scoring 22 points, making 7-of-12 field goals, and nailing all eight of his free throws, plus playing an almost flawless floor game with nine assists and two turnovers. Harrell had played only 13 combined minutes in the two games and taken two shots with zero assists.

During the ACC Championship Game, the fifth-ranked Blue Devils, who had moved two spots ahead of Carolina in the polls by virtue of their win the week before, could get only 33 percent of their field goals to drop against a fresh and fired up UNC defense and went to the dressing room trailing 31–25. The Tar Heels were attacking the Duke zone with crisp passes and dribble penetration. Most of the 15,753 capacity crowd were Carolina fans who had found their way into the building and loved what they saw.

Duke rallied to tie the score at 39 on a basket by Gminski, who had hardly touched the ball in the first half and took only four shots against Carolina's sagging man-to-man defense. "They were collapsing on me—fronting and backing me—and it was hard to get a pass in there," Gminski said afterward. "In the second half, they didn't do it as much."

Then came the turning point of the game. Bradley, Carolina's long-armed senior guard, who had made the regular season's most famous play when he stripped State's Clyde Austin and dunked over the Wolfpack at the buzzer, had the ball in the right corner as the Duke zone extended. Averaging only 4.4 points for his career and not known at all for his offense, Bradley decided to challenge Gminski, the 1979 ACC Player of the Year on his way to a 19-point, 16-rebound game. It was more like he surprised the G-man.

Bradley took two dribbles and appeared to be moving back out to the perimeter when he instead darted toward the basket, elevated, and two-hand slammed the ball over the front of the rim and a stunned Duke center. It was only two points, but it underscored how aggressively Carolina had come out to play after seemingly being afraid to attack the Blue Devils the week before in Durham. A photo of the play was on the cover of *Sports Illustrated* the next week with the headline: "Stealing the ACC Title: Dudley Bradley Dunks Duke."

The Blue Devils actually played gallantly and only lost 71–63 by making four fewer field goals than the Tar Heels, as both teams hit an identical 19-of-25 from the line. Bradley had his best collegiate game with 16 points and four assists. Most of the stars on both teams came out to play and played well. The exception was Dennard, who had only two points and fouled out after 23 minutes on the court. Duke lamented its poor shooting early, but the Blue Devils were in it until the last few minutes when UNC capped its fourth ACC championship of the decade. "Dudley had his best game as a Carolina player, and it couldn't have come at a better time," Smith said. "This is a great basketball team and so is Duke. Either of us could go on to win it all."

"Coach should get as much credit for this game as he got abuse for the last one," O'Koren said after he and his teammates celebrated on the court and cut down the nets. Bradley, O'Koren, and point guard Dave Colescott (who had succeeded Ford) joined Gminski and Spanarkel on the All-Tournament team.

Bradley won tournament MVP. "Give Dudley a lot of credit," Banks said. "He missed making the All-ACC first team, and I thought he should have been on it. He proved it tonight."

After a bitter season in which the teams split four games and the programs picked at each other constantly, some civility seemed to return to the rivalry as both awaited the NCAA pairings on Selection Sunday, thinking, of course, they would be sent to different regions and had seen the last of each other except possibly at the Final Four.

There were no rules about who could go where or rhyme or reason (as if there is today) of what the NCAA Selection Committee would do. And with either diabolical glee or inability to truly decide which team deserved it most, both were assigned to the East region, given a top two seed, and—after getting byes in the 40-team field—scheduled to play second-round games in Reynolds Coliseum on the following Sunday. The excitement and anxiety returned immediately, awaiting the unique circumstance.

Top-seeded Carolina would face the winner of Ivy League champion Penn and Iona College, ironically coached by Jim Valvano, who in two years would make his home in Reynolds. Second-seeded Duke would await the winner of Temple and the same St. John's team that had beaten the Blue Devils in Madison Square Garden over Christmas. Few expected either Tobacco Road teams to lose, and most anticipated both returning to the Greensboro Coliseum for the Sweet 16—two wins away from a fifth Duke-Carolina game of that season.

As Franklin Street and Chapel Hill bustled with the exhilaration of March Madness and the Tar Heels getting to play in their home state all the way through the regional, the Duke campus was more solemn over the physical condition of its basketball team, which that week began to look more like a M*A*S*H unit. Ruled out for the weekend but hopeful of returning for the regional rounds, Bender remained in the hospital. On Tuesday night Dennard severely sprained an ankle playing pickup ball and horsing around with some inebriated buddies and Duke football players.

Dennard was lying in room 204 at Duke Rehabilitation Center, sobbing, nursing his tender right ankle, and wanting to somehow be ready to play on Sunday but knowing it wasn't possible. Just down the road in room 4507 at the Duke Medical Center, Bender was still convalescing from last Saturday's appendectomy.

While Dennard was in the bed with his swollen ankle elevated, Bender was allowed to leave the hospital for a few hours and wandered down to Cameron Indoor Stadium to shoot free throws and jogged lightly. "When I stop and go, my side starts to pull," he said, wincing in pain. "But I want to keep my wind up. I'm going to try to shoot free throws and jog constantly."

Dennard and Bender were released from the hospital Wednesday night, but neither was cleared to play. Foster made plans to be without them on Sunday and prepared freshman Vince Taylor to take Dennard's spot and Harrell to start at point guard for the second straight game.

Most of practice on Saturday was spent working with Taylor and Harrell and the other three starters. Bender and Dennard had been keys to the chemistry of this Duke team the past two years—part of the fine mix of stars who had each sacrificed their personal stats for the sake of the team.

With Bender and Dennard out, the Blue Devils had to learn a new mix with Harrell and Taylor. Unlike Bender, the true set-up point guard who ran the offense and looked to pass first, Harrell was a quick-moving shooting guard who had been reduced to a role player. Taylor was much more of a scoring forward than Dennard, who was known for his ability to rebound, do dirty work underneath, and hit an occasional jumper from the corner.

So practice in Reynolds Coliseum on Saturday afternoon was spent getting this new starting lineup to work together at the most crucial time of the year, when one loss ended the season. The team stayed at the Velvet Cloak Inn in Raleigh, located on Hillsborough Street, and after an early team meal at the hotel, several of the players, including Gminski, headed to Brothers Pizza for a late-night snack.

Gminski's nickname was "Mikey," a moniker taken from the Life cereal commercial where Mikey ate the cereal that all the kids were scared to eat.

Mikey Gminski was a big boy with a big appetite. Al McGuire called him the "Aircraft Carrier" because of his wing span and the space he took up inside. At 6'11", 250 pounds, he had become a brilliant basketball player, possessing a soft touch and an instinct for the ball when it came off the rim. His size was definitely a plus on the defensive end as a threat to block any shot taken inside the paint.

Meanwhile, the Tar Heels had stayed in Chapel Hill, as was Smith's policy for any game played within 90 minutes the campus. He wanted his players to go to class like normal students and sleep in their own beds the night before the game. But the night before this game was Saturday night, and some of the Tar Heels did what normal students do on Saturday night. That included juniors O'Koren and Rich "Chickie" Yonakor hitting Franklin Street and a few of their favorite haunts.

No one was injured, but some missed the soft curfew of midnight. Smith reminded the team to get a good night's sleep at the end of Saturday's practice, but none of the Carolina coaches stopped by Granville Towers for bed check because they knew some players would still be out at midnight and they would have to report a violation of team policy to Smith. Besides, it was a mid-afternoon game in Raleigh, and any Tar Heels who did miss curfew had plenty of time to sleep it off before the 10:00 AM pregame meal on Sunday morning.

Party animals O'Koren and Yonakor were most likely to miss curfew, and a story that has lived forever in Chapel Hill was of one of them piggybacking on top of the other as they left the Mad Hatter bar at 2:00 AM. O'Koren was a three-year starter who had scored 31 points against UNLV in the Final Four as a freshman and was a two-time All-ACC player since then. The 6'9" Yonakor had become a part-time starter as a freshman after senior Tom LaGarde tore up his knee in February and never played again. They were two of the biggest characters on a team full of them.

On Friday night Guthridge, Eddie Fogler, and first-year assistant coach Roy Williams had gone to Reynolds Coliseum to scout the first-round doubleheader. They watched Penn defeat Iona 73–69 and came away believing the Quakers were much better than a No. 9 seed. Their best player was Tony Price, who had 27 points and 12 rebounds against Valvano's team.

And at the time, Penn had a strong tradition in basketball, winning eight of the last 10 Ivy League titles and regularly registering 20-win seasons. Only UCLA, Notre Dame, and Marquette reached as many NCAA Tournaments in the 1970s as the Quakers. Entering the 1979 season, Penn had won 213 of its last 272 games, closely approximating what UNC had done. Penn coach Bob Weinhauer considered the ACC overrated and resented how many ACC games were televised into the Philadelphia market. His team felt the same way and was poised to shock the basketball world.

Did the Tar Heels take Penn too lightly and were they ready to play? Those questions would be asked throughout the offseason after Price scored 25 more points and pulled down nine rebounds, and Penn constantly held off Carolina comebacks. Finally, the Tar Heels inched ahead in the last minute, but a foul call that was hotly protested by the UNC bench sent Keith Hall to the free throw line, where he made both shots to seal the 72–71 upset. Penn proved its worth by going on to beat Syracuse and St. John's before falling to Magic Johnson and Michigan State in the Final Four.

The Duke players had watched the first half of the Carolina-Penn game from under the basket at Reynolds, which by now was packed with blue-clad fans of both schools. At halftime the Blue Devils went downstairs to get in uniform for St. John's. They could tell from the vibrations of the crowd above them that it was close and going down to the wire. They were ready to take the court for warm-ups as the game ended and came up the stairs as the Tar Heels were about to go down. Spanarkel and O'Koren, the old Hudson Catholic teammates, stopped to embrace. O'Koren was in tears; his junior season was over. In the stands the fans in light blue sat stunned. Some got up to leave; others stayed in their seats. Duke fans, who had cheered wildly for Penn in the second half, were giddy but also well aware that the same thing could happen to their depleted team.

Smith and his staff left Raleigh unhappy with their team's play and the last foul call. He mentioned in his postgame press conference that he thought Penn was much better than a ninth seed, something he would do periodically throughout his career. But Smith had no real excuses because his team was healthy and rested after a week off.

By the time Duke and St. John's tipped off, the Tar Heels were on the bus back to Chapel Hill, their 23–6 record in the books. There would be no next game in Greensboro, no return to the Final Four for the second time in three years. Roy Williams was the most disconsolate, having experienced for the first time how suddenly the season ended with a loss in the NCAA Tournament. He was making $2,700 as UNC's restricted earnings coach and drove a beat-up Mustang with a broken window. As the bus came up Route 54 and approached campus, Williams asked the driver to stop at the Glen Lenox Apartments, where he and his wife, Wanda, and their baby daughter, Kimberly, lived. "That was the first time, and every year since when the season ends with a loss, I am still affected by the swiftness and suddenness of it all," he later said. "You play all season to get into the NCAA Tournament, and if you lose, there is no next game, no practice the next day. It's over just like that, and there is nothing you can do about it."

Almost as suddenly, things had gone from bad to worse for Duke. Dennard and Bender would be sitting on the bench in street clothes with a wrapped ankle and a stitched side, while Gminski, who said he could play, had placed a bucket under his chair to throw up into during timeouts or when he came out of the game. He had been upchucking most of the morning after apparently eating some bad pizza before going to bed.

Hard to believe that after all this team had been through, another shot at the national championship might be lost because of pizza, a pickup basketball game, and a nearly ruptured appendix all in the span of one week.

St. John's entered the game with a 19–10 record; its likable coach Lou Carnesecca and Foster were good friends from Foster's eight years at Rutgers. "We never played St. John's when I was at Rutgers, so maybe that's why Lou and I are friends now," Foster said, chuckling.

Carnesecca was well aware of the sixth-ranked Blue Devils, having won their earlier match in December at the Garden. Duke had a big lead in the second half, only to fall in a furious comeback by the Redmen. "I'm quite aware of who we're playing and where we're playing," Carnesecca had said before the game. "But the crowd doesn't put the ball in the basket. I like my position at any time. And at my age, I like my position of just being alive."

Carnesecca also knew exactly what St. John's would have to do to survive and advance. "When you play a great center, you have to take risks," he said of Gminski, who entered the game averaging 18.9 points and 9.2 rebounds. He was going against the man-to-man defense of St. John's 6'8" sophomore Wayne McCoy, who averaged 14.7 points and 7.8 rebounds and had scored 20 against Gminski in their earlier match-up. "If you win, it's a calculated risk. If you lose, it's sheer stupidity."

Following their pregame warm-ups, the Blue Devils went back to their locker room and talked about this tournament now being their tournament with Carolina out and if they could win today through all their adversity they would be on the way to playing again for the national title.

Things started well for Duke, which took an early 10-point lead with its makeshift lineup. St. John's strategy didn't work against the G-man, who played 31 minutes despite being sick to his stomach, scored 16 points, pulled down eight rebounds, and blocked two shots. He kept puking into the bucket behind the bench during timeouts.

McCoy got in early trouble with three fouls, but when the Redmen switched to a 1-3-1 zone to protect him, he made some great defensive plays. St. John's again rallied in the second half, and it was evident that Duke was just hanging on. With the game tied, Reggie Carter hit an eight-foot jumper, and the Redmen ended the Blue Devils' season 80–78.

Now the fans in royal blue had their chance to sit in stunned silence. How could it happen that both teams lost? A few Carolina fans had remained for the second game, and to them it was some consolation that at least their archrival would not be advancing either.

Duke actually played one of its best games of the turbulent season, shooting 55 percent from the floor and making 14-of-19 free throws. St. John's was just a little better, making 12-of-14 from the line and having the ball for the last shot.

Playing in his final game in a Duke uniform, the senior Spanarkel scored 16 points in 38 minutes, several at point guard to spell Harrell. "When I go home, I'll go home proud," Spanarkel said. "It's just like walking out of this locker room. I'm not going to hang my head. We may not have won the national championship, but I know there aren't many teams in the nation better than us. We could have used our players...Kenny and Bobby, and Mike wasn't feeling well. If we had all our horses ready, it would have given us more depth. But the effort on everybody's part was fabulous. Luck wasn't on our side, but you can't depend on luck to fall your way all the time. The game tonight wasn't because we didn't have luck on our side. It was because St. John's played very efficiently."

Harrell and Taylor did well in their emergency action. Harrell played 27 minutes, hit all three of his field goal attempts, scored seven points, and had seven assists to only one turnover. Freshman Taylor played all but one minute, scoring six points and grabbing two rebounds in place of Dennard.

But sophomore Banks almost single-handedly kept Duke in the game with 24 points, 10 rebounds, and six assists in 38 minutes. It was perhaps his best performance of an otherwise checkered second season. After being named Duke's third straight ACC Rookie of the Year in 1978, enduring a death threat phoned in to a local TV station before the National Championship Game, and appearing regularly in the national media, Banks suffered what might be called a sophomore slump. His scoring average fell off by almost three points, and he was left off the All-ACC first team.

Somewhat like his frontcourt running mate Dennard, Banks filled his life with off-the-court activities, working with kids in inner city Durham and often appearing at a local restaurant where he would grab the microphone and sing with the band. He irritated Duke fans for the first time when, after the team fell from the No. 1 ranking, he said, "Some people are going to get hurt falling off the bandwagon."

After the loss to St. John's, Banks sat with his head down and jersey pulled halfway over his head. "This season has been brutal—mentally and physically," he said. Banks' scoring average would improve his last two years at Duke, but he had now ended a second straight season with a loss, and this one was far from any kind of championship game.

Banks' college career was suddenly half over, and his own personal honeymoon period had ended. The school's most ballyhooed recruit, who drew a standing room capacity crowd to Cameron for his first public appearance in the preseason Blue-White Game as a freshman, Banks now knew that every season wasn't going to end with a championship like it did at his West Philly high school. He had literally helped Duke go from worst to first in the ACC, and what had been accomplished in 1978 was suddenly the new standard for the Blue Devils.

Foster's staff followed the coach to the postgame press conference in the ROTC room in Reynolds Coliseum. Sports information director Tom Mickle said to make sure there were no weapons in the room that Foster could use to kill himself. Luckily, there weren't any because Foster indeed looked suicidal.

The usually quick-witted coach was anything but that after this loss. His face was ashen and drawn. The pressure of being No. 1 for the good part of an entire season and the disappointment of seeing it all fly away so quickly was etched in every corner of his face. The walk from the locker room on one side of the building to the ROTC Room on the other side of the arena was agonizing. "Can you believe it ended like this?" He said as he shuffled down the long red and white concrete hall way. "After all we went through this year, it's hard to believe it ended like this."

In the pressroom with his head bowed, he took a deep breath and began his postgame statement. "We had some problems, but that's no excuse," he said to the assembled media. "It came down to an eight-footer by Carter that went in," said Foster. "We had good position on defense, but he just went up over us for the shot and made it. I thought about using the zone, but St. John's seemed to be hitting well, so we went man-to-man."

He stopped and just shook his head. He took a few more questions, but by now most of the writers who covered Duke knew when enough was enough with Foster. Like Carolina, Duke dressed in almost deadly silence and got back on the bus to Durham with its 22–8 record also in the books. There would be no fifth meeting with the Tar Heels. In a strange way, the civility that seemed to return after the ACC Championship Game was now a shared sorrow among fans from both schools. "It's a big jump for the East," said St. John's guard Bernard Rencher, "because nobody thinks we're as tough as the ACEC, or whatever you call it."

On the same day, at the same site just a short bus ride from both campuses, Duke and Carolina, the pride of Tobacco Road, had each lost its final game of the season in the NCAA Tournament. For both of them, it was over, and—like Roy Williams said—there was nothing either could do about what was dubbed as Black Sunday.

. . .

Each school had a Black Sunday of its own the following season in 1980, which ended in disappointment and criticism for Coach Smith and Carolina and in great sadness for Foster at Duke.

The Tar Heels, who had been ranked as high as No. 6 in the country before star freshman James Worthy broke his leg and was lost for the season, split four more games with Duke, and they were all unique in their own way.

The Blue Devils opened the season ranked No. 3 based on everyone returning except Sparnarkel, who completed his transformation from a pudgy, nonathletic-looking high school player to a svelte college superstar who was MVP of the 1978 ACC Tournament, a two-time All-ACC selection, and an All-American. He was replaced in the Duke lineup by the sophomore Taylor.

Sixth-ranked Carolina, meanwhile, had lost only Bradley, who despite averaging less than 10 points in college, was still the 13th pick in the NBA draft by the Indiana Pacers, three spots ahead of Spanarkel, who went to the Philadelphia 76ers. But the Tar Heels had the 6'8" Worthy, an explosive and versatile freshman who had been a man among boys since he was a high school sophomore in Gastonia, North Carolina.

For the second straight year, Duke whipped Carolina in the Big Four Tournament and was 12–1 and ranked No. 1 when UNC arrived at Cameron on January 12, 1980, with a 1–2 ACC record and had plummeted to No. 15 in the rankings. With Worthy spinning and dunking over a stunned Dennard, the Tar Heels somehow blew out the Blue Devils by 15 points in the second half and climbed back to No. 9 after the shocking upset.

Learning to play without Worthy, who slipped on a fast break against Maryland on January 20, Carolina was still in the top 10 by the regular season finale against Duke in the last home game for O'Koren, Colescott, Jeff Wolf, and Chickie Yonakor. Distracted by pervasive

Final Four Drought

The Duke-Carolina brand remains stronger than ever, but the twin stranglehold the two programs once had on the Final Four is clearly over. Both are in somewhat of a slump.

Connecticut has now won two national championships and three other schools (Kentucky, Louisville, and Michigan State) have been to at least two Final Fours since the last time either the Blue Devils or Tar Heels were there. They have reached three Elite Eight games but have lost all three.

UNC still has the most Final Four appearances at 18, while Duke has 15. Those combined 33 began with Carolina's undefeated national champions of 1957. In the 1960s each school went to the final weekend of the season three times when only about half the ACC schools took basketball seriously. (Virginia, for example, used coaches of spring sports as basketball assistants as late as the 1960s and did not have cheerleaders at basketball games until 1971.)

That was the last full decade when only the ACC Tournament champion advanced to the NCAA. After the tournament expanded from 25 teams in 1960 to 32 in 1975, a second deserving team from a conference could receive an at-large bid.

The dominant stretch for Duke and Carolina came between 1986 and 2001, a span of 16 years when only two Final Fours were played without one of the blue bloods (1987 and 1996).

Some Final Four slippage has occurred since Duke and Carolina combined for three trips in the 1970s and went back up to five in the 1980s, doubling that to an astonishing 10 (five each) in the 1990s. Since 2000 Carolina has been to four Final Fours and Duke three—all in the first 10 years of the new century. Carolina won national championships in 2005 and '09 under Roy Williams, who also led the Tar Heels to the 2008 Final Four, where his team lost embarrassingly to his old school, Kansas. Duke also went to three Final Fours during that decade, winning Krzyzewski's third and fourth titles in 2001 and 2010 and losing in the semifinals in 2004.

Both have been noticeably absent in recent years.

Duke's four national championships in 15 Final Fours is about the same percentage as UNC's five titles in 18 trips. But the Blue Devils have a much better rate of reaching the National Championship Game, having played in 10 compared to only seven for the Tar Heels, who had four frustrating losses on Final Four Saturdays from 1995–2000. Getting back to the last weekend of the season is going to be on both programs' radar more sharply than ever, as Krzyzewski and Williams continue to load up on five-star recruits, no matter how long they plan to stay in school.

rumors that Foster was leaving for South Carolina after the season, Duke had lost four of its last six games going to Chapel Hill. With O'Koren and his senior mates getting a wild send-off in Carmichael Auditorium, the Heels absolutely destroyed the Devils 96–71 behind 18 points and a career-high 12 rebounds from O'Koren.

Foster announced that week that he had agreed to replace retiring South Carolina coach Frank McGuire, who ironically had been honored at halftime of the blowout of Duke 23 years after he had coached UNC to the undefeated national championship season of 1957. Foster seemed distracted before, during, and after the game, prompting his revelation the week before the 1980 ACC Tournament.

Although Foster had fussed with athletic director Tom Butters over upgrades to Cameron, more money for his assistant coaches, and reportedly the school's refusal to pave the muddy lot where the coaches parked every day, all that seemed to lift off his shoulders when the team arrived in Greensboro as a No. 6 seed in the ACC Tournament.

Unranked after having been No. 1 two months earlier, the Blue Devils dispatched No. 19 N.C. State in the first round and faced the 10th-ranked Tar Heels in the Friday night semifinals. With a chance to win three straight from Duke, Carolina fell behind early and despite 32 points from Wood never was in contention. Gminski saved his best game against Carolina for last with a dominating 24 points and 19 rebounds.

After the Blue Devils edged regular season champion Maryland and All-American Albert King in a thrilling championship game— witnessed by barely 10,000 people because of a blizzard in North Carolina—Gminski joined Banks and Wood on the All-Tournament team but lost out to King's 27 points for the MVP. It was Gminski's best season statistically, as he finished second in the ACC in scoring (21 points per game) to King and rebounds (11) to Virginia freshman Ralph Sampson while also making his third straight All-ACC team. But Duke's midseason swoon kept him from repeating as a first-team All-American.

For the third straight season, Carolina was a one-and-done in the NCAA Tournament, losing on another Black Sunday to Texas A&M in double overtime as unfounded criticism of Smith's style of play engulfed the UNC program. The loss of Worthy had kept the Tar Heels from being a great team, which would be proven in the next two years.

After starring on national TV in UNC's run to the 1977 Final Four, O'Koren and his classmates never got back to even the regional round. The Jersey City rowdy, who was often moody over his brief, secretive marriage to a Carolina cheerleader, had consistent career averages in points, rebounds, and assists. After being drafted sixth in the first round by his home state New Jersey Nets, he was featured by *USA TODAY* as the most complete basketball player in the NBA.

Duke rode the momentum of its second ACC championship in three years and a win-one-for-Foster attitude to a pair of NCAA victories, including a stunning 55–54 upset of fourth-ranked Kentucky on its home court in Lexington in which hometown kid Taylor hit 7-of-9 for 15 points. But two days later, the Blue Devils could not contain Purdue All-American center Joe Barry Carroll and missed a chance to return to another Final Four in Foster's last season at Duke. Foster, who looked out of it on the bench during the final minutes and squirmed disconsolately on a training table in the locker room after the game, may have known that he was trading an annual shot at the national championship for what he believed was more peace of mind and an easier schedule at then independent South Carolina.

He returned to Durham on his own personal Black Sunday and started clearing out his office. In six years in Columbia, South Carolina, followed by a dismal seven seasons at Northwestern before retiring from coaching, Foster never returned to the NCAA Tournament. "I guess it was just time to leave. I don't know," Foster reflected a few years later. "Those were my most memorable days in coaching. But I never did enjoy it. I don't know what it was. It didn't really sink in, and that's my own fault. I don't blame anybody for that. I certainly don't blame Duke. I just never relaxed."

Chapter 6

Double Standard

*I*t was late in the evening when Curry Kirkpatrick of Sports Illustrated *and I arrived at Mike Krzyzewski's hotel room at the old Adam's Mark in Winston-Salem. The Blue Devils had just shocked the world by handing the No.1 team in the nation its second loss of the season and knocking them out of winning the 1984 ACC Tournament.*

This was a Carolina team loaded with talent—Michael Jordan, Kenny Smith, Sam Perkins, and Brad Daugherty for starters—all eventual NBA stars.

I told Curry we needed to bring a bowl of ice cream to Mike to persuade the coach to be forthcoming, and we secured the dessert from the restaurant downstairs.

Going up the elevator, I remembered how we sat in a Waffle House in Atlanta a year ago, following an embarrassing loss to Ralph Sampson and the Virginia Cavaliers by 43 points in the first round of the ACC Tournament. Now I was taking the lead college basketball writer for the nation's most popular sports publication to see our coach about an Earth-shaking victory. But here we were standing at the door with a bowl of ice cream as a peace offering to get 10 minutes with Mike for an interview as he tried to prepare for Sunday's ACC Championship Game against Maryland.

The door opened and Mike's wife, Mickie, stood there beaming with pride from the win and then grinning when she saw the ice cream. She welcomed Curry, and as we walked over to the sitting area we could see another bowl of ice cream on the table. Mike quickly said that two bowls were perfect with a sly grin and sat down. The ice cream worked, and the coach took time from his preparation to talk with Curry—the start of hundreds of interviews with national journalists about Duke basketball.

—JM

The 1983–84 basketball season marked the turning point for Mike Krzyzewski in the Duke-Carolina rivalry. While Duke still struggled to recapture the preeminence it enjoyed in the 1960s under coach Vic Bubas, UNC was perched on the mountain top of college basketball under legendary coach Dean Smith. The Tar Heels had won the national championship in 1982 and began the season ranked No. 1. Senior Sam Perkins and junior Michael Jordan graced the cover of *Sports Illustrated*, with both smiling and wagging their index fingers in the public's face. Carolina also had sophomore center Brad Daugherty and precocious freshman point guard Kenny Smith, whom they called "The Jet." All four of those players would go on to be first-round NBA draft choices, and in 1984 they were given a chance to be the first undefeated college basketball team since Indiana in 1976.

The Blue Devils were at the bottom of the mountain, working their way back up the incline with a head coach under heavy fire that reminded him of being behind enemy lines during his active service in the U.S. military. Meanwhile, Smith had already been elected to the Naismith Hall of Fame, and ground was broken at UNC on a 22,000-seat, light blue arena—the largest privately funded college stadium—that would eventually be nicknamed the "Dean Dome."

Duke had a short resurgence in the late 1970s, losing to Kentucky in the 1978 NCAA Championship and spending most of the 1980 season as the No. 1 team in the nation. But the Blue Devils, still clearly in the shadow of the state university led by the "Dean" of college basketball, lost their head coach Bill Foster to South Carolina. Foster had left only three players on the roster from their ranked teams—seniors Gene Banks and Kenny Dennard and junior Vince Taylor.

The job did not attract much interest because, despite Foster's brief three-year run in the top 10, the cupboard was left bare, and the perception existed that Duke was cheap. A popular and funny story about Foster's departure was that Duke refused to pave the muddy lot outside Cameron Indoor Stadium where the coaches parked. And South Carolina offered Foster a lot more money than he was making at Duke—plus better parking.

Despite having pitched for the Pittsburgh Pirates before a serious car accident derailed his major league career, Duke athletic director Tom Butters, who had taken over the athletic department in 1977 and held the dual role as head of the Iron Duke's fund-raising foundation, was a basketball junkie who had a yardstick for the school's basketball program. "We sat in the middle of the ACC, a small school trying to figure out how to compete in the changing world of college basketball," Butters said. "Eight miles away sat a legend, perhaps the greatest coach of all time. He cared about his school and his kids and he kicked ass every day. I was inundated with thoughts of beating Dean Smith. If we couldn't beat him, we could never get to what we were thinking about."

Butters was from Delaware, Ohio, near Massillon, the hometown of Bobby Knight, the legendary Indiana basketball coach who had led the Hoosiers to an undefeated season and national championship in 1976. Butters idolized Knight, even though they were about the same age, and called him for his recommendations, beginning the conversation with the perfunctory offer to coach Duke and take on Carolina and Smith. Knight politely declined and recommended several of his former assistants and sitting head coaches such as Ole Miss' Bob Weltlich, Tennessee's Don DeVoe, and Dave Bliss at SMU, all of whom had fairly high-profile jobs in the Southeastern and Southwest Conferences.

Butters, who had someone else in mind, asked about "the coach at Army." "Oh, him," Knight said of the 33-year-old Mike Krzyzewski, laughing slightly over the phone. "He has all of my good qualities and none of my bad."

Krzyzewski had played for Knight at Army, where he was a defense-minded guard and captain of the Cadets his senior year, holding South Carolina All-American John Roche under double figures in a 59–45 upset of the nationally ranked Gamecocks in the 1969 NIT at Madison Square Garden. Knight became a lifetime mentor when Krzyzewski's father died his senior year.

Knight, who moved on to Indiana in 1971, said Krzyzewski was far from his best player but knew he would make a great coach if he chose that profession following active duty. Krzyzewski coached service teams for five years and after spending one year as a graduate assistant with Knight at IU took over the Army program from Dan Dougherty in 1975. He was 28 at the time, three years older than Knight when he became the head coach at Army.

Krzyzewski had also served on Knight's staff at the 1979 Pan American Games in Puerto Rico, where Knight caused an international incident by allegedly striking a San Juan policeman and getting handcuffed and arrested. The U.S. won the gold medal easily, but that was probably an example of what Knight meant when he said Krzyzewski had only his "good" qualities.

At Army, Krzyzewski did about as well as Knight, compiling a five-year 73–59 record, including two appearances in the NIT and putting together three winning seasons. But his team finished the 1980 season at 9–17, which dropped him off the radar of most schools looking for a new coach.

Butters interviewed Krzyzewski at least four times without offering him the job because he wasn't sure how the proud Duke alumni would accept an unknown coach from Army coming off a losing season. Assistant athletic director Steve Vacendak, a former Blue Devils star in the 1960s, had seen Krzyzewski's Army teams play when he was the Converse shoe rep in the Northeast. "I went to a pregame meeting before they played Navy one year," Vacendak recalled. "I was impressed with how he had everything organized. I watched him coach. It was just good basketball, really good basketball. He was in control."

While Butters procrastinated, Krzyzewski went to Ames, Iowa, to interview at Iowa State, whose athletic director, Max Urich, was a classmate of Butters at Ohio Wesleyan. Ames was closer to Chicago, where Krzyzewski had grown up and still had family, and Knight actually told him his Midwestern roots might make it a better fit. Urich called Butters and asked him if was going to hire the Army coach because "if you are not, we are." At one point Butters thought he had lost the candidate that "I couldn't get off my mind." But with no commitment from Duke, Krzyzewski withdrew his name at Iowa State and rolled the dice on Duke.

Finally, after sending the candidate back to the Raleigh-Durham Airport without an offer, Butters had him paged and told him to come back to Durham.

It was a surprise selection, to say the least.

Krzyzewski's name had not been mentioned in a single speculative story by the local media trying to find out whom Duke would pick as UNC's and Smith's next punching bag. This secrecy seemed to delight Butters, who at least had snookered the media before revealing his new head coach at a press conference in May of 1980. Krzyzewski, who earned a reported $10 million in 2010, started at $48,000.

Butters walked out with a funny-looking young man—a pointy nose under a jet-black comb-over and thin lips, from which came perhaps the most amusing line he uttered in what would be a four-decade career at Duke. "My name is pronounced Sha-shef-ski," he began, "it is spelled K-R-Z-Y-Z-E-W-S-K-I. And you should have seen it before I changed it. My players call me Coach K."

Three years later the Blue Devils had become the laughingstock of ACC basketball, while UNC—and N.C. State's upstart funny man, Jim Valvano—had won national championships. Meanwhile, after reaching the NIT with Foster's holdovers in 1981, Duke's second and third seasons under Coach K were insufferable sixth- and seventh-place finishes in the ACC and two of the worst records in the school's history, 10–17 and 11–17. Already a group of disgruntled boosters calling themselves the "Concerned Iron Dukes" had formed. "What were they concerned about?" Krzyzewski deadpanned years later. "Me as their basketball coach."

• • •

Heading into the 1983–84 season, there wasn't much left of the Duke-Carolina rivalry, as the Blue Devils had lost six of the last seven games to the Tar Heels. Since Bubas retired, Smith's record against Duke was 26–9.

But 12 days in January of 1984 proved to be a defining period in Duke basketball history and in the rejuvenation of what became known as the "blue blood rivalry."

Buoyed by a surprising recruiting class the determined Krzyzewski had seemingly signed out of nowhere, the Blue Devils had put together an impressive 14–1 start to the season with the one loss a two-point defeat to Southern Methodist at the Rainbow Classic in Honolulu.

On January 14 the Devils faced fifth-ranked Maryland in Cameron Indoor Stadium. Although Duke lost 81–75, the real fallout came from how the student body had acted before and during the game. Maryland senior Herman Veal had been accused of improper sexual advances toward a female the prior spring. The charges were dismissed, but the oft-creative, sometimes-crude Duke students had not forgotten. They greeted Veal with vulgar taunts and peppered the playing floor with women's underwear and condoms when he was introduced.

Not only was Duke seeking respect for its basketball program, now the student body was being lambasted by newspapers near and far for its crass actions at the game. Amidst what had become a national embarrassment, the Blue Devils were crushed four days later by No. 12 Wake Forest in the Greensboro Coliseum 97–66.

The great start to this critical season was beginning to fall apart for the Blue Devils and Krzyzewski. The Concerned Iron Dukes were meeting regularly, discussing who would be their next basketball coach. Even Krzyzewski thought it might be his last season at Duke.

The morning following the loss to Wake Forest, Butters stuck his head in the basketball office just past 8:00 to see if Krzyzewski was in yet; he wasn't, having spent most of the evening and early morning watching film of the Wake Forest disaster. It was a Krzyzewski coaching ritual to spend the evening immediately after a game going over the film with his assistants. He eventually earned the nickname of "Mole Man" from his own family for pulling these all-night sessions at home or in the office.

These film sessions in the early morning hours began in the small coaches' locker room at Cameron with the staff hanging over the back of chairs or the side of the couch after going over and over the tape, looking for ways to improve this team. The coaches usually hit the bed—or couch—around 4:00 or 5:00 AM. By then a player who had 12 points and six rebounds in the game could be in the doghouse for not switching on defense, being in the wrong spot on certain plays, or not hustling and supporting his teammates. All this meticulous preparation would eventually lead to ACC and national championships. But in 1984 Krzyzewski was still crafting a program. He wanted to be ready the next day to discuss with each player what he did well and poorly during the entire game and make the necessary adjustments.

Butters asked the secretary to have Mike come to his office when he arrived. A somber Krzyzewski entered Butters' suite later that morning. Butters could tell by how thin Krzyzewski's lips looked that he was uptight about his job. The embarrassing losses of the past two seasons were supposedly behind the program, but the 31-point wipe-out to Wake Forest rekindled that hurt, and Krzyzewski didn't know exactly what to expect in the middle of January of his fourth season as he walked into his boss' office.

Butters was about to answer that question. "I looked right at Mike and told him, 'The fans, the media, even you don't know how good of a basketball coach you are,'" recalled Butters, then in his seventh year as Duke athletic director. "'But I know how good you are.' And I opened my drawer and pulled out a new five-year contract and slid it across the desk."

When Krzyzewski realized what it was, his eyes filled up, and a tear trickled down his cheek. Someone did believe in him and what he was trying to do to make Duke basketball what it once was. And fortunately for the beleaguered coach, that person was his boss—Tom Butters—the guy with the strongest belief in him. "Only thing," Butters said, "I want you to announce this when you are ready."

Krzyzewski would wait a while, but it gave him an ace in the hole he needed when the time was right.

ROUND ONE—UNC AT DUKE

The first meeting between Duke and North Carolina in 1984 came on Saturday, January 21, in Cameron Indoor Stadium. A strange side note was that for the first time in several years the game would not be televised. It had been scheduled for the Season Ticket package that ESPN and the ACC discontinued on the prior Tuesday after controversy surrounding the pay-per-view model was being addressed in area courtrooms.

The Duke student body would be on its best behavior as well after a weeklong chastising from the media. Appeals from university officials from president Terry Sanford to Butters to Krzyzewski, who met with the students two hours before the game, assured that.

The letter written by Sanford and delivered to each student's mailbox has become legendary. Sanford wrote: "I don't think we need to be crude and obscene to be effectively enthusiastic. We can cheer and taunt with style; that should be a Duke trademark. I suggest that we change. Talk this matter over in your various residential houses. Think of something clever but clean, devastating but decent, mean but wholesome, witty and forceful, but G-rated for television, and try it at the next home game."

He signed it "Uncle Terry."

Duke University
Durham
North Carolina 27706

Office of the President   January 17, 1984

AN AVUNCULAR LETTER

To My Duke Students:

The enthusiasm of Duke students in Cameron Indoor Stadium during basketball games is legendary, especially at ACC games. That's great! It is as if we had a sixth man (maybe seventh, eighth, or tenth sometimes) playing on the floor.

But hold a minute--I have a reservation about all that. There is a recognizable line between enthusiasm and cheapness.

It is generally assumed that a person resorting in conversation to profanity and obscenities is short of an adequate vocabulary. That is doubly true in public utterances.

Resorting to the use of obscenities in cheers and chants at ball games indicates a lack of vocabulary, a lack of cleverness, a lack of ideas, a lack of class, and a lack of respect for other people. We are, I am sorry to report, gaining an unequaled reputation as a student body that doesn't have a touch of class.

I don't think we need to be crude and obscene to be effectively enthusiastic. We can cheer and taunt with style; that should be the Duke trademark. Crudeness, profanity, and cheapness should not be our reputation--but it is.

I suggest that we change. Talk this matter over in your various residential houses. Think of something clever but clean, devastating but decent, mean but wholesome, witty and forceful but G-rated for television, and try it at the next game.

We have too much going for us as an outstanding university to tolerate the reputation we now have for being so crude and inarticulate that we must resort to profanity and obscenities at ball games.

I hope you will discipline yourselves and your fellow students. This request is in keeping with my commitment to self-government for students. It should not be up to me to enforce proper behavior that signifies the intelligence of Duke students. You should do it. Reprove those who make us all look bad. Shape up your own language.

I hate for us to have the reputation of being stupid.

With best wishes,

Uncle Terry

President Terry Sanford

There was much discussion from all corners of the basketball world about the Duke student body, which was not yet coined the "Cameron Crazies" by TV announcer Al McGuire.

Prior to the game, UNC senior forward Matt Doherty said exactly how he felt about the Duke crowd, which would soon be the model—good and bad—for fan behavior across the country. "They are all just a bunch of rude northerners who study too much and release it on the opposing players," said Doherty. "Seriously, I don't think it shows much class. If I was a university official, I wouldn't let it go on like that. What they did last Saturday and what they have done in the past is pretty rude, and I think if any of the fans put themselves in the players' shoes, they wouldn't like it either. It's my last trip over there, and they can do what they want. But they need to just look at themselves. I haven't seen too many things over there that seemed clever. It's been pretty crude, some of the things...I could accept as fun or as a clever cheer, but not what they do...Over there it looks like it's supported by the university."

The loud but well-behaved Cameron crowd witnessed a superb first-half performance by the Blue Devils. Sophomore Johnny Dawkins came out of his weeklong shooting slump; fellow sophomore Mark Alarie and the rest of his teammates played inspired man-to-man, in-your-face defense against the nation's No. 1 team. "I think our defense caught them off-balance," said sophomore David Henderson, who with Jay Bilas, Dawkins, and Alarie comprised the underrated recruiting class Krzyzewski had put together the year before. "I think they were expecting a fight from us, but I don't think they expected us to play them so tough straight up."

Duke led at the half 40–39, but the best show was not put on by the players—rather the coaches on the sideline. Smith worked the officials hard. The crew was made up of two experienced officials, Dr. Hank Nichols and John Moreau, and the third, the youngest of the group, whom Smith went after. Mike Moser, the son of veteran ACC official Lou Moser, would be the target of the majority of Smith's officiating criticism. Nine years before during the ACC Tournament in Greensboro, Smith accused Lou Moser of intentionally making calls against his team, calling him "a cheater" after the game.

At the end of the first half, Smith pointed at Moser and yelled harshly, "You, you!" Moser walked from the court unharmed, while Krzyzewski went off screaming into the ear of Nichols.

Smith was as mad at his own team as the officials. Jordan had played lackadaisically, and seven-foot sophomore center Brad Daugherty had not taken a single shot. After also scolding freshman Kenny Smith, who had been featured in *Sports Illustrated* the week before, the Tar Heels prepared to go back out. Assistant coach Bill Guthridge shouted, only half-jokingly, about the refs, "Let's go out there and beat all eight of those guys!" But the drama would not end at halftime.

With 4:26 left in the game, Smith was at the scorer's table, trying to stop play for the second time in the game. Yes, stop play. The game was going on, and Smith was banging on the table trying to hit the button for the horn to stop play so he could get a substitute in the game. Veteran Duke scorekeeper Tommy Hunt said he could not blow the horn until the refs blew the whistle.

But Smith was trying to stop the game on his own, inadvertently hitting the visiting team's score button and adding 20 points to Carolina's total. When UNC manager Greg Miles tried to restrain Smith by pulling at his coat, the Tar Heel coach slapped Miles' hand away.

After the dust settled, Jordan hit a 15-footer from the baseline and cut Duke's lead down to one 67–66. "With five minutes left, I thought we were going to win," said Duke junior forward Danny Meagher. "Then Michael took off."

Jordan scored six consecutive points, but the most important baskets of the game may well have been scored by Kenny Smith, who tallied 10 points in the final four minutes of play.

Meanwhile, Duke hit just two of six shots and turned the ball over on two critical possessions. The Devils could not get the ball to Alarie, who had scored 16 points, missing just one of eight shots, but did not attempt a shot in the last 16 minutes of the game. "We showed we could play with anybody," Alarie said. "We confused them with our defense at first. We played a hard, aggressive man-to-man. I don't think they are use to not being able to run their offense."

The 78–73 loss was a tough pill for the Blue Devils, but even tougher on their young head coach. Krzyzewski's eyes flashed with the fury that had just taken place on the floor only a few steps away as he entered the press room following the game. "I want to tell you all something," he said as he addressed the assembled media. "When you come in here and you start writing about Duke having no class, you better start getting your heads straight because our students had class, and our team had class. Nobody connected with Duke was pointing at officials, nobody connected with Duke was banging on the scorer's table, and nobody from Duke was running around the bench area. So let's get some things straight around here and quit the double standard that sometimes exists in this league. All right? Let's just get that kind of thing straight. We can laugh and joke and do all those things, but there's a room full of kids who just played their hearts out, and they showed a hell of a lot of class. Any questions?"

Krzyzewski was referring partially to the flak Duke caught during the past week over student conduct at games, but his anger was more directed at a technical foul called on him with five seconds left in the game and to a Carolina bench that had one of its more active nights. Smith had rarely been more vocal and demonstrative on the sideline.

The first question he received was about the technical at the end of the game. Krzyzewski started by characterizing the technical as a "terrible call" but stopped himself in mid-sentence: "Let me correct that. I think I deserved a technical foul at the end of the second half and I think the coach on the opposing bench deserved a technical at the end of the first half...You cannot allow people to go around pointing at officials and going out on the court and yelling at them without technical fouls being called. That is just not allowed."

This was Krzyzewski's first public outburst since arriving at Duke, and despite his justified anger, it seemed out of character for a coach on the brink. But only he and his staff knew about his new contract and the vote of confidence from his boss and university. For the first time, it became apparent that Krzyzewski was not only interested in keeping his job and building a basketball program, but also going after the top man in the college game, the leader of the Tar Heels—Dean Smith.

The public announcement of Krzyzewski's five-year contract extension was not made until Thursday, January 26, five days after the home loss to Carolina. Although the Devils were 14–4 at the time, consecutive losses to Maryland, Wake Forest, and UNC weren't sitting well with a lot of the Duke faithful.

He had systematically and at times stubbornly stuck to a plan, a virtual construction process from the ground up. Man-to-man defense had been the staple of his coaching philosophy, and at times over his first few seasons, the critics wanted him to play some zone, slow it down, and do something that at least gave Duke a chance to win. The Concerned Iron Dukes, who were after his head, thought of him as a stubborn military man. But the ability to apply pressure never before seen in the ACC was now a key to the Blue Devils' success and indeed would be the foundation of redefining defense in Coach K's conference, if not all of college basketball.

For Krzyzewski the contract was a red badge of courage, justifying his efforts to rebuild the Duke program his way. "It shows a strong general commitment to what we're doing from our athletic and regular administration," Krzyzewski said. "I've always known it, but it's nice to know again we're doing it the way they want us to do it both on and off the court."

"He deserved it, he's earned it, and the university is extraordinarily pleased with him as a man and as a coach," Butters added. "For years I've been asked my yardstick on a coach, and Mike measures up to it."

Butters said that Krzyzewski's original five-year contract called for a review after the fourth year. "We just moved up the schedule about 45 days," he said. "We offered the first five on what I thought he could do. Now this five is on what I know he can do and what he's in the process of accomplishing."

The night Duke announced the new contract, the Blue Devils lost to defending NCAA national champion N.C. State and Jim Valvano 79–76 in Cameron, bringing Krzyzewski's three-and-half year record at Duke to an even 52–52. His team then ripped off eight consecutive victories, and his record would never dip below .500 again. Far from it.

ROUND TWO—DUKE AT UNC

It was Senior Day in Chapel Hill, and the Blue Devils, who had not won at Carmichael Auditorium in 19 years, were scheduled to be the sacrificial lambs to fete seniors Perkins and Doherty and Jordan, the junior who was likely going pro after the season. But before it was over, the No. 1 ranked Tar Heels had to scrap and claw for the win.

The reason for the scrapping and clawing was discussed and noticed by everyone well before the leaves had fallen from the trees and winter's cold grip had settled on the Triangle. It was early August, and Krzyzewski was in his office, discussing the upcoming season's team with a couple of reporters and friends.

Johnny Dawkins, Duke's freshman All-American guard of a year ago, continued to come up in conversation. Dawkins was one of the top backcourt players in the nation. Krzyzewski pointed out there were other quality players in his program and said, for example, "Just wait till you see Mark Alarie play this year." It was a simple statement, but it was one delivered with an all-knowing smile that had proven to be prophetic.

In this game Alarie, who scored 28 points, would prove to be the difference maker.

Duke was able to break Carolina's gambling defense in the first half for some easy baskets, pulling to within one at intermission 41–40.

With 2:04 left in the game the Tar Heels took a 71–68 lead, but Jay Bilas came back with a bucket, and Jordan missed a 12-footer to give Duke a chance with 1:12 remaining. With 40 seconds left, freshman point guard Tommy Amaker was called for a charge, trying to bust out of a double-team trap by Doherty and Jordan. But Amaker deflected a pass seconds later, and Dawkins headed straight to the basket on a breakaway. Only a last-second save by Jordan, who batted the ball away, kept Duke from going ahead.

The Blue Devils retained possession, and Alarie scored underneath with 20 seconds left, was fouled, and converted the three-point play that put Duke ahead 73–71. A miss by Steve Hale on the Carolina end sent the capacity crowd into panic, as it appeared Duke would win.

Danny Meagher was fouled by Brad Daugherty, his fifth of the game, and with nine seconds left went to the foul line to close out the win for the Devils. While Carmichael was a bandbox like Cameron, Smith had tried to discourage hand waving or distractions by the Tar Heel fans behind the goal when opponents shot free throws. It was commonplace in college basketball, but Smith considered it poor sportsmanship and could usually control the crowd by waving for the fans to stop.

That wasn't the case with this free throw attempt. The No. 1 ranked Tar Heels were about to lose a game to Duke—a team they had beaten in 23 of their last 29 meetings. In the section behind the basket, the frantic faces in the stands, the yelling, screaming, and waving of their hands confirmed that the rivalry was back.

It is not a rivalry if one team wins all the time. A rivalry comes not just from two schools sitting eight miles apart but from a mutual respect and distaste for losing to your arch enemy. The eyes of the Carolina faithful in the end zone told the story. Duke, the school they truly hated, was about to ruin their Senior Day.

Meagher took aim and missed, the ball falling off the rim to Matt Doherty, who took off dribbling the length of the floor, as Duke players rushed to double-team Jordan and Perkins. Doherty pulled up in the lane and hit a 14-foot jumper that tied the score at 73 as time ran out. "I didn't realize the importance of the Duke-Carolina rivalry until this game," Meagher said. "In the past they had always been so good they just beat us. When we started getting close to beating them, you could see in the Carolina players and fans something different. They did not want to lose to us. Suddenly the learning curve for me about the Duke-Carolina rivalry clicked in, and I understood they really thought they were better than us."

In the first overtime, Dawkins made a twisting, underhand shot with seven seconds left to tie the score at 79. Following a timeout by Carolina, the teams broke from their huddles and as they walked back onto the floor Duke's Henderson, a native of Drewery, North Carolina, walked directly toward the man he had to cover, Michael Jordan. "You know you aren't going to get the shot off," said Henderson, bumping up against his friend from Wilmington.

"We'll see," Jordan retorted with a sly grin. His reputation as one of the NBA's biggest trash talkers actually grew out of how competitive he became in college, constantly challenging his own teammates to games of one-on-one and his coaches to billiards matches.

The ball went to Jordan in the left corner, and with Henderson draped all over him, his shot hit the side of the backboard.

Overtime No. 2.

Carolina wasn't about to lose this game. The second extra period opened with an alley-oop, three-point play by Jordan, and the Tar Heels never looked back, outscoring Duke 17–4 to finally secure the 96–83 victory. "You have to understand, UNC was our measuring stick," explained Bilas, the current ESPN broadcaster. "This wasn't one of those losses where the coaches come in and say, 'Okay, this is what we did wrong tonight, here's what we have to work on.' The locker room was just devastated. Quiet.

"Coach K finally comes in and sticks his fist out. He says, 'We will play them again, and we will beat them.' And he leaves the room."

In his six previous losses to North Carolina, the average margin of defeat was 15 points. In the two 1984 meetings, the Blue Devils had lost by five at home and taken the second game into double overtime on the road.

And while the Duke-Carolina rivalry was again becoming a serious affair, there were still moments of levity. The day after the loss in Chapel Hill, Meagher checked his mailbox and found an actual brick with his name on it. The brick had been placed there by Duke assistant coach Tom Rogers. The brick, symbolic of Meagher's missed free throw, made him grin. Later that same mailbox would bring him solace in letters from Duke fans who told him to hang in there and not worry about missing the one against Carolina. "It really made me feel good that so many people cared about me and believed in me," Meagher said. "All the notes and letters I got made me understand how big the game was and how people really wanted us to win. It was actually a great experience."

One of the more interesting facets of the 1984 season was the closeness of the Duke and Carolina basketball teams off the court. During the spring or summer, players from both programs held pickup games regularly on either the Duke or UNC campus. "We knew that Johnny and Michael were friends, so we would let them set up the games," Alarie said. "Johnny would call Michael, or Michael would call Johnny, and we would set up a pickup game in Woollen Gym at Carolina or in Cameron. We would let the guys from State know as well, but they didn't come over as much. Jordan was always there, working on his game. We all knew each other pretty well and were friends, but when game time came, that was all over."

ROUND THREE—ACC TOURNAMENT

"The three games we played against Carolina in 1984 were a microcosm of the Duke basketball program at the time," Alarie recalled. "We were continuously working to make our team better. We had won a lot of games but had not played well against ranked teams. In 1984 we played well in the first game against Carolina and then had them beat in Chapel Hill before letting it slip through our hands. We knew we could beat them if we got another shot in the ACC Tournament."

Newspaper stories about the Duke-North Carolina basketball game in the semifinal of the 1984 ACC Tournament showed some simple stats and facts about how the game unfolded and concluded. Alarie scored 21 points and held Sam Perkins to nine. Dawkins scored 16 points and twice—with the score tied in the final three minutes—hit crucial go-ahead baskets. Henderson, the conference's most effective sixth man, had 14 points, hit four critical free throws in the final minute, and survived a defensive encounter with Jordan on the Tar Heels' best chance to force the game into overtime.

But there was a lot more to this game.

For a team gunning for the national championship, the Tar Heels did not take to heart the two close losses to Duke. To them the Blue Devils were still also-rans in the ACC compared to N.C. State, Maryland, Virginia, and Wake Forest. And truth be told, Carolina was not nearly the team that had started the season 21–0 despite Kenny Smith missing eight games with a broken wrist suffered against LSU in early February.

Dean Smith was peeved at his team before the game ever started, having been told by his assistants and managers that the players were bickering over how many tickets they could get from each other to give to family, friends, and girlfriends. Sophomore guard Steve Hale had played splendidly in Kenny Smith's absence, and Coach Smith gambled by putting his freshman point guard back in the lineup with a protective cast on his left wrist. The Jet was never the same player that season. And Smith, who majored in math at Kansas and always played the percentages, never liked the odds of beating a good team three times in the same season. His players may have not thought so, but Smith knew Duke had become a very good basketball team. He had seen it before anyone else during the infamous "double standard" day in Durham.

Sometimes the biggest games turn on the little plays and the smallest moments. *The* play that defined this Duke-Carolina game and solidified the return of rivalry took place long before the climactic final seconds.

With the score tied at 67, Henderson had just bounced the ball off his foot and out of bounds followed by a TV timeout with 3:42 remaining in the game. In the UNC huddle, Smith set up a play designed to get Jordan the ball in the lane close to the basket. Henderson would be guarding him for Duke.

Jordan worked for position on Henderson down in the lane and when he finally secured his spot, placing Henderson in an apparent hopeless defensive position behind him, Doherty fed Jordan the ball. Given that he was at a disadvantage, Henderson did what any good defensive player would do and reached over Jordan's shoulder and swatted the ball away. He got a pretty good piece of the ball and an even better chunk of Jordan's shoulder.

For some reason nothing was called. The whistles of Hank Nichols, Joe Forte, and John Clougherty, three of the best in the business, were silent. Nine times out of 10, officials will call that a reaching foul but not this time. As the UNC bench exploded in protest, play continued to the amazement of even Duke fans who knew they had gotten away with one. "I leaned on him," Henderson explained, "and when the ball came in, I reached over and knocked it away. You never know how the officials are going to call that, especially an official behind you who may not have a good view of the play. That's the reason I jumped back and raised my arms—to show that there had been no contact. But I know they normally call the foul on a play like that."

The loose ball wound up with Alarie, who quickly moved down the court. He shot and missed, but Dawkins tipped the ball in to give Duke a 69–67 lead. Following the game UNC's Smith vividly remembered the steal by Henderson. "Henderson fouled him, and it wasn't called," Smith said, "and that's the way it goes."

This game would come down to a free throw contest for the Blue Devils. The first to be tested was the most logical from UNC's standpoint, brick-mason Meagher, who had missed the critical free throw just a week earlier in Chapel Hill. "Dean was always going off on me about being a flopper and a tough player," Meagher said. "I learned quickly to hate Carolina. I knew he was coming for me in the tournament and I wanted them to foul me. Krzyzewski leaving me in the game gave me a lot of confidence."

Meagher got two chances at the foul line late in the game and hit both of them. When Henderson converted a one-and-one free throw opportunity with 17 seconds left, the Blue Devils led 77–73. A rebound basket by Jordan with five seconds left pulled the Tar Heels to within two points.

Then Henderson opened the door by missing a one-and-one with four seconds remaining, and the Tar Heels had a shot to tie. Carolina took a timeout with three seconds left.

Doherty inbounded the ball in the backcourt in front of the Duke bench. After using most of the allotted five seconds looking for teammate to get free, Doherty tried to hit Jordan in the left corner near the sideline, but the ball landed beyond Jordan's grasp near a water bucket at the Tar Heels bench.

Jordan, who scored 22 points in the game, had run from near midcourt from right to left behind several picks to the left corner; Henderson stayed with him. "There were so many seven-footers around the lane it was tough guarding him," Henderson said. "We headed toward the basket, and someone slowed me up a little, and he got a step on me. If the pass had been there, he probably would have caught it because I wasn't going to foul him. But he couldn't reach it."

Following the game Smith told a small group of reporters that Jordan actually was a decoy, and the play was set for someone else but that he couldn't tell all his secrets. Instead freshman forward Joe Wolf told everyone the real play was designed to go to Perkins. "I got him [Henderson] a little bit coming back by," Wolf said. "Then I was supposed to set a pick on Sam's man, and Sam was to pop out toward the hash line, but with the five seconds, we didn't have enough time to do that."

Carolina fouled immediately on the Duke inbounds play, and Dawkins went to the free throw line with a one-and-one opportunity. When he missed with two seconds left and with Carolina out of time-outs, Perkins grabbed the rebound and heaved the ball down court toward the basket, missing by the wide margin that once separated these two basketball programs. "When Dawkins missed I thought there was a chance Perkins was going to bank it in," Krzyzewski said. "It's never over until it's over, especially in this game."

"We got outhustled," Smith said. "That should never happen."

"It is the greatest win any of these players have realized," said an exhausted Krzyzewski outside the jubilant locker room in the bowels of the Greensboro Coliseum.

"I still can't believe it," said a smiling and sweaty Meagher, sitting in a small metal locker with a towel wrapped around his neck. "I looked up and saw all the fans go crazy. I just keep hearing how that the Heels are so good. I've heard so much talk, but we're the good ones."

Just maybe the "double-standard" speech by Krzyzewski earlier that season had not fallen on deaf ears. Just maybe someone heard his pleas to even up the calls, to give other teams a chance against the Tar Heels. Just maybe the Henderson steal of the ball from the nation's premier college player was a sign of a new era, where his Blue Devils would be getting the calls going their way.

Just maybe that's where it all started.

Chapter 7

Blood and Roses

On practice day of the 1989 ACC Tournament in Atlanta, I witnessed two separate conversations involving Dean Smith and Mike Krzyzewski within minutes. Both were fascinating talks and personified each of the Hall of Fame coaches. And both conversations involved an incident at the UNC-Duke game in Cameron Indoor Stadium on January 18, a full seven weeks earlier.

Smith was incensed over a sign in the Duke student section about the intellect of one of his players, a sign he considered subtly racist. It had bothered Smith all season and on the pre-ACC Tournament teleconference—a few days after the Tar Heels lost Jeff Lebo's senior game to Duke—Smith mentioned the sign again and called it not only racist, but also wrong. He said two of his African American players had a higher combined SAT score than two of Duke's comparable white players. "And I know," Smith said sharply, "because I recruited both of them." In doing so he had seen their academic records. He also started a media hailstorm.

So there I was, walking through the tunnel of the old Omni arena and into the bowels of its bottom floor. In the distance I saw Smith talking with Bill Brill, the veteran and very partial sportswriter to Duke. Brill was a Duke graduate and made no apologies for his affection for all Blue Devil teams.

As I approached them, I heard Brill say to Smith, "You can't do that. You can't go public with private information about any students—even yours."

"Why not?" Smith said to Brill. "I never said the particular score of any one player. I knew exactly what I was doing."

Smith was defending one of his players, something he had done in the past after the rowdy Duke students had crossed what he considered a line of decency. Smith was quick to jump on a legitimate cause and especially one that involved race.

I kept walking and thought about what Smith had done and I figured he needed a combination of two scores, instead of just one score, to prove his point. As a mathematician Smith was always thinking that way: analytical, thoughtful, almost never saying something he regretted, no matter how opinionated.

As I entered the court area at the Omni, Duke happened to be working out on the playing floor. It was basically a shoot-around because the public always watched the practice day. The Duke assistant coaches ran the shoot-around while Krzyzewski stood just outside the baseline with a small group of media. Among them were two sportswriters I expected to see, Duke alum and best-selling sports author John Feinstein and Durham Morning Herald sports editor Keith Drum, who had befriended Coach K just after he arrived at Duke.

I wasn't going to join in but had to pass the group on my way to the press room on the other side of the building. No one noticed me as I walked by. All eyes were glued to what Krzyzewski was saying. And what was he saying as I passed by? "It really pisses me off that he would talk about two of my players in public," Krzyzewski said angrily. "Fuck him."

Four days later in the absolutely brutal ACC Championship Game between Duke and Carolina, Smith and Krzyzewski would have a lot more to say—and some of it to each other.

—AC

To fully understand the animosity that had grown between Dean Smith and Mike Krzyzewski by that 1989 season and would go on for eight more years, one must trace back recent history a bit and have a pretty good understanding of human nature.

Just after Krzyzewski had taken the job at Duke as a 33-year-old unknown, he was in the Duke Gardens for a family picture. One of the sports information directors, who had set up the photo shoot and was there, mentioned to Krzyzewski that his blue suit wasn't quite dark enough and in the sunlight could turn out to be light blue in the photo. Krzyzewski smiled and said: "I'm not going to get caught up in all of that Carolina stuff."

Yeah, right.

It did not take Coach K long to break his vow once his first season began and he saw how pervasive and suffocating the ramped-up Tar Heel fan base could be even in the city of Durham, where more UNC alumni and fans resided than their Duke counterparts. The Blue Devils actually did defeat Carolina in his first season, on Smith's 50th birthday, thanks to a bravo performance by Krzyzewski's holdover senior Gene Banks.

But the losses got so lopsided the next two years that even Krzyzewski's oldest daughter, Debbie, was being harassed by students and several teachers who were die-hard Heel fans at her middle school.

One late morning, Debbie called her father at the Duke basketball office in tears. She told him they were teasing her, and even some teachers were writing "Go Heels!" on her papers when she got them back. She wanted her father to come pick her up and take her home. "I'm coming," Krzyzewski said, "but I am not picking you up. I am bringing you something."

Before leaving the office, Krzyzewski grabbed a Duke T-shirt from the storage closet. When he arrived at Debbie's school, he pulled her out of class and handed her the T-shirt. He told her to put it on and wear it for the rest of the day. "No Krzyzewski ever turns away from a fight," he said, hugging her and kissing her on the cheek before leaving.

By the time he had recruited enough good players to compete with Carolina, Krzyzewski and his family had become as obsessed with Dean and his Tar Heels as other coaches at Duke and N.C. State whom Smith had driven away. Years later, acknowledging that the rivalry made him a better coach and suspecting that it motivated UNC as well, Krzyzewski had built a program that in many ways emulated Carolina, but it also was markedly different. There were things that

Smith and the Tar Heels did that he felt Duke could do better, such as giving players more individual freedom within the team concept.

It truly began during the epic 1984 season, when Krzyzewski first took on Smith publicly and finally upset the Tar Heels of Michael Jordan, Sam Perkins, and Kenny Smith in the ACC Tournament. Duke sophomore guard Johnny Dawkins said that convinced the Blue Devils they could beat any team in the country. And as the two schools began battling head-to-head for recruits, almost all the niceties of Coach K's early years were gone.

Before then players and coaches from both schools were friendlier than most fans would have believed. In the early 1970s, several Blue Devils and Tar Heels actually lived together during the summer, and Bucky Waters brought his squad to Chapel Hill to scrimmage before both teams went to New York for the 1971 NIT. (UNC defeated Duke in the semifinals at Madison Square Garden.) Carolina's Mike O'Koren would party regularly at Duke with former high school teammate and Duke star Jim Spanarkel. In the early 1980s, Jordan and Dawkins had each other's phone numbers and arranged pickup games in the fall before practice began.

That all changed by the end of the 1984 season, when during a double-overtime thriller won by UNC in Chapel Hill, Duke's Jay Bilas and Carolina's Perkins shoved and cursed at each other. From that point on, the Tar Heels were the establishment, and the Blue Devils were the announced challengers coming on strong until they caught what had been the ACC's model program over the last 20 years.

Important steps included the recruiting victory for Danny Ferry in the spring of 1985; the decisive win over Carolina at Carmichael Auditorium in January of 1985, snapping Duke's 20-year losing streak in Chapel Hill; the 1986 honor, in a strange sort of way, of being the opponent on the day the 22,000-seat Dean Smith Center opened on the UNC campus. The final step was the start to a stunning run of ACC championships and Final Fours, putting the Duke program in the same elite category as the Tar Heels and eventually surpassing them for a while.

And surely it was getting under the skin at Carolina, which was in the process of winning more games in the 1980s than any other program and won or shared six ACC regular season, if not tournament, titles. The Tar Heels were perennials at the NCAA Tournament, working on an amazing record of 13 consecutive trips to the Sweet 16. Smith knew Duke had become a player, but few had expected the Blue Devils to gain national prominence so quickly.

After defeating Duke in the Smith Center opener in 1986, Carolina was undefeated (18–0) and ranked No. 1 in the country. But Duke won the rematch and its first ACC Tournament in six years, as the Tar Heels faded with key injuries to senior Steve Hale and junior Joe Wolf. The Blue Devils got the favorable draw in the NCAA East regional and then went all the way to the national championship game in Dallas before losing to Louisville in the last minutes.

The Tar Heels went undefeated in the ACC regular season for the second time in four years in 1987 but lost their two most important games, the ACC Tournament championship to N.C. State (whom they had beaten twice by a combined 35 points in the regular season) and the Elite Eight game to No. 10-ranked Syracuse at the Meadowlands, where Smith cut short his postgame press conference in tears. Five years after winning his first NCAA title in New Orleans, when it seemed like it was his turn again, Carolina came up short. "Yeah, we have a really bad basketball team. We were 32–4," assistant coach Bill Guthridge said sarcastically after criticism of the season was pointed at Smith for blowing such big games.

But Duke wasn't blowing many games. In 1988 the Blue Devils defeated the Tar Heels three times (prompting the sale of hundreds of T-shirts celebrating the "Triple Play Season"), including the ACC Tournament championship game, which Carolina led late by five points. "To beat them once in a season is great," said Blue Devils guard Kevin Strickland, a native of Mt. Airy, North Carolina. "To beat them three times is something we can always remember."

That bitter ACC Tournament loss also cost UNC the No. 1 seed in the NCAA East regional, where the first two games were scheduled for the Smith Center. Imagine how pissed off the Tar Heels were, having to vacate their own arena for two games at the West region in Salt Lake City while the Dukies pretty much laughed their way through two double-digit wins in a half-empty Dean Dome.

And even though Carolina went on an NCAA roll to reach its second straight Elite Eight game in Seattle, the Tar Heels lost to Arizona while Duke was winning the East region by beating top-ranked Temple as senior Billy King shut down the Owls' freshman sensation Mark Macon. Fortunately for UNC fans, Duke stumbled in the Final Four to unranked Kansas, which was coached by Smith protégé Larry Brown, who led the Jayhawks to the 1988 National Championship.

• • •

By the 1989 season, the graying 57-year-old Smith was under fire for not winning a single ACC championship since 1982, and the youthful 41-year-old Krzyzewski seemed like the young stud in the office pushing the established old dog out to pasture. This delighted a Duke fan base that had had it for years with Smith and his program, and it threatened Tar Heel fans into developing a newfound hatred for the Dukies, especially their pointy-nosed, ninth-year coach, who had become a villain in his own right and already been given the squirmy nickname of "Rat Face."

By now Krzyzewski's wife and three daughters and their small entourage were visible and audible at all Duke games, cheering and yelling at the officials, often using sailor's language that they picked up from the family patriarch who grew up on the mean streets of Chicago. Under Coach K, Duke had introduced an aggressive, in-your-face brand of defense to the ACC that had opponents believing the Blue Devils were subject to the same double standard that back in 1984 Krzyzewski claimed Smith had enjoyed. Wake Forest coach Bob Staak, who lasted four losing seasons in Winston-Salem, had the best line of all. "Duke plays great fucking defense," he said, "five guys fouling all the time."

Why would Duke not be the preseason favorite again in the ACC? The Blue Devils had Ferry playing his senior year after his consensus All-American junior season when he led the ACC in scoring, was unanimous All-ACC, won ACC Player of the Year and tournament MVP honors, and set the single-game Duke scoring record with 58 points at Miami. Ferry would end his career as the first ACC player to compile more than 2,000 points, 1,000 rebounds, and 500 assists, mostly a product of playing in Krzyzewski's motion offense and not camped at the low post.

Senior Quin Snyder was coming off his best college season, when he shot 48 percent from the floor, 46 percent from the three-point line, and 78 percent from the foul line; averaged eight points and 5.7 assists per game; and led the Blue Devils in steals.

Also returning was the unsung leader of the team, 6'5" junior Robert Brickey, who could play guard and forward and was both a ferocious inside scorer and rebounder. Krzyzewski loved it when people called Brickey undersized or—better—a misfit who couldn't shoot from outside and was too small to play power forward. Despite his size, though, Brickey was one of the most physical antagonists in the Carolina rivalry. "He came to Duke and became a hell of a player," Coach K told Barry Jacobs in the *Fans' Guide to ACC Basketball*. Duke was installed as the prohibitive favorite to win the 1989 regular season, if not the NCAA title.

Carolina had eight of its nine top players returning, including junior All-American J.R. Reid and his inside running mate Scott Williams. Jeff Lebo was the soul of the team, coming off a junior season in which he made 47 percent of his three-pointers (including five in a row to rally the Tar Heels from a 13-point deficit against Georgia Tech) and was now comfortable as a shooting point guard. Senior Steve Bucknall, junior Kevin Madden, and even sophomores Pete Chilcutt, Rick Fox, and King Rice had all played in every game the prior season. The Tar Heels were pretty packed and gunning to break a six-year drought of ACC championships and trips to the Final Four. They knew all that went through Duke, and all the guys on both teams now hated each other.

As expected, Duke blew out of the gate, winning its first 13 games and rarely by less than 10 points. As the preseason top-ranked team, the Blue Devils were even more solidly sitting atop the polls on January 18 when the No. 13 but hobbled Tar Heels arrived in Durham, having lost two of their last three games. Even worse for UNC, Lebo was sidelined with a sprained ankle—and was sardonically handed a dozen roses by the Duke cheerleaders when he came out on the court in street clothes and on crutches. Lebo laughed and gave the long stems back.

Among the many games for which Smith has been hailed a great coach, this was one of the most forgotten. He believed his big men Reid and Williams could dominate underneath since Ferry roamed in Duke's offense, and there was no other size to match the Tar Heel twin towers. Smith made a rare appearance at the team's pregame meal to pull Reid and Williams aside. Despite not having Lebo, he said Carolina could pull the upset if they rebounded like mad men and the Tar Heels hit some shots.

Gameplan executed. Carolina clobbered Duke on the boards 43–27 and shot 53 percent from the field. Despite great nights from Brickey and Phil Henderson (a combined 36 points on 16-of-23 shooting), Duke fell behind early and lost its first game of the season 91–71. Reid and Williams both had double-doubles, scoring 35 points to go along with their 21 rebounds.

In a late timeout, Smith smiled wryly and said, "Don't you love how quiet this place is right now?"

Smith was thrilled with the victory but angry about something he saw in the Duke student section—a placard that read, "J.R. Can't Reid." It pressed Smith's hottest buttons, as he believed the sign would have never been made had Reid been white. In the postgame press conference, he called the play on words racist and scolded the Duke administration for not monitoring its student behavior better. Complaints about the student-section behavior at Cameron Indoor Stadium were not new, and Krzyzewski defended the young fans for having cleaned up their act in recent years.

The Tar Heels went on a roll and climbed to No. 3 in the polls, while Duke lost three more of its next four games and free fell to No. 12. This had been an overconfident team that did not play a ranked opponent until Carolina. Smith had pointed out a rebounding flaw that would dog Duke for the rest of the season. And without Lebo, Smith had played sophomore Rice at point guard and let the poor shooter dribble drive on the Blue Devils, making seven assists and 10-of-11 free throws when Duke tried to stop him with the ball. It became the new way to play Krzyzewski-coached teams.

By the rematch at the Smith Center, the Blue Devils were the underdog, but such odds generally mean nothing in the Duke-Carolina series. Snyder decided a close game down the stretch by draining three clutch three-pointers to seal an 88–86 upset road win. Smith, who invented the tradition of Senior Day, hated when his players lost their last home game and was edgy all week, leading to his SAT research and pointed remark in the pre-ACC Tournament teleconference.

Hosting its last ACC Tournament, Atlanta's Omni Coliseum was a tight arena by today's standards with funky angles and narrow aisles between the seating sections. Despite knowing how the Duke-Carolina rivalry was festering since their first game in Durham, the ACC foolishly assigned fans from the schools to adjacent sections separated by one of those thin aisles. Krzyzewski's family entourage was in its customary position a few rows behind the Duke bench, and they had their game faces on long before the opening tip. It was a mild March 12 afternoon, and the body heat in the building was stifling and almost unbearable for some. The action on the court began aggressively and escalated from there.

Duke's Snyder was dating Larry Brown's daughter, who was a UNC coed. The two eventually married (and divorced), but in their senior years, Kristi Brown alternated her time between Snyder and her homies in Chapel Hill. Among them was a close friend of Lebo. (We'll refer to him as Steve.) As the starters shook hands in the center circle, Lebo leaned over to Snyder and told him Kristi was spending a lot of "quality" time with Steve and that they were together in Chapel Hill the entire weekend while they were playing in Atlanta. The ball went up, and the game was on. Snyder shot 1-of-9, missed all seven of his three-pointers, and fouled out.

Ferry, who had added the Naismith Award nomination to his resume, was playing for the last time against the school he once loved and he was now loathed by its fans who chanted "Fer-ry! Fer-ry!" every time he did anything on the court. Some eye-popping statistics helped Duke overcome a dismal shooting day of 39 percent from the floor and only 3-of-23 from the three-point line. There were 59 free throws attempted on 49 total fouls called by officials John Moreau, Dick Paparo, and Lenny Wirtz.

The Tar Heels shot just under 50 percent, but they turned the ball over eight more times than Duke, which also had 14 steals compared to Carolina's eight. The play under the basket and hand-to-hand combat on the perimeter was so aggressive that both coaches wound up yelling at opposing players to take it easy. Smith was the first to shout down the sideline to Krzyzewski, who thought Scott Williams was roughing up his players on the way to fouling out with 11 points and 11 rebounds—and told him so.

It had escalated less than two and a half minutes into the second half. Williams challenged an inside shot by Duke freshman Christian Laettner and was charged with a foul that sent Laettner to the free throw line.

Smith called Williams to the Carolina bench, and as the 6'10" UNC junior walked past the Duke bench, Krzyzewski gave him an earful, telling him he thought it was a dirty play. "I thought it was a flagrant foul and I don't care for that," Krzyzewski said later. "That's when somebody gets hurt."

Smith didn't like Krzyzewski talking to his player. "Hey, don't talk to my players," Smith yelled in his Kansas twang to Krzyzewski just 30 feet away.

"Hey, Dean, fuck you!" Krzyzewski yelled back, and his words traveled on a light rail along the scorer's table between the benches. Almost everyone sitting there heard the exchange.

Six minutes later came the next confrontation involving Duke's Henderson and Carolina's Rice and Madden. "I was cutting through the lane, and Phil caught me in the throat with an elbow," Rice described it. "The ball went out of bounds, and timeout was called."

The players headed for their respective benches, and they bumped shoulders. To Henderson it looked like Rice threw his shoulder into him on purpose. Henderson then walked to the Tar Heel huddle and pushed Madden, causing both benches to erupt and earning Henderson a technical. "I think Phil retaliated, and that's not what the officials called," Krzyzewski said.

"There were cheap shots out there all day. I just got caught," Henderson said. "It was a retaliation thing, but I shouldn't have done it."

The physicality went on the entire game. Ferry received a long, bloody scratch from his left cheek to his ear, and Reid had a large bump under his right eye. "I went up for a shot on the wing, and J.R. tried to put a hand in my face on the way up and scratched me," Ferry said.

The powerful forwards also spent a lot of time trash talking to each other. With 4:20 left in the game, Reid hit a jumper from the lane as

Ferry crashed to the floor. Reid looked down and shouted at Ferry, "Take that, Mr. Naismith!"

"Coaches get on me a lot about talking when I play," Reid said, "but that's just the way I play. It gets me into the flow of the game. I realize there are times to do it and times not to do it, but our guys are very emotional."

Ferry walked off the court with a bloody face after also missing all seven of his three-pointers, the last a 75-foot heave that would have tied the score. It was right on line but hit the back rim and bounded high into the air as the buzzer went off. "The ball did all it could to go in there," Reid said. "It was close. If it had gone in, I think it would have been their game. But it was our day in the sun."

Carolina hung on to win 77–74 and cut down the ACC Tournament nets for the first time since 1982. The game is still remembered by those in attendance as among the most intense sporting events they ever witnessed in person.

So the hatred was in full force, on and off the court. Duke continued to have the best of it by building a new belief system that March meant a brand new season and going to five straight Final Fours and seven out of a possible nine between 1986 and 1994. The 1989 team lost a semifinal to Seton Hall in Seattle, and the '90 Blue Devils were blown out by undefeated UNLV in the championship game in Denver.

Duke's first national championship in basketball came after Carolina had avenged two regular season losses in 1991 by blowing out the belligerent Blue Devils in the championship game of the ACC Tournament in Charlotte. Duke came in cocky after having swept the Tar Heels in the regular season and only needing one victory to reach championship Sunday. Maryland was on a probation that banned it from playing on TV and forced it to sit out the tournament, giving regular season champion Duke a first-round bye. The Blue Devils easily dispatched N.C. State in the semifinals while the Tar Heels survived close games against Clemson and Virginia to get their third shot at Duke.

Since the Blue Devils were fresher, they figured they would easily handle Carolina again. But UNC had steely focus and, led by Rick Fox's 25 points, jumped out to a double-digit lead, as Duke began bickering with the officials and each other. Krzyzewski drew an early technical foul from referee Wirtz, who heard profanity from the Duke bench. Krzyzewski was actually yelling at one of his players, and the T further unraveled the Devils, who trailed by 13 at the half and eventually lost 96–74. By the end Laettner was sulking on the bench after having drawn his own technical foul for mouthing off to official Gerry Donaghy. King Rice held Bobby Hurley without a field goal for the second game that season.

It was a bad day all around for Krzyzewski, who saw his frustrated family leave the Charlotte Coliseum early after being mercilessly heckled by the UNC pep band sitting nearby, and he was rebutted by Smith as they were coming and going from the postgame press conference. Rice had accompanied Smith, and Krzyzewski, looking at a stat sheet, said, "Nice game, King, 12 points and seven assists."

Smith butted in and said, "The way we keep it, King actually had 11 assists."

"However the hell you keep it, nice game, King," Coach K said as he walked away and met some media outside the Duke locker room.

He was asked about his players' on-court demeanor, particularly Laettner, and acknowledged that, as great as he was, Laettner could be a "real asshole" at times. It looked like his team was in tatters heading into the NCAA Tournament.

But Duke had learned to reset for the postseason and cruised to its fourth straight Final Four by romping through four Midwest region games by an average victory margin of more than 18 points. The Tar Heels had walked a similar path in the East region, winning four games over unranked teams and having to oust Temple and its now senior star Macon in the Elite Eight game in New Jersey.

It was the first time Duke and UNC had reached the same Final Four. Smith had not been there in nine years and found out just what a celebrity Krzyzewski had become. At the banquet on Thursday night, Smith kiddingly slipped into a line, waiting to get Coach K's autograph. This was already Krzyzewski's fifth Final Four. At the time Smith had only seven in 15 more years of coaching. Still, Smith and his Tar Heels were just happy to be back. And they played with a far different focus than Duke.

The weekend in Indianapolis could not have turned out more differently for both fan bases.

From hoping their team could win Smith's second NCAA title and anticipating top-ranked UNLV pummeling Duke in the Final Four for a second straight season, Tar Heel fans got exactly the opposite. Ragged play against mirror-image Kansas left Carolina down nine at the half and scrambling to get back in the game. The Tar Heels shot 38 percent and lost the rebounding battle to the smaller Jayhawks. Kansas won 79–73 for its third-year coach Roy Williams, who was in his first Final Four as head man after leaving as Smith's assistant at Carolina.

And Duke shocked the Rebels with a performance as brilliant as it was brave. Krzyzewski had harped all week on how UNLV had not been in a close game all season and said "if we keep it close, we will win at the end."

Hurley made a three-pointer with Duke down five and less than three minutes to play. The Rebels, now facing the scenario Krzyzewski had predicted, did not score again as Laettner's two free throws finished the monumental 79–77 upset that kept UNLV from winning back-to-back national championships after crushing the Blue Devils in 1990 by a record differential of 30 points. This was the true milestone for Krzyzewski and his program as he won the school's first national championship with a team that was supposed to be a year away from greatness. It added the element of confidence that helped make the 1992 season so special.

For many Duke fans, it remains the greatest weekend of their lives, whether they were at the Hoosier Dome or watching on TV. They were treated to a first-game feast when the Tar Heels not only lost, but Smith was also ejected on a second technical foul late in the second half. The Carolina coach walked off the court, passing through the tunnel right under where the Duke contingent sat high on natural ecstasy. UNC losing and Dean getting tossed would have been enough for most of them, but vanquishing Vegas and then winning it all against Williams, the Tar Heel lifer, two nights later left the Duke fan base giddy and their team in rarified air.

The 1992 Blue Devils of Laettner, Hurley, Grant Hill and a solid seven-man rotation are considered one of the greatest college basketball teams of all time. They lost only twice by a combined six points on the way to a second straight NCAA title—punctuated by Laettner's 15-foot jump shot off Hill's 80-foot pass that beat Kentucky in the

East regional championship. One of Duke's defeats was in Chapel Hill, where a struggling Tar Heel team demonstrated why the rivalry should never be overlooked in any year. Carolina pulled the upset in the middle of a five-game winning streak but soon collapsed to lose five of its last six regular season games.

The Tar Heels finished with double-digit defeats (23–10) for the second time in three years and only the fourth in Smith's 31 seasons as head coach. Something was wrong, especially since the 1992 squad had statistics worthy of a better record, including 50 percent shooting from the floor and the second best field goal defense (.434) in Smith's tenure. Turnovers were up, and they gave up more three-pointers than in any season since the 19-foot, 9-inch arc was established in 1987. Smith decided it was a lack of focus on offense and a lack of quickness on defense that allowed opponents to break UNC's double teams and find wide-open shooters.

Upsetting top-ranked and undefeated Duke still made it a special season and carved the image of a bloodied but unbowed Eric Montross forever in the minds of Tar Heel fans. After getting a few minutes off the bench as a freshman, sophomore Montross was learning to play the college game with a fervor that belied his almost gentlemanly demeanor off the court. He would simply not give up the paint, banging bodies with Dukies and Tar Heels alike. He had to go to the bench several times, looking for UNC's answer to Angelo Dundee to close the wounds under his left eye and on his closely cropped head, several of which were inflicted by Laettner's flailing elbows and one head butt in traffic. Double zero ran to the training room for stitches and returned to a huge roar from the Smith Center crowd. "They were just stronger than we were on the boards," Krzyzewski said after the 75–73 loss in Chapel Hill, "and they used it to their advantage. That's good coaching."

But *real* good coaching came the next year, when Carolina had virtually its entire team back—with the exception of leading scorer Hubert Davis, who became somewhat of a Cameron legend in the 1992 rematch by scoring a career-high 35 points, including six three-pointers in an 89–77 defeat to end the regular season.

The Tar Heels, who had lasted three NCAA Tournament games in '92 while Duke rolled to its second straight national championship—this time against Michigan's Fab Five in Minneapolis—would have the extraordinary season in 1993 when their sum added up to more than their individual parts. Montross was the center around whom they worked, but their spiritual leader was senior George Lynch, whose nose for the ball and quickness made him UNC's third-leading career rebounder (behind Tyler Hansbrough and Perkins) and second all time in steals (only six behind 1993 teammate Derrick Phelps), a rare stat combination for a rare player.

Lynch led Carolina to first place in the ACC standings and No. 1 in the polls, displacing a Duke team that had lost Laettner and was hampered by a foot injury to Grant Hill, whose value to the team was underscored as the first ACC player to exceed 1,900 points, 700 rebounds, 400 assists, 200 steals, and 100 blocked shots

After the Blue Devils' streak of five consecutive Final Fours ended with a second-round loss to California and Jason Kidd, the Tar Heels moved on to the Final Four in New Orleans with a determination that admittedly Duke helped build over the last two years. "All I heard was them being tired of us, and if I were them, I would have been tired of us, too. Actually, I'm now tired of them," Krzyzewski told *Sports Illustrated* shortly after as a CBS commentator he got a bird's-eye view of the Tar Heels avenging the loss to Kansas in 1991 and then denying Michigan's Fab Five again. Montross and Lynch went on to become NBA journeymen, but no one else on that team even sniffed the league, including Final Four Most Outstanding Player Donald Williams, who nailed 10-of-14 three-pointers over the weekend.

But Carolina had gotten back to playing better team defense and began a seven-game winning streak against Duke that covered the Blue Devils' seventh Final Four season in nine years, the two games Krzyzewski missed in 1995, and the two after he came back in 1996, where the rivalry picked up where it left off before his 19-game sabbatical.

• • •

When Krzyzewski returned for the 1996 season, both teams were mediocre by their own lofty standards. But that did not keep them from staging two more classics—close if not necessarily well-played.

The Tar Heels won both, rallying from 12 down at the half to escape 73–72 at home and then surviving a wild scene at Cameron that included 45 fouls and 54 free throws, the ejection of Carolina's Jeff McInnis, and the Crazies again crossing the line in Smith's mind. There had been nasty rumors about the personal life of UNC assistant coach and legendary player Phil Ford, and the Crazies were relentless in their cheers and chants aimed at Ford. Smith was furious and said so, following the 84–78 victory, as the two programs harped at each other until the forgettable season ended for both early in the 1996 NCAA Tournament.

When Smith retired in October of 1997 after his 11th Final Four team lost in the national semifinal to Arizona in Indianapolis, Krzyzewski began his royal praise of the former rival that has continued to this day. Calling him a great competitor who he would miss going against, Krzyzewski was also about to regain his mantle as America's coach, and his program began putting together the most dominating stretch in the history of the ACC.

There was one bitter season remaining, however, when Guthridge took over a loaded 1998 team that played three epic games against Duke, the last ending in controversy that moved Krzyzewski to defend his family in public.

The Tar Heels won the first meeting in 1998, when they actually blew out Duke twice in the same game. Before a Smith Center crowd, they ran off to a 16-point halftime lead behind Duke-killer Antawn Jamison, who averaged 23 points and 11 rebounds in going 5–2 against the Blue Devils in his career. After Duke rallied to within four points, the Tar Heels exploded again—highlighted by sophomore Ed Cota lobbing the ball against the backboard for a Vince Carter dunk during a fast break that had the home fans in frenzy. The final score was 97–73 with four starters in double figures and Cota adding 12 assists to his 12 points.

Carolina had a veteran team with four future NBA players and several others who would have long pro careers in Europe. But under the affable Guthridge, who referred to it as "Dean's Team," the No. 1-rated Tar Heels lost to unranked Maryland and N.C. State and went to Cameron Indoor Stadium, having to sweep the Blue Devils to claim first place in the ACC regular season race. Duke's one league loss had been the double-digit blowout in Chapel Hill, and its only other defeat all season was at Michigan back in December, which relinquished the top ranking to UNC. During the amazing 1998 season, the Blue Devils and Tar Heels each spent seven weeks at No. 1 in the polls.

On Saturday afternoon, February 28, it was 70 degrees outside and sweltering inside Cameron. Behind Jamison, who had scored 35 and 33 points in his last two games against Duke, the Tar Heels raced to a double-digit lead in the first half that was 12 at the break and grew to 17 with 10 minutes remaining. Freshman Elton Brand, who had missed two months with a broken foot, stormed off the bench in the second half to score 13 points and spark a rally that overcame Carolina with less than two minutes to play. The Blue Devils hung

Hurley and the Heels

Mike Krzyzewski has called Bobby Hurley the "most daring" player he ever coached, but their relationship was rocky from the start—as it is with many Duke players who don't know how to play hard enough to meet the Blue Devils' standards. "Obviously, there was accountability," said Hurley, now the head coach at the University of Buffalo, "but he gave me the power and freedom out on the court and did not manage every move I made. That's why I had so much success my last three seasons."

Hurley was baptized into the Duke-Carolina rivalry as a freshman, when he committed 10 turnovers and was dogged aggressively by UNC point guard King Rice. At one point Hurley left the game in tears, as the Smith Center crowd roared with its approval.

Rice, now the head coach at Monmouth in New Jersey, acknowledges how rugged the Duke-Carolina games were in the late 1980s and early '90s. "There was a lot of trash-talking on the court," Rice said. "Both teams wanted to win because it made their seasons."

"King was very frustrating to play against," Hurley said, "but he helped me raise my game and to understand what the rivalry meant. I learned to love the rivalry. The weeks and days leading up to the two games, it was all over campus and town. Two days before every Carolina game, I went over to the football stadium and ran the steps. I wanted to sharpen my focus and not disappoint our fans. I built up as much anger as I could inside to channel toward that game because I knew how important it was."

Hurley, who is the all-time NCAA assists leader with 1,076, also had a less-celebrated rivalry with All-American teammate Christian Laettner, who was known to be tough on his fellow Blue Devils when they made mistakes or did not hustle. "We didn't see eye-to-eye all the time. We were both very competitive players," Hurley said. "But I had the ball in my hand for most of the time, so I had some control over him."

on to win 77–75 for Krzyzewski's 500th career coaching victory, a feat celebrated on the retired Dean Smith's 67th birthday.

The victory gave Duke, which became the first ACC team to win 15 games (15–1), a big advantage in the revamped ACC Tournament in Greensboro. The conference eliminated the dreaded play-in game on Thursday night. Instead the No. 1 seed played Thursday and (if it won) got Friday off while the No. 2 team played back-to-back on Friday and then Saturday. In the Friday game, No. 2 seed UNC demolished eighth-seeded N.C. State. With so much anticipation of a third Duke-Carolina game Sunday for the ACC championship, both teams barely made it through the semifinals. The Blue Devils edged Clemson by two points, and the Tar Heels needed overtime to survive Maryland.

That night, word spread that Jamison had injured his groin against Maryland and was doubtful for the championship game. Carolina fans fretted and wondered whether Jamison should try to play or sit out and be healthy for the NCAA Tournament. They got their answer Sunday when Jamison ran out to warm up, running and jumping without a problem. The problem would be for Duke, which had the game tied at 57 with eight minutes remaining when Jamison led a decisive 13–0 spurt that triggered a huge celebration amongst the thousands of UNC fans who remained in the Greensboro Coliseum after the game. For a guy nursing a sore groin, Jamison scored 22 points and grabbed 18 rebounds and had enough left to jump up on the press tables with several teammates to wave to the fans.

Carolina's Makhtar Ndiaye stayed on the table to dance as senior Shammond Williams went over to play several instruments with the Carolina pep band. The sociable Williams had made news 10 days earlier by visiting the Krzyzewskiville tent city before the regular-season finale. "They treated me great," he said. After scoring 15 and 19 in his last two games against Duke, he did not want the music to stop.

The party ended, and all awaited the NCAA pairings, which gave both Duke and Carolina No. 1 seeds and sent the Blue Devils to the South region for two games in Lexington, Kentucky, and the Tar Heels to the East and Hartford, Connecticut. Krzyzewski was angry that the two marquee programs weren't assigned more glamorous first-round sites like Atlanta and Washington, D.C., but by his Monday NCAA press conference was mad about something else.

His family had stayed in their seats after the game in Greensboro, very close to where Ndiaye was cavorting on the press table. The Krzyzewski women believed that Ndiaye knew who they were and made throat-slitting and dagger-to-the-heart gestures directly at them. Of course, these gesticulations were prohibited in any sport, but it is not generally meant to be a death threat or vow of violence. It's more a sign of supremacy because the Heels just hammered the Devils 83–68.

During a timeout earlier in the game, Ndiaye had walked by the Duke bench and made a slashing motion across his throat at the Blue Devils, particularly senior Ricky Price, who was in Krzyzewski's doghouse all season and never got off the bench in this game and instead jawed at the Tar Heels. That so infuriated Krzyzewski that he made the game officials call Guthridge to midcourt to complain about Ndiaye's actions. Guthridge didn't know what Krzyzewski was talking about or else was playing dumb.

Krzyzewski didn't hear about the incident with his family until well after his postgame press conference. "I'm not sure I would ever see that as part of a celebration," he said Monday when asked about Ndiaye allegedly taunting his family. "If it ever happens at our place…that would never happen at our place. That kid would never play. Certainly people should celebrate, but they should do it with their own fans. I don't think that you jump on the scorer's table and yell at the opposing fans. I don't think you can put a dagger in the heart of the opposing fan."

Krzyzewski had called out Ndiaye and the Carolina program but got no response from either—other than seeing Ndiaye's public response that he didn't mean to offend anyone.

The story died after a day or two but ramped up the expectation that Duke and Carolina would again make it to the Final Four, where they could meet for the 1998 National Championship on Monday night, March 30. However, Duke squandered a 17-point lead to Kentucky in St. Petersburg, Florida, while Carolina defeated Connecticut back in Greensboro the previous day and denied UConn coach Jim Calhoun his first Final Four. (The Huskies went on to win three national championships over the next 13 years.)

Disappointed by losing and how he lost, Krzyzewski was still zinging the ACC Tournament episode by complimenting Kentucky and coach

Tubby Smith for a "classy celebration" after such a dramatic comeback win. Coach K got over it more quickly after the top-ranked Tar Heels had shooting problems in the Alamodome in San Antonio, making only 39 percent of their field goals and missing 20-of-23 three-point attempts in a 65–59 upset loss to seventh-ranked Utah. And maybe Coach K felt some form of justice when Ndiaye was caught lying about hearing a racial slur from one of the white Utah players. Carolina had its fourth embarrassing Saturday semifinal loss in the 1990s and was further embarrassed afterward by Ndiaye's foolish claim.

Guthridge, who had discussed stepping down after the season with heir apparent Roy Williams, decided he could not leave on such a sour note and returned for the 1998–99 campaign, when Duke continued its rule over the ACC that lasted a full 10 years until Williams returned to UNC in 2003 and got the Heels back to where they'd been before.

• • •

Duke went 16–0 in the 1999 ACC race, becoming the first team to go unbeaten with the expanded schedule. (Over a three-season stretch, the Blue Devils would go 46–2 in conference play.) They also swept through the first three games of the 1999 tournament virtually untouched, winning only one of the 19 ACC games by less than 10 points. It was the first of five straight ACC tourney titles for Duke, which won seven out of eight between 1999 and 2006.

Connecticut won its first national championship for Calhoun in 1999 by beating Duke on the same St. Petersburg court where the Blue Devils had succumbed to the Kentucky comeback the year before. Richard "Rip" Hamilton's 27 points bested Trajan Langdon's 25 in the 77–74 UConn victory, as Duke—after being ranked No. 1 the last seven weeks—finished 37–2 to tie its own NCAA record for victories in a season.

During that post-Smith span, Carolina lost 15-of-17 games to Duke under Guthridge, Matt Doherty, and Williams. The Tar Heels' only wins were in Doherty's first and last regular-season games against the Blue Devils: the upset at top-ranked Duke that led to an 18-game winning streak and their own No. 1 ranking and Senior Day at UNC in

2003, when Doherty and Duke assistant Chris Collins almost started a brawl in front of the Duke bench.

Doherty had come onto the court to check on his fallen player, Raymond Felton, and to also complain about the foul by Dahntay Jones that floored his freshman point guard. "Mike, he's a dirty player. He threw an elbow at my guy," Doherty said to official Mike Wood about Duke's Jones, who committed what Doherty thought was a flagrant foul.

"That's not what happened, Coach," Wood said to Doherty, who was standing over Felton but talking loud enough for the Duke bench to hear him.

Collins responded, "Hey, Mike, did he come out here to check on his guy or bitch and whine about the play?"

Doherty approached Collins and said, "Shut the fuck up, motherfucker!"

As Collins was saying the same thing, the 6'7" head coach chest bumped the 6'3" assistant and raised both palms as he backed away. Duke reserve Andre Buckner got between the two coaches and shoved Doherty, and for a split second, it looked like an actual fight would start.

The officials finally got control of the scrum after pulling bodies apart and brought both head coaches to the scorer's table. Wood said, "This is wrong. This is embarrassing to a great league, two great universities, and two great basketball programs. It has to end now."

It did, along with the game, which Carolina won 82–79 to snap that six-game losing streak. Duke finished third in the ACC but went on to win another ACC Tournament with a furious second-half rally to defeat N.C. State. The Blue Devils lost to Kansas—and the coach they would be facing at least twice a year moving forward—in the Sweet 16. The Tar Heels were invited to the NIT, won two games at home, and then ended their 19–16 season by losing to Georgetown in the third round and missing a chance to go back to Madison Square Garden, where they had won the preseason NIT by beating Kansas. The Jayhawks went all the way to the national championship game before missing 18 free throws and losing to Syracuse. Ten days later and a week after Doherty was ousted at UNC, Williams left his 15 years at KU behind and was introduced as the new head coach at his alma mater.

Having been away from the ACC so long, Roy Williams got along much better with Krzyzewski than Smith had. They served on various NCAA committees together, had been on the same Nike trips, and knew each other away from the sideline. Duke was still ruling the ACC, but Williams' Tar Heels took the Blue Devils to the wire in their first three meetings, losing by a total of eight points. The 2004 Duke team reached Krzyzewski's 10th Final Four and had UConn beaten in the semifinals before turnovers against the Huskies' press lost the game.

Carolina finally broke through in March of 2005, rallying from nine points down with less than three minutes to play to defeat Duke on a put-back by freshman Marvin Williams in a deafening Smith Center, the loudest moment Williams said he has ever heard in any arena anywhere.

The Tar Heels went on to win the national championship against Illinois in St. Louis and then lost seven players to graduation or the NBA. They had a freshman coming in who would not only break the all-time UNC scoring and rebounding records and lead UNC to a second NCAA title in four years, but Tyler Hansbrough *never lost* in Cameron Indoor Stadium. It was a four-year reign that ruined Senior Nights for J.J. Redick, Duke's all-time leading scorer, and the Blue Devils' 2008 top scorer, DeMarcus Nelson.

But it was a game the year in between at the Smith Center that has become the most memorable moment of Hansbrough's four-year career. Late in the Senior Day for Reyshawn Terry and Wes Miller that the Tar Heels controlled from the outset, Duke freshman Gerald Henderson went up for a rebound and came down with an elbow that caught Hansbrough squarely on the nose and split open his face. To some it looked intentional and out of frustration over Duke losing its third straight to the Tar Heels. To others it looked like Hansbrough's face got in the way of Henderson's elbow as he was coming down with the ball.

As Duke bussed back to Durham, Henderson texted his best friend and former Philadelphia high school teammate, Carolina freshman Wayne Ellington, to say he was sorry and that he hoped Hansbrough wasn't injured too badly.

His nose was broken and his face and uniform so bloody that Hansbrough wouldn't hit the showers until a picture could be taken, and the photo has become one of the most famous in Carolina athletic history. Both head coaches snipped at each after the game as to why the two starters were still playing in the closing minutes of UNC's 86–72 victory. And Hansbrough had to wear a protective mask at the ACC Tournament in Tampa that the Tar Heels won for the first time in nine years and in a first-round NCAA game against Eastern Kentucky in Winston-Salem.

By the time Duke was ousted in the first round by VCU and Hansbrough threw off the mask early in UNC's second-round game against Michigan State, the incident had been tucked away in Duke-Carolina lore. The Tar Heels were headed for the Meadowlands to win two games and reach the Final Four in Atlanta. They won one and almost two, blowing a 10-point lead late in the second half against Georgetown, and finished the season one game short of their goal.

Chapter 8

Decades of Transition

A s a rookie reporter for The Atlanta Constitution in 1972, I was given the assignment of trying to get legendary Kentucky coach Adolph Rupp on the phone. Although that was supposed to be a tough assignment, it turned out to be a practical joke: anyone could get Rupp on the phone, and no one could get him off.

After becoming Durham Morning Herald sports editor, I remembered how easy it was, when outlandish rumors began that Duke would hire the retired Baron of the Bluegrass in 1973 to succeed Bucky Waters, who resigned just weeks before the new season was to begin.

I had kept Rupp's number in my black book and called him. He answered the phone—just like the last time.

"Coach, I am calling from Durham and…" I began before he cut me off.

"Are you in Durham?" Rupp asked abruptly, and I told him I was. "Do you know Carl James? Can you reach him for me? We've had an electrical storm, and I can't make any calls from my phone. Would you give him a message?"

"Yes, Coach, but what would you like me to tell him?"

"Tell him not to send that plane for me tomorrow for his press conference. My farm manager, Carl Yazell, dropped dead here this afternoon, and I can't leave this 500-acre cattle farm to coach the Duke basketball team."

"Yes, Coach, I will call him and tell him that."

Rupp hung up.

I telephoned James, the new Duke athletic director, at his home and said I had a message from Adolph Rupp: "Don't send the plane because he can't make your press conference in the morning."

James was silent on the other end for about 10 seconds before he said, "Thank you, Art...but I don't really know what you are talking about."

James hung up.

The Duke press conference went off as scheduled at 11:00 AM, only James introduced former assistant Neill McGeachy, who told me later he had been offered the job that morning at 9:00, as his new head coach.

It was an absolutely true story, though James denied it until his death in 2004, and some old guard at Duke still insist that McGeachy was to be named interim coach all along and that Adolph Rupp was just a wild rumor.

—AC

———————

Most Duke-Carolina fans who love the rivalry would admit they prefer both basketball teams to be good at the same time. Yet, that hasn't always happened, creating a different kind of great curiosity across the blue divide. Like wealthy owners of adjacent beachfront property, the Duke-Carolina rivalry is one of true voyeurism in which both alumni and fan bases want to know what's going on, right or wrong, at the neighbors' house.

Although many alumni and fans under 50 look to the 1980s as the tipping point of the rivalry, the hatred had started more than 20 years earlier. Tar Heel fans, who knew the Duke Chapel had chimed their fight song in congratulations after UNC's 1957 National Championship and had long considered N.C. State their archrival in basketball, suddenly had a new obsession.

There became essentially another team to cheer for—besides their own, which was not doing very well after Frank McGuire resigned and was replaced by his three-year assistant, the unknown Dean Smith. That other team was whoever played against Duke.

While the on-court competition remained hotly contested, Duke dominated the early 1960s as Smith struggled to escape McGuire's long shadow. Tar Heel fans loathed Art Heyman, who had originally signed with UNC, and cheered against other stars that followed, such as Jeff Mullins, Jack Marin, Steve Vacendak, and Bob Verga, who combined to win three ACC championships and reach three NCAA Final Fours from 1963–66.

Toward the end of the decade, the feeling became very much mutual, and ardent fans were not sure what made them happier—a victory for their team or a defeat for the other shade of blue.

That question has remained in vogue for both schools ever since nationally ranked UNC teams of the late 1960s also won three ACC titles and advanced to three Final Fours. By the end of the decade, Smith had rebuilt a Carolina program that would surpass Duke and cause Blue Devils coach Vic Bubas to step away from coaching at age 42.

Despite a respectable 66–47 record through his first five seasons with two second-place finishes in the ACC, Smith could not avoid the specter of McGuire and the Duke juggernaut of the early '60s. Under Bubas the Blue Devils made the Tar Heels look like laughingstocks. Duke not winning a national championship was the only saving grace for UNC fans and students, who longed for the glory days of McGuire and hung Smith in effigy early in the 1965 season.

Smith survived because of support from chancellor Bill Aycock, who promoted the 30-year-old assistant in 1961 with a mandate to clean up the program the arrogant McGuire had left on NCAA probation. Smith inherited recruiting limitations placed on UNC and N.C. State when consolidated university president Bill Friday cancelled the celebrated Dixie Classic in the wake of point-shaving scandals that hit both schools. Friday, who reigned over all of the UNC system campuses, also ruled that Smith and State's Everett Case could only sign two players outside of the ACC area in 1962 because the gamblers had migrated south from New York, and Friday wanted to cut off any more bad influence.

With the signing of UNC's first black scholarship athlete, Charlie Scott, the Tar Heels became the team that Duke followed with as much fervor as its own. Scott replaced the graduated Bobby Lewis in the 1968 starting lineup that won a second straight ACC championship and this time went all the way to the NCAA Championship Game before losing to Lew Alcindor and UCLA, the same school Duke had lost to in its one trip to the title game in 1964.

Thus began the habit by the most zealous Duke and UNC fans of knowing as much about each other's roster as they did their own, while paying far less attention to any other teams in the ACC.

Bubas announced late in the 1969 season that he would be stepping down as basketball coach for a position with the Duke administration. His 10-year record of 213–67 gave him a .761 winning percentage. With the gradual integration of southern state universities in the wake of the Civil Rights Act, it would be increasingly difficult to bring in black players at the rate of other public ACC institutions. And in his last game on the Blue Devils' bench, he got a firsthand confirmation of his suspicion.

While hovering around a .500 record for most of the season, Duke won three straight to advance to the championship game of the 1969 ACC Tournament in Charlotte, upsetting 13th-ranked South Carolina in one semifinal when both teams used their starters for all 40 minutes. That had never happened before—or since—in the history of the ACC Tournament.

In the championship game, the Blue Devils led Carolina 43–34 at halftime behind sophomore guard Dick DeVenzio and senior forward Fred Lind. And the Tar Heels had received a devastating blow when three-year starter Dick Grubar suffered a season-ending knee injury. Despite 12 first-half points from Scott, Carolina was in trouble.

With his team still ahead by double figures when UNC forward Bill Bunting fouled out midway through the second half, Bubas remembers "looking down at the Carolina bench and thinking everyone knew the game was over. But on the court, Charlie Scott was yelling at his teammates to give him the ball."

The Tar Heels ran away with the victory and needed a Scott buzzer-beater in the NCAA East regional final to make their third consecutive Final Four. The gifted Scott's spectacular 28 points in the final 20 minutes of the ACC championship not only turned the game in Carolina's favor, it affirmed to Bubas that the black athlete was coming to the ACC, and with Duke sticking to certain entrance requirements and quotas, he would have had a harder time fielding championship teams. "That's not why I left, though," Bubas said. "We had always adjusted to recruiting the players that fit our program. There are times in your life when you know it is time to move on. I never envisioned myself as a lifer as a coach. I admire the coaches who can do that. I always felt I could do other things and was fortunate enough to serve as a vice chancellor at Duke, be the first commissioner of the Sun Belt Conference, and work with the NCAA."

For reasons occurring on both campuses, the rivalry lost its luster in the early 1970s as one school attracted new arch enemies, and the other struggled to stay relevant.

• • •

At West Virginia former Duke assistant coach Bucky Waters had a new arena coming out of the ground and a big time recruit in 6'1" guard Will Robinson, who would go on to earn All-American honors in 1972 and become the Mountaineers' third all-time leading scorer. Fred Brown was the athletic director who had the guts to hire a young 29-year old assistant from Duke, and West Virginia was big time in basketball thanks to its greatest former player, Jerry West, Zeke from Cabin Creek.

Waters knew there would be an opening at Duke University before anyone else. He had beaten the Blue Devils two of the three times they had played and had a 1–0 record against Carolina, so it was logical that his old boss would want to talk with him about the job. But not so soon. "It was a surprise when Vic called in the middle of the season and told me he had something important to discuss with me," recalled Waters, who has since retired in Durham. "He said he'd fly to the airport in Pittsburgh, which is only 60 miles from Morgantown, [West Virginia,] we'd meet there for two hours, and he would get back on the plane and go back to Durham. It was February, and Vic flew to Pittsburgh. I drove up, and we met at the hotel at the airport, and he told me what his plans were for the end of the season.

"He said it was time for him to walk away from the game. He said he was tired of getting on another plane and chasing another high school kid. And because of our past relationship and what I had done against Duke at West Virginia, I was going to be in the bull's-eye. He wanted me to have a chance to think about what I wanted to do."

Waters thought about it and decided he had a better job at West Virginia and told his wife, Dottie, they were staying in Morgantown.

He and Brown went to see West Virginia president Dr. James Harlow. "We were in Dr. Harlow's office, working on the wording of the statement—the love of the school, the new arena, and the phone rings," Waters said. "The secretary says it's for me. It was Eddie Cameron and president Doug Knight. I had sent them a telegram and thanked them for the honor of being offered the Duke job, but for professional reasons, I was staying at West Virginia."

Dr. Harlow made everyone leave the room while Waters talked with Cameron and Knight. "They started telling me how they needed me to come back to Duke," Waters said. "No increase in money or anything, just that they really needed me to come back. I loved Duke; they knew I did in my heart. I told them I would get right back to them. When the West Virginia people came back in the room, they asked if I was ready to begin the press conference to announce I was staying. I told them I had changed my mind and I was going to take the Duke job. Dr. Harlow could tell I was still confused. He asked me what was in my heart, and I told him going back to Duke. He looked right at me and asked if Sonny Moran, my assistant, could coach. I said he could, and he turned to Fred and told him to announce Moran as our new head coach."

Duke hired the crew-cut Waters to replace Bubas in the turbulent, demonstration-marred early '70s. Having served under Bubas for six years and with head coaching experience, Waters seemed like a logical successor. Like Bubas, Waters played at N.C. State and then became his protégé. But he was precisely the wrong man at the wrong time, as protests and pot-smoking became the activities of choice on a campus with a mostly Northeastern student body.

Waters had early recruiting victories in the New York area, but several of those key players—Don Blackmon, Jim Fitzsimmons, Richie O'Connor, and Illinoisan Jeff Dawson—wound up transferring because they chafed at Waters' disciplined style of coaching.

After twice reaching the NIT (losing to eventual champion UNC in the 1971 semifinal at Madison Square Garden), Duke suffered its two worst seasons in 13 years despite upsetting the No. 3-ranked Tar Heels on the day Duke Indoor Stadium was named for retiring athletic director Eddie Cameron. By then, Cameron had become so unpopular for hiring Waters that hecklers in the upper deck interrupted the halftime ceremony by yelling, "Stop! Don't do it!"

After the season in which Duke finished 14–12 and Carolina made its fourth Final Four in six years, Waters asked the school for a new contract and public vote of confidence to quell speculation over his job security that he said was killing recruiting. He did not get it and asked again, somewhat foolishly, after Duke went 12–14 in 1973. Duke refused and told Waters to coach through the last year of his contract and then the school would make a decision on his future in the spring of 1973.

Waters did not wait that long. He was offered a fund-raising position at the Duke Medical Center by his friend Dean William Anlyan, and the Blue Devils suffered a September surprise when Waters stepped down less than a month before practice opened for the 1973–74 season, similar to what Dean Smith did 24 years later at UNC. "I knew I wasn't coming back," Waters said, "so I waited until September, hoping my assistant Neil McGeachy would have a chance at the job."

Since school was already in session around the country, it gave new athletic director Carl James few options. The job was still attractive to several sitting head coaches, even though Duke had fallen behind UNC and the David Thompson-led N.C. State teams, but no coach was going to bolt a college or professional team as the new season was just beginning.

James had a brainstorm that in retrospect was not a bad idea. Duke was expecting another mediocre record, and interest was so low that season tickets to Cameron Indoor Stadium cost $40 or $4 a game. James needed something, anything, to draw the attention of the local and national press back to Durham. He offered the job to retired coach and legend Adolph Rupp, who had been put out to pasture at age 70 by the University of Kentucky. James' idea was for Rupp to be a figurehead coach and entertain the media while holdover assistant McGeachy ran practice every day and really coached the team. And Rupp agreed to do it.

Duke had called a morning press conference for October 17, 1973, to introduce Rupp. But the death of his cattle farm manager caused Rupp to change his mind, and McGeachy, a former three-sport star (football, basketball, tennis) at tiny Lenoir-Rhyne College, was introduced to the press corps after literally a last minute change of plans. He had just turned 30.

McGeachy became either a trivia question or a footnote to history when he coached Duke to a 10–16 record, including the school's 1,000[th] victory, and to two of the more memorable losses to UNC in the series.

The first, on January 19, 1974, occurred after Carolina All-American Bobby Jones stole an inbounds pass at Cameron with the game tied and laid it in to beat the final buzzer. "That was one of the finest college games I've ever seen or taken part in," McGeachy said. "But when Jones made that steal, my whole life flashed across my mind."

The other came a month later and remains the most famous comeback in college basketball history, as the Tar Heels rallied from eight points down with 17 seconds to play in Chapel Hill to send the game into overtime, where they won 96–92. Blue Devils guard Pete Kramer missed a free throw before the legendary long shot by UNC's Walter Davis tied the score at the end of regulation. "Sometimes I think at that time there was a disease hanging over Duke basketball," Kramer said.

The bitter endings to both games obscured a great coaching job by the personable McGeachy, who got his last-place team (2–10 in the ACC) ready to upset its top 10 rival twice. Winning both games, or perhaps either, might have helped him get the job permanently. But James, who barely talked to his interim coach that season, was already out scouting candidates from other schools. He announced shortly after Duke's first-round ouster in the 1974 ACC Tournament that McGeachy and the staff would not return.

In April, Utah coach Bill Foster took the Duke job. The 44-year-old Foster had led the Running Utes to the NIT championship game before losing to Purdue. (Twenty-six years later UNC would hire Matt Doherty after his Notre Dame team lost in the NIT finals to Wake Forest.)

Foster needed three seasons to rebuild the Duke program, during which Carolina had developed more serious rivalries, particularly an N.C. State program that went undefeated in the ACC for two straight years and won the 1974 NCAA Championship after upsetting seven-time champion UCLA in double overtime at Greensboro Coliseum

Jabari Parker, part of Coach K's recent trend of bringing in talented one-and-dones, drives on Carolina big man Brice Johnson during 2014, a turbulent year for both teams. (AP Images)

As part of his 25-point, 11-rebound, four-steal performance, Shane Battier blocks UNC's Joe Forte, which was part of a five-point swing that fueled Duke's road win during its 2001 championship season.

J.J. Redick, Duke's all-time leading scorer, receives advice from his mentor, Coach K.

Sean May, who scored 26 points while going 10-of-11 from the floor, shoots over Jack Ingram during the 75–70 victory against Illinois in the 2005 national title game.

North Carolina celebrates its first title since 1993 and the first of the post-Dean Smith era.

Roy Williams and Coach K wait for the officials to sort out the fouls and penalties, following Tyler Hansbrough's bloody injury in UNC's 86–72 home victory.

After Duke's Gerald Henderson broke Hansbrough's nose during a controversial foul, the Carolina big man looked like something out of a horror movie. (Jim Bounds)

Because of the broken nose, Hansbrough briefly wore a plastic mask, which he ditched early in UNC's second-round tournament game against Michigan State in 2007.

Hansbrough dunks at Cameron Indoor Stadium, where he never lost during his four years.

Roy Williams chats with Ty Lawson, whose toe injury became a growing concern to the Tar Heel faithful.

The Tar Heels celebrate their 2009 National Championship at the White House with President Obama, who once scrimmaged with the team.

One year after UNC won the national title, Kyle Singler celebrates Duke's 2010 NCAA Championship, mirroring how Carolina won in 1993 following Duke's 1992 title run. (AP Images)

The center of one of the most hotly contested Duke-Carolina recruiting battles, Harrison Barnes is taunted by the Cameron Crazies.

Though he only stayed in school a year, Austin Rivers earned a permanent place in Duke-Carolina lore with his last-second shot over Tyler Zeller to win the 2012 road contest 85–84. (AP Images)

Dean Smith sits next to
his coaching protégé,
Roy Williams (left),
and his former player,
Michael Jordan (right),
two pillars of UNC
tradition that hold Smith
in the highest regard.

Announcing the ESPN telecast
during November of 2011,
Bob Knight congratulates his
protégé, who surpassed him
as the all-time winningest
basketball coach in Division I
history. (AP Images)

They've had their contentious
moments, but Roy Williams
and Coach K became somewhat
friendly after serving on various
NCAA committees together
and traveling on the same
Nike trips.

A mere eight miles separate the two schools, and the proximity is part of what makes Duke-Carolina such a special rivalry.

on Final Four Saturday. The Wolfpack of coach Norm Sloan then defeated Al McGuire's Marquette Warriors Monday night for State's first national title in basketball.

Also getting more of UNC's attention were the Maryland teams of Lefty Driesell, who had led Davidson to consecutive NCAA Eastern regional finals, losing both times to Dean Smith and Carolina. Driesell's mantra was to make Maryland the "UCLA of the East," and he recruited high school stars to help him. His biggest coup was stealing Tom McMillen of Mansfield, Pennsylvania, away from Smith on the day of enrollment at both campuses. McMillen had committed to Carolina, but his parents refused to sign the letter of intent and he spent the summer weakening to family pressure to play closer to home in College Park. Even after McMillen, Len Elmore, and Jap Trimble graduated, Maryland continued to have great teams and marquee match-ups with Carolina, pushing the Duke rivalry further into the background.

A Durham native named John Lucas had spurned his home-town school and was not offered a scholarship by Smith; he went to Maryland to become an All-American and No. 1 pick in the 1976 NBA Draft. Had Foster been at Duke when Lucas signed with Maryland, the loquacious lefty with the push-jump shot might have stayed home for college.

So through the mid-1970s, the Duke-Carolina rivalry waned such that players from that era do not recall the rivalry as it once was and became again. Former Dukies were bitter about what had happened to the celebrated program they expected to play for, while dismissive ex-Tar Heels remember the classic comebacks but little else about the games each year, when Carolina won 16-of-17 renewals. Much of the same thing happened during Mike Krzyzewski's first three seasons at Duke, when UNC won two ACC championships and one NCAA title behind players named Jordan, Perkins, and Worthy.

Coach K's omnipotent program overshadows almost everything that came before him at Duke, but it's clear the importance of the Foster years, which produced three NCAA teams and Blue Devil legends Jim Spanarkel, Mike Gminski, and Gene Banks, along with a legion of fans that jumped back on board when Krzyzewski got it rolling in the mid-1980s.

Under Foster's regime students began camping out the night before the UNC game to get the best seats, which eventually morphed into Krzyzewskiville, and their team went from trying to emulate the Tar Heels' enthusiasm on the court to beating them at their own game. There was no greater example than the first home-and-home meeting on January 14, 1978, at Cameron, the senior season of UNC All-American point guard Phil Ford.

Guard Bob Bender, a mid-season transfer from Indiana, turned eligible and was the missing link in an otherwise star-studded lineup that had won nine of its next 11 games since a loss to UNC in the December Big Four Tournament. Included was a 10-point victory at Maryland in the ACC opener, no small feat for a Duke program that had won exactly one ACC road game in the previous six seasons. That accomplishment, along with scoring 212 points and winning by a total of 64 in its two games before Carolina came to Cameron, left the Blue Devils confident against the No. 2-ranked but actually overrated Tar Heels on a Saturday afternoon on regional television.

Duke would no longer play into Dean Smith's hands, pushing the tempo early and, while holding a narrow lead late in the game, answering Carolina's pressure defense by taking the ball all the way to the hole for layups and dunks. As the lead grew, Cameron erupted through the final horn of the 92–84 triumph that snapped an eight-game losing streak to the Tar Heels and propelled Duke into national prominence for the first time in a decade. Some joyous Duke students actually cut down the nets after the regular season game.

Nine more classic encounters followed through the 1980 season, when Foster decided to bolt Duke for the University of South Carolina, a move he regretted for the rest of his coaching career that ended at Northwestern without another trip to the NCAA Tournament.

Whereas Duke's record versus Carolina had been 3–19 from 1970–77, the Blue Devils finished the Foster regime 5–6 against the Tar Heels and revived the rivalry to the point that Krzyzewski losing eight of his first nine games to Smith did not matter. Had Foster not produced those three great teams and seasons, Duke's record against UNC over 11 years would have been far worse than even 8–25. "What he said touched us very much," Banks said of Foster's parting comments to the team. "I'm sure we'll get a good coach, but he'll never be another Coach Foster."

The next coach turned out to be pretty good, but without Foster's rebuilding job, Krzyzewski may have gone to Iowa State instead of Duke, and the Blue Devils would have likely continued to struggle no matter who their coach was. The rivalry with Carolina could have been irreparably harmed.

• • •

While Krzyzewski built his own dynasty, surviving personal and physical trauma that is chronicled in the next chapter, Dean Smith was winding down a Hall of Fame career in which he won 879 games and eventually retired with the most victories of any major college coach. Well into his 60s, Smith had rebounded from losing his first seven games to Bubas by dominating Duke with a 59–35 career record against the Blue Devils, finishing 24–14 against Krzyzewski-coached teams.

Despite reaching the Final Four in four of his last seven seasons, Smith was dogged by speculation during the 1990s over how long he would coach the Tar Heels. It never subsided, even though what many consider to be his best coaching job ever took place in 1995, when he took a three-guard, two-forward lineup to a four-way tie for first place (with Maryland, Virginia, and Wake Forest) in the ACC and defeated John Thompson's Georgetown Hoyas team and Rick Pitino's Kentucky Wildcats in the Southeast regional at Birmingham, Alabama.

After losing to defending national champion Arkansas in the Final Four at Seattle's Kingdome, star sophomores Jerry Stackhouse and Rasheed Wallace bolted to the NBA a year before expected. Smith was caught short with talent and experience the following season, needing to boost the morale within his program while the constant buzz over his retirement hovered over Blue Heaven.

One afternoon, he walked out of his office into the main lobby of the basketball suite, sensed a downbeat atmosphere, and overheard conversations about exactly who was going to play for the Tar Heels during the 1995–96 season. Atypically, he snapped at secretaries and others in the conversation. "We *will* field a basketball team this season," he said sharply and told everyone to get back to work.

Although it was a rare role, no one was better than Smith as the underdog, and his young team with two freshmen in the starting lineup surprised the ACC by going 7–1 in their first trip around the league. But after defenses cramped freshmen Vince Carter and Antawn Jamison inside, the Tar Heels shot poorly from the perimeter and went 7–6 in their last 13 games, losing to Clemson in the ACC Tournament opener on a dunk at the buzzer by Greg Buckner. UNC went out quietly to Texas Tech in the NCAA second round, and for the first time in many years, it appeared Smith's program was in trouble while talk of his retirement escalated from a buzz to a dull roar.

Duke, meanwhile, barely made the 1996 NCAA Tournament in Krzyzewski's return to the bench and lost its first-round game to Eastern Michigan. It marked the first time in 16 years that neither of the blue bloods reached the Sweet 16 and threw both programs into a state of wild speculation over their coaches, one getting too old and the other unable to regain command of his team. Indeed, changes were on the horizon for both of them—only going in the opposite directions.

Despite winning nine of its first 10 non-conference games the following season, Carolina went 0–3 to start the ACC schedule for the first time in Smith's tenure, and the same old doubts and speculation resurfaced. The Tar Heels were blown out at Wake Forest, squandered a double-digit lead at home to Maryland, and lost at unranked Virginia. "When are we going to start playing like a fucking team?" yelled senior center Serge Zwikker in the locker room after the loss in Charlottesville.

They very nearly went 0–4 in the ACC but rallied from nine points down with two minutes to play against N.C. State at home. The true turnaround game came against Clemson, which had climbed to No. 2 in the national polls. Tigers coach Rick Barnes had become a villain to Carolina fans after his scorer's table confrontation with Smith at the 1995 ACC Tournament, when Barnes got in Smith's face about yelling at several Clemson players for dirty tactics.

But the Tar Heels shot 57 percent compared to Clemson's 27 percent, thanks mainly to the 6'5" Carter smothering 5'10" Clemson point guard Terrell McIntyre, and won 61–48 to preserve Clemson's all-time winless streak in Chapel Hill (which has since reached 57).

Despite going 3–5 in the first trip through the ACC schedule, Smith had watched endless tape and worked hard with his players to restore their confidence and felt much better about the second half of the season. After a hard-fought loss at Duke, Smith said smugly, "Duke knows it was in a game tonight."

Krzyzewski was even more confident in his opponent's resurgence. "That's a team that will not lose very much for the rest of the season," Coach K told his own players, following the 80–73 victory secured by a Trajan Langdon three-pointer that left the Blue Devils with 5–3 first-half record.

Both teams had great second halves with each winning seven straight in the ACC before their regular-season rematch in Chapel Hill. Both had one close game during the undefeated stretch. Duke survived a dismal shooting performance and rallied for a 62–61 win at Virginia, and the very next night, Carolina earned a pulsating 45–44 victory at State on freshman point guard Ed Cota's teardrop basket, forever dubbed as the "Cota Flota" in Carolina lore.

Smith had settled on a rotation that began working like a charm. Cota did not start, sitting on the bench to study how the game unfolded but entered shortly thereafter to become the steadying influence on the team. Cota went on to lead the Tar Heels in assists (with a 2:1 turnover ratio) and steals, and Carolina proved Krzyzewski's prediction true long before the season finale rematch.

Duke had clinched the ACC race three days earlier with a home victory over Maryland, and Krzyzewski worried that his players would not have the proper edge going to the Smith Center against their steamrolling rival. His concerns were born out, as the Tar Heels shot out to a 49–40 halftime lead behind a monster game in the making from Jamison, who poured in 33 points to lead the Tar Heels to a gritty 91–85 victory.

For Duke, Steve Wojciechowski had his finest college game with 18 points and five assists in 37 minutes, earning high praise from both coaches. "What a game Wojciechowski had," Smith gushed. "Not just defensively, but I knew he was a good offensive player. I saw him shoot well in high school."

Krzyzewski was even more effusive about Wojo's performance in a jam-packed Smith Center. With 21 seconds left in the game, Wojo picked up his fifth foul. As the guard left the floor, Krzyzewski embraced him with a big bear hug. For some players that acknowledgement of a job well done is more valuable than a win. But don't confuse the tough play of Wojo and the leadership of Langdon as to who turned the program around.

Langdon was a natural leader, and without him there is no telling how long it would have taken Duke to get back in the national limelight. When Langdon—hardly a screamer—spoke, everyone on the team knew to follow. He was exactly what Krzyzewski needed at that point in the program and the coach's stalled career.

After the defeat to UNC, Krzyzewski was so proud of his team's refusal to quit and wrapping up the ACC regular season that he mentioned his fear that the Blue Devils would come out flat. Listening on the Tar Heel Sports Network postgame show, thousands of Carolina fans lost all sympathy for Krzyzewski's hardships of the past two seasons and quickly realized that the rivalry had been re-stoked.

N.C. State upset Duke in the first round of the ACC Tournament in Greensboro, and Carolina went on to win the title by defeating Tim Duncan and two-time defending champ Wake Forest in the semifinals and then beating State for the third time that season. Just as importantly, it was the Tar Heels' 12th straight win and moved Smith within one of tying Adolph Rupp's record for all-time victories. After the so-so 21–11 record in 1996 and Carolina's 3–5 ACC start, reaching Rupp that season seemed like a long shot.

Former Tar Heel players and fans heard Smith's claim that he did not care about passing Rupp and his threat to "quit before he ever got close." So they wanted him to get it over with while he was still the UNC coach in 1997. He would have his chance in the first two rounds of the NCAA Tournament the following weekend on Wake Forest's home court in Winston Salem.

Three days before Duke lost a second-round game in Charlotte to Providence, the top-seeded Tar Heels played tight in the East regional in the first-round win over 16 seed Fairfield. But they relaxed in the second round and blew out a Chauncey Billups-led Colorado team for Smith's 877th career victory, surpassing the Baron of the Bluegrass.

Despite tickets to the 14,000-seat Joel Coliseum going for more than $500, dozens of former UNC players and their families found their way into the building and assembled in the hallway outside the locker room after the game.

Smith was stunned and close to tears as he emerged on his way to the press conference and walked through a gauntlet of familiar faces from his 36 years at Carolina. Shaking hands and nodding to players' wives and children, Smith was truly amazed by the reception. His office had fielded hundreds of requests for tickets, but the NCAA allotment was sparse, and, as always, the first priority went to the current players and their families. Yet, Smith saw Mitch Kupchak and Bobby Jones, who had flown all night from Los Angeles and Denver, respectively; George Karl from Milwaukee; and Sam Perkins from Dallas, plus players from four decades who barely got off the bench. If anyone was thinking it's time, this was truly the way to leave a legendary coaching career.

• • •

Even a loss to eventual national champion Arizona in the Final Four at Indianapolis did not deter Smith from changing the plans that had been in his mind for more than a year. He had found it increasingly more difficult to get himself recharged for a new season even after a summer of golf and spending time with his five children and five grandchildren. He had long promised to retire *before* the next season instead of *after* the last because he always felt like quitting when the last game ended. And in doing so, he could control the succession plan in his program, which was very important to him.

So it was a shock to the system of Carolina basketball, but not a big surprise, when on October 9, 1997, Smith told rookie athletic director Dick Baddour that he was retiring and that Bill Guthridge would take over the program for as long as he wanted it. Though such a move was what UNC opponents had been waiting for, Baddour or chancellor Michael Hooker could not fight the powerful Smith on his intention to leave another top 10 team to Guthridge, who was given a five-year contract. And while Guthridge won an ACC championship and took two teams back to the Final Four, the plan all but killed recruiting because rivals were telling prospects that Guthridge would not be their coach for four years, and they could not know who they would end up playing for.

Despite the fact that Guthridge won an ACC championship and led the Tar Heels to two more Final Fours, Joseph Forte was the only high-caliber recruit signed by Guthridge and assistants Phil Ford, Dave Hanners, and Pat Sullivan. And that may have played into Roy Williams' decision not to succeed the retiring Guthridge in 2000; it certainly left the man who did—Matt Doherty—with less young talent than the program had had in 30 years.

Doherty's hire was a gamble and a product of Baddour's inexperience as an AD and his desire to please incoming chancellor James Moeser, who was still packing up from his old job as chancellor at the University of Nebraska. Moeser wound up playing a much larger role in the successor to the Dean Smith era than he should have. What happened that July, 2000, resulted in the first of several hiring blunders by Baddour and Moeser that cost UNC millions of dollars as well as extensive collateral damage.

After Williams told Baddour and Smith he was remaining at Kansas, the athletic director and head coach went on separate paths to form the Plan B that had not existed. Baddour called Moeser to deliver the bad news, and much to the AD's surprise, Moeser had stronger opinions on the matter than a new chancellor with no ties to UNC should have had. Moeser had allowed Nebraska's Hall of Fame football coach Tom Osborne to name his successor, Frank Solich, because, according to Moeser, Osborne had promised Solich the job. Moeser said, "Tom pleaded with me to honor his commitment, which didn't turn out to be the best choice."

The fact that Solich—though he finished with a 58–19 overall record, including three double-digit-win seasons and three first-place finishes in the Big 12—did not live up to Osborne's legacy apparently contributed to Moeser's belief moving forward that: "Coaches should not determine their successors." However, Moeser knew far less about the Dean Smith era at UNC and how difficult it would be for the coach who followed Guthridge, the man who signaled the end of that era.

"Larry Brown was Dean Smith's choice, strongly delivered to me, and I just put my foot down," Moeser recalled in 2014. "I said I was not going to hire any coach who put two schools on NCAA probation, Kansas and UCLA. I remember it vividly; I felt very strongly about it. I was still in Lincoln [Nebraska], and this was done from a distance, but I was adamant about it. I wouldn't even consider it."

Smith and Brown, the former Tar Heel who was having his own Hall of Fame coaching career in the NBA and college, had already spoken. And Brown told Smith he would come back to help the man he had idolized his entire adult life and fulfill his dream of coaching at Carolina. Smith told Baddour it was a done deal and "to just schedule a press conference and tell Larry when to be here." Brown confirmed that, saying, "After Roy turned it down, Coach Smith called me and said he wanted me to take the job for five years. I told him I would."

Brown, then 59, was making about $3 million coaching the Philadelphia 76ers and, having banked millions more from eight previous coaching jobs, would take a significant pay cut to move to Chapel Hill. Smith knew Brown's history of having left the UCLA and Kansas programs on probation after leading both to the Final Four (and winning the 1988 title at KU) would bring resistance from some circles at UNC, but still the most powerful man in Chapel Hill knew how to answer all objections. Or so he thought.

After all, Carolina basketball was almost at Defcon status because of the widespread assumption that Williams would eventually come home. Smith's plan to resign in October and for Guthridge to take over for as long as he wanted, earning the larger salary and all the other benefits Smith had enjoyed, had worked so far. But the next step—Williams following Guthridge—had fallen apart. Now, UNC was left with Larry Brown, not a bad Plan B. "Larry was a great coach, and if it hadn't been for the probations, I would have been open to it," Moeser said. "I also had the view that Larry never stayed in a place for more than three years, and that's proven to be absolutely true."

Well, not exactly.

Although Brown seemed to jump from job to job, his record shows that to be overblown. He coached the Denver Nuggets for five years, Kansas for five years, the San Antonio Spurs and Indian Pacers for four years each, and was beginning the fourth of six seasons with the Sixers when Smith asked him to come back to UNC, where he had been the point guard on Smith's first two teams in 1962 and '63 and his assistant for the 1966 and '67 seasons.

(After being nixed by Moeser, Brown reached the NBA Finals in Philly and then won the NBA championship in his first season with the Detroit Pistons. He was inducted into the Naismith Hall of Fame in 2002, served as the USA Olympic coach in 2004, and remains the only coach to win an NBA championship and NCAA title.)

Brown stayed mum for a few years but eventually talked to the media about the bizarre meeting he had with Baddour and UNC faculty athletic chairmen Jack Evans at the Bel-Air Country Club in Los Angeles in July of 2000, after Moeser had already made his decision. Ostensibly, Baddour and Evans (neither of whom had ever played or coached basketball and were neophytes about the game) went to California to interview Brown. Moeser said he thought the trip "was strictly in deference to Dean. They felt they had to do that out of respect for him and their relationship with him."

"The first hour Baddour spent telling me how perfect Roy Williams was for the job," Brown said when he finally broke his silence. "The second hour he spent telling me that I was too old, that I couldn't accept less money, and why I shouldn't take the job. I agreed that Roy was a great coach and how much I wanted him at Carolina but that I can coach a little, too. And it's up to me to decide whether I'm worried about the money, not you."

Baddour has long maintained the decision on who to hire was a collaboration between him, Smith, Guthridge, and Moeser. Smith said at the time that Brown would stay five years, if not longer, because his protégé loved Chapel Hill and would do anything to help his school.

Moeser, coincidentally, had been a provost at Kansas when Brown led the Jayhawks to the national championship but also was cited for several minor violations by the NCAA. Kansas had been on probation in football and, according to Brown, "They hired an in-house attorney whose job it was to keep them from getting the death penalty. She really didn't even defend the basketball program."

The choice not to overlook Brown's past discretions with the NCAA was an unpopular one with those who cared about continuing the tradition of Carolina basketball. Brown had, and still has, many supporters among Tar Heel alumni who believe he—despite his foibles—would have been the answer to Carolina's crisis after Williams turned the job down.

"James did have a strong feeling about Larry," Baddour said in 2014 after he and Moeser had both retired from their positions. "He was intensely concerned about the NCAA issues, as we all were. And that was one of the things we [he and Evans] went out there to talk to Larry about."

After the meeting in California, Brown called Smith and said, "Coach, they don't want me." Brown continued, "Coach got angry and said, 'Larry, you wait, you hang on a couple of days, you'll be the next coach at North Carolina.' I said, 'Coach, I don't want to put you in that position.' And that's basically where it ended. I was devastated because I didn't know there were any obstacles. Coach Smith ran the program. I thought that if he said you should have the job, you were going to get the job. Later, I learned that Moeser had something to do with it. I was so aligned with Coach Smith. The reason the five years came up was he told me Phil Ford was going to be the next coach, and that was fine with me. I told Coach I would hire Phil and Dave, and whenever he said it was time for Phil to be the coach, I would step down."

"As we talked about it and worked through it," Baddour explained, "we decided that Larry wasn't a good fit."

Meanwhile, Baddour had his eye on a coach who would turn out to be a total *misfit*. He contacted UNC alumnus and first-year Notre Dame coach Matt Doherty in South Bend and invited him to Chapel Hill for an interview. Smith sat in on part of the six hours Doherty and Baddour spent together and, despite apprehensions raised by former UNC players and coaches about Doherty's readiness for such a job, did not stand in the way of Doherty being hired to coach the Tar Heels. Smith did grow very angry after learning Doherty planned to bring his four assistants from Notre Dame and not retain anyone from the Smith-Guthridge staff. "That was the first of many mistakes Doherty made, and that was a huge mistake," said Moeser, adding he had nothing to do with that part of it. "I didn't get into the hiring of Doherty. Dickie was the athletic director, and I let him do that."

Smith seethed at the back of the room as Doherty was introduced as UNC's new head coach on July 14, 2000. "This feels more like a funeral because three very capable coaches are losing their jobs," Smith said between clenched teeth.

Almost immediately, Doherty rubbed some people the wrong way despite *looking* like a good fit. Doherty had little professional equity after only one season as a head coach, and his methods to motivate his first Carolina team were in stark contrast to the mild-mannered Smith and Guthridge. But the Tar Heels did have veteran talent left, and an 18-game winning streak and ascension to the No. 1 ranking camouflaged serious problems within the program.

After a 3–2 start, Doherty put junior Ronald Curry in as point guard, the Tar Heels upset second-ranked Duke in Durham, and kept winning all the way to No. 1 in the polls. But it proved to be a house of cards, and the season collapsed after a halftime tirade at Clemson on the same day Dale Earnhardt died at Daytona. The Tar Heels went 4–4 over their last eight games, and by the time they were blown out by Duke twice in seven days, rumors, some perpetuated by office staff Doherty had fired, were already swirling about player unrest within the program.

Forte, a sophomore sharpshooter who clashed with Doherty throughout the season, turned pro, and seven-foot center Brendan Haywood graduated. Curry and Julius Peppers, football players on loan to the program, skipped the 2001–02 season to prepare for the upcoming NFL draft. A team—left short on talent from recruiting misses during Guthridge's three seasons—lost its first three games. By January it was apparent that Carolina's streaks of consecutive 20-plus win seasons (31), top-three finishes in the ACC (37), and 27 straight appearances in the NCAA Tournament were over. The 8–20 washout ended with a fifth straight loss to Duke in the first round of the ACC Tournament, when Doherty tried a slowdown to keep the game close. Even Mike Krzyzewski felt compassion for Doherty during the disastrous season in Chapel Hill.

At a timeout in a lopsided win at the Smith Center in February, when several of his players were literally laughing their way to a huge lead, Coach K snapped at them. He had known such embarrassment himself early in his career. "Hey, there has been great basketball played in this building and there will be great basketball played here again," he shouted. "So don't be assholes out there. When the game is over, just shake their hands and walk off the court without saying anything to anyone."

The record was one thing, but reports of player unhappiness were blasphemous in a program with the tradition of Carolina. Baddour said he was "riding this horse as far as it could go," and Board of Trustees member Paul Fulton befriended Doherty to counsel him on his relationship with the players.

Fortunately, three high school stars, whose recruitment had begun before Doherty arrived, were already signed to enter school in the fall of 2002, and the presence of freshmen Raymond Felton, Sean May, and Rashad McCants would improve the talent level of the 2002–03 team if not the internal strife.

After May suffered a stress fracture following a 5–0 start that included beating Roy Williams and Kansas on the way to the preseason NIT title, the Tar Heels could never climb to 10 games over .500 and were left out of the NCAA Tournament for a second straight season. Under almost any other circumstances and considering the loss of starting center May, the 19–16 record would have been labeled as progress. But thanks to the Internet message boards and the beginning of what is now known as social media, too much unhappiness among players and their families had reached the public.

Ballsy alumni and fans had also gotten involved; several passed secondhand information to Moeser's office using pseudonyms. They warned of players threatening to transfer if Doherty remained the coach, as the school faced a rash of bad publicity about a basketball program that had been built into a national model by the man whose name was on the building and who still went to his office in the basement of the Smith Center almost every day. Dean Smith and Bill Guthridge had always believed Roy Williams would come home to continue the legacy, and their silence in not supporting Doherty was deafening.

On April Fool's Day of 2003, instead of simply issuing a statement that Doherty had resigned, Baddour and Moeser held an awkward press conference on the floor of the Smith Center with a funereal black curtain behind them and stumbled their way through the rhetoric. Every member of the media and most listening on a statewide broadcast of the event knew the university was moving to correct a terrible mistake it had made. "Dean never forgave me for that," Moeser said. "When Doherty flamed out, Dean said, 'I told you so' and reminded me if I had done what he said none of this would have happened." Moeser added, somewhat naively, "Other than that, Dean and I had a great relationship."

Luckily, Williams had changed his mind about staying at Kansas for the rest of his coaching career, thanks to some of KU's own administrative missteps that had taken arguably the most beloved figure in the Jayhawk state out of his comfort zone. Jettisoning Doherty was only half the problem at UNC. What to do next was the rest of the equation. Smith went after his protégé for the second time in four years, and this time he brought Williams back to take over a lilting program. By his second season, Carolina basketball was looking the rest of the ACC, including powerful Duke, directly in the eye again. The two-year nightmare—the biggest scar of a phenomenal 50-year run—had ended.

Chapter 9

The Good, the Bad, and the Ugly

*F*or years after games, Mike Krzyzewski would sit and talk with a group of guys in the back of the coaches' locker room. Basically, it was his assistant coaches, sports information director Tom Mickle, myself, and Durham Morning Herald's Keith Drum, whom Krzyzewski befriended just after arriving in Durham in 1980. We'd all listen to Mike break down the game, pointing out places where certain individuals could have done better and just sit and talk basketball.

With Krzyzewski out in 1995, it was a much smaller group. It was usually just Mike Brey, Tommy Amaker, and me sitting in the back. After one tough loss, we were trying to figure out how to get this team on track from another losing streak during the dismal season, when suddenly the phone in the coaches' lounge buzzed.

No one knew this number. Wait—one person knew the number—Krzyzewski. But he was home flat on his back recuperating and supposedly incommunicado with any of the coaches—by order of his wife, Mickie.

We all looked at each other. I sure wasn't going to touch the phone. Finally, Brey picked up the receiver—"Yes, sir," he said.

It was Krzyzewski, the Captain, on the other end.

—JM

After Mike Krzyzewski survived the lynch mob his first four seasons at Duke and built 11 straight NCAA teams, reaching seven Final Fours and winning back-to-back national championships in 1991 and '92 to surpass Carolina's success and replace the Tar Heels as America's team, the Blue Devils' blip in the rivalry came in the 1994–95 season that nearly sunk the program.

The season, which did not get off to a good start for Duke by Krzyzewski standards, was surrounded with questions and frustration. But the seeds were actually planted for the forthcoming nightmare the year before, which ended with the seventh Final Four for Coach K.

The 1993–94 season had been almost Cinderella-like for Duke. Taking the fairy-tale analogy further, it was more like the prince turning into a frog, the beautiful princess kissing the frog, and turning the frog into a prince again. To say the least, 1994 was an up-and-down season, especially toward the end and in large part due to Wake Forest star guard Randolph Childress.

The Blue Devils won their first 10 games before falling to Wake Forest at home on a last-second Childress jumper but staying ranked among the top six teams in the country with the defending national champions down the road right on their preferable heels.

Five straight wins—following the Wake Forest loss—including a 75–62 victory against No. 18 Maryland, coupled with UCLA's first loss to Jason Kidd and California, vaulted the Blue Devils to the No. 1 ranking, heading to Chapel Hill and their first meeting of the 1994 season with No. 2 North Carolina.

This was the first time in the 191-game history of the series that Duke and Carolina had faced each other ranked No. 1 and 2 in the nation.

On January 18, 1986, when the old rivals had carried a combined 33–0 record into the opening game at the Dean E. Smith Center, Carolina was No. 1 and Duke No. 3 with Michigan in between. Because Michigan had lost to Minnesota on the prior Thursday night, the Duke-Carolina match-up on national television in the largest on-campus basketball facility in the country was actually a de facto

No. 1 vs. No. 2—where they would be ranked on Monday after UNC's 95–92 victory before 22,000 fans in the new Blue Heaven.

So their first meeting in 1994 was coined the "Game of The Year"—Duke and Carolina—No. 1 vs. No. 2. The old senior Grant Hill vs. the young freshman Jerry Stackhouse. It was a battle between the two schools that had won the last three NCAA championships and was so highly anticipated that ESPN decided to offer the game on its new channel ESPN2, forcing fans to add "The Deuce" to their cable subscription if they wanted to see it.

The Blue Devils shot the lights out in the first half, hitting 64 percent from the floor but held just a two-point lead at 40–38. The second half belonged to Carolina when Duke would hit just 35 percent while Carolina sizzled with 58 percent shooting to pull away to the 89–78 win.

Smith Center fans flooded the court in celebration of toppling their top-ranked rival while the Duke locker room remained silent after the game. The Blue Devils played so well for 20 minutes but could not make anything happen for the final 20. "We were getting good looks at the basket in the second half," said an exhausted Hill with his head in his hands after scoring a game-high 20 points. "We were getting the same looks that we were getting in the first half. The ball just wouldn't go down."

Hill also blamed the loss on the Blue Devils' lack of changing defenses. "The first half we did a really good job of dropping back on defense and confusing them," he said. "In the second half, they realized what we were doing and after they started hitting their shots they got rolling."

As usual the positive-thinking Mobile, Alabama, native Tony Lang had a different look at the outcome. "UNC players felt a lot of pressure because it was their home game and they were behind in the standings," Lang said. "We know why we lost the game. We played well in the first half and didn't keep our intensity up in the second half. We have to learn to play hard for both halves."

So Round One of the game of the year was over with both teams knowing they would meet again a month later at Cameron Indoor Stadium in the regular season finale with eight games in between for each of them.

Round Two took place on March 5 with the Blue Devils ranked No. 2 in the nation, losing just once more again to Childress and Wake Forest in Winston-Salem. The Tar Heels were ranked No. 5, having gone 3–3 in their last six games as chemistry problems emerged between the holdover stars of the 1993 NCAA title team and the talented freshman trio of Stackhouse, Rasheed Wallace, and Jeff McInnis.

Except for it being Duke and Carolina, the second meeting of the season had little meaning to any of the metrics of college basketball except possible NCAA seeding. The Blue Devils had already captured the ACC regular season, and Carolina was hoping to finish alone in second place and complete a prestigious sweep of Duke.

It was senior night for Hill, Lang, and Marty Clark, who didn't get the home curtain call they coveted. Despite Hill, Cherokee Parks, and Erik Meek combining for 53 points, Carolina outplayed the Blue Devils and rolled to an 87–77 victory behind 20 points from 1993 Final Four Most Outstanding Player Donald Williams and a couple of monster dunks by Wallace in the closing minutes.

The Blue Devils appeared to be reeling and were upset in the semifinals of the ACC Tournament by Virginia, quashing a chance to avenge the two losses to Carolina and opening the door for the Tar Heels to defeat the Cavaliers in the championship game.

For a team ranked sixth in the nation heading in to the NCAA Tournament, it suddenly seemed like a lackluster season for Duke. Losing both meetings to Carolina and being sent home early from the ACC Tournament had placed a black cloud over this team. There was a widespread belief among the media and fans that Duke's best basketball had already been played, and the Blue Devils were done.

However, March had come to be known as Duke's month with Krzyzewski resetting the team and its priorities the week of practice before the Big Dance. As they had after getting blown out of the 1991 ACC Tournament title game by Carolina, the Blue Devils were starting over and believed they could turn their season back around.

Behind Hill's outstanding play, they went on a very special four-game run in the NCAA Tournament with wins over Texas Southern and Michigan State in the first two rounds. The Monday after beating the Spartans by 11 points, Krzyzewski rode in a long black limo along Duke University Drive, taping a promotional spot for CBS and the Final Four.

Krzyzewski appeared as the limo driver in a takeoff of the Bud Light "Dr. Galazkiewicz" commercial featuring Eddie Jemison, the original "Yes, I am" guy. The spot, with Jemison riding in the limo and recognizing Krzyzewski as the chauffeur and asking him if he was Coach Krazooskie and getting the "Yes, I am" answer, first appeared before Duke's regional final against third-ranked Purdue and Glenn "Big Dog" Robinson.

The Blue Devils came through with their best game of the season in the South regional final in Knoxville, Tennessee. Parks had 15 points and 10 rebounds, three others scored in double figures, and freshman Jeff Capel was sensational with 19 points, seven assists, and one turnover. Great defense keyed by Lang frustrated the Big Dog into 6-of-22 shooting, and Duke broke a halftime tie to win going away 69–60. When the Devils arrived in Charlotte for the Final Four, "Yes, I am" was the buzz phrase, and "Yes, we can" was the belief among Duke players, coaches, alumni, and fans.

There were "Yes, I am" buttons and T-shirts galore—and not just for Dukies. A UNC fan was spotted in Charlotte with a shirt that read: "Are you still a Heels fan? Yes, I am."

Johnny Harris, the powerful real estate developer and UNC alum who led the move to bring the Final Four to Charlotte, was a close friend of Carolina coach Dean Smith, hoping to use the Queen City as an appropriate backdrop to celebrate a second straight Tar Heel national championship and Smith's third.

Harris had worked Duke athletic director Tom Butters, a member and chairman of the NCAA Basketball Committee, very hard to land the Final Four with site visits not only to the Charlotte Coliseum but rounds of golf at Butters' favorite course in Charlotte—plush Quail Hollow Country Club.

But the 1994 coronation of Tar Heel basketball on home soil wasn't to be. Of all teams, Duke made it instead. Carolina had lost a second-round game to rugged Boston College in Landover, Maryland. The Eagles were a No. 9 seed but were big and tough enough to rough up the Tar Heels and snap Smith's amazing streak of having reached 13 consecutive Sweet 16s.

The sudden end to UNC's season devastated hundreds of thousands of Tar Heels in North Carolina and Charlotte, the biggest light blue city in the state. This had been a Final Four carefully constructed for the Tar Heels, who were loaded that season and gunning to match Duke's back-to-back NCAA titles.

In a preseason article in *Basketball Times*, Kansas coach and former UNC assistant Roy Williams thought his old school was such an overwhelming favorite that he was quoted as saying, "The only team that can beat them is themselves."

That was prophetic, as Smith remained adamant about not starting the three freshmen over veterans who had led Carolina to the 1993 NCAA title, even though future NBA stars Stackhouse and Wallace were better than seniors Brian Reese and Kevin Salvadori, and McInnis *believed* he was better than senior point guard Derrick Phelps. It created friction all season, as the three UNC frosh chafed at not starting and getting on a fast track to the NBA.

So the Tar Heels were already home when their archrivals opened the Final Four with a victory over No. 14-ranked Florida, setting up a meeting with Nolan Richardson's "40 Minutes of Hell" Arkansas Razorbacks for the national crown. Chief Hog and native Arkansan president Bill Clinton wanted to be there, requiring all 20,000 fans to pass through metal detectors before entering the Coliseum.

It was a match-up of two of the best teams in the country in 1994; Arkansas had spent more time ranked No. 1 that season than any team. The battle came down to two big time shots, the last one with only seconds remaining. After Duke blew a 10-point lead midway through the second half, Hill nailed a 22-footer, giving the Blue Devils the lead going into the final minute. With a hand in his face, Arkansas' Scotty Thurman drilled his three-pointer from the right side to put his team ahead by two. Duke missed its last-chance shot and barely missed winning its third national title in four years.

It was an incredible run—four national championship games in five years. As the overachieving Blue Devils left the floor, Duke fans and basketball fans in the Charlotte Coliseum gave them a loud and appreciative ovation, not knowing that Duke's dominance was about to end with an earth-shattering thud.

• • •

To stay in shape, one of the 47-year-old Krzyzewski's avocations was playing racquetball with former Duke assistant football coach and wrestling coach Carmen Falcone. Coach K pulled a muscle in his butt in one of those racquetball games and aggravated his back by not getting the appropriate treatment.

On October 15, 1994, the first day of basketball practice, the pain in Krzyzewski's back was so severe that he turned the drills over to his assistant coaches and watched them while lying on the playing floor of Cameron Indoor Stadium.

Tests showed a ruptured disk but no nerve damage. On October 19 he met with doctors, who asked him to walk on his toes when his back began to hurt. "When I stepped with my right foot, I was fine," Krzyzewski explained. "When I stepped with my left foot, I collapsed because I had lost 50 percent of the strength in my lower left leg, and my foot went numb."

Two days later Krzyzewski underwent back surgery to ease the pain enough for him to return to practice and continue getting the Blue Devils ready for the season. Once again he never gave his body time to rest despite strong suggestions from his doctors that he stay out longer so he would be able to finish the season, if not start it. In his mind he knew they weren't delaying anything for him and that the college basketball season waits for no one.

But the problems began piling up early.

From Krzyzewski's back surgery, which caused him to miss three weeks of early practices and conduct others sitting on a stool, to junior Chris Collins injuring his foot on the first day of practice, to not knowing the academic status of Jeff Capel for the spring semester, to Erik Meek giving up his redshirt year, to Joey Beard transferring, to Ricky Price injuring his ankle, to losing their ACC opener—Friday, January 6, seemed like a normal day by this team's problematic standards.

The Blue Devils had played in the Rainbow Classic after Christmas, and Krzyzewski ignored orders from his doctor to avoid the transcontinental flight and stay home to rest. Assistant coaches Mike Brey and Pete Gaudet, Coach K's Army associate and former head coach of the Cadets, were more than capable of leading the 6–1 team while Coach K remained in Durham to recuperate further. But his military background of never leaving his troops made him go on the trip to

Honolulu, lying on the main cabin floor of the Delta commercial flight for much of the eight-hour trip from Atlanta.

With Krzyzewski popping painkillers, he was not himself when Duke lost to Iowa in the first round of the Rainbow Classic. The Army-tough coach suffered what some people in that traveling party and a few others who spent time with the Blue Devils in Hawaii saw as an emotional and physical breakdown from a lack of sleep. He canceled all of the team's non-basketball events and rested in the bed in his hotel room between team meetings and practices and, of course, the games.

Duke wound up defeating Boston University and No. 17 Georgia Tech, and Krzyzewski was again stretched out on the plane's floor as the Blue Devils went home to defeat South Carolina State and climb to No. 7 in the national polls. Their record was 9–2 with the ACC opener against Clemson on January 4.

Beginning that week everything in the world of Duke basketball came to a startling halt in 1995, when Carolina would go on to reach its third Final Four of the decade, and Smith would regain the mantle of America's best college coach.

There was an implausible home loss to perennial ACC doormat Clemson. After four straight losing ACC seasons, Clemson had a new coach in Rick Barnes and a new attitude. Some new players Barnes brought in had led the Tigers to eight straight wins to begin his first season. They came to Duke intending to pull off an upset.

The top-ranked Tar Heels, who had opened the season with nine victories, lost their first game at N.C. State the same night, and Smith seemed shocked when told afterward that Duke had lost to Clemson at Cameron. (Earlier in the week, Smith had made an offhand comment about how Clemson and its new head coach were in for another tough season.) "That's remarkable," Smith said, shaking his head. Even more remarkable was the news that followed two days later.

Duke faced a weekend trip to Georgia Tech. Doctors and Mickie Krzyzewski pleaded with Coach K all week not to get on another bus or airplane until his back healed. His distraught wife issued what was close to an ultimatum: get on that bus, and she wouldn't be there when he returned. Mickie was as stubborn as Mike in many ways, and her stance convinced him that he should stay back and get a complete examination at the Duke Medical Center.

Late Friday afternoon the Blue Devils found out they would be without their head coach for the next game, perhaps longer. Lack of sufficient time to recover from the October back surgery had actually caused Krzyzewski to regress. Doctors say normal patients who undergo the kind of procedure he had would typically stay out of work for three months. But guess what? They weren't going to postpone the Final Four until June to accommodate Krzyzewski's problems; so he returned to practice after recuperating at home for less than a month.

Prior to flying to Atlanta to face Bobby Cremins and his Georgia Tech Yellow Jackets for the second time in eight days, the Duke coaching staff met as usual in the conference room on Friday. This meeting only lasted 10 minutes. "It was Mike telling us he was leaving—doctor's orders," recalled Brey, now head coach at Notre Dame. "Luckily, we had just played Tech in the Rainbow Classic so we didn't have to go over much preparation."

Brey and Gaudet were the only members of the coaching staff traveling with the team to Atlanta; the third assistant, Tommy Amaker, was on the road recruiting and got a surprise phone call from Brey. "You're not going to believe this," Brey said to Amaker from his hotel in Atlanta, "but we're on our own tomorrow night."

"Friday was the definition of chaos for us," Brey went on. "It was one thing after another. As adults we can handle distractions, but I think for the players some of the distractions were hard to manage."

Gaudet, who was handed the interim head coaching title almost by default, was the most shocked because he had known Krzyzewski for years and knew how strong and strong-headed he was. It was logical for Krzyzewski to let the "next in command" take over because he thought his absence would be short term. "He was such an intense person I don't think anyone thought it was going to hold him back," Gaudet said years later. "Nothing held him back. He didn't get much sleep anyway. The combination of that, the trip to Hawaii, game after game after game—there comes a point when you don't know how much you can endure. But none of us saw him stepping aside."

"It was different looking over at the bench and not seeing him there," sophomore guard Capel said, among varied reactions from the team.

"I really tried not to think about it," said senior Meek. "I just tried to go out there and play. He's coached me and the older players for so long now that we know what he expects. I just wanted to go out there and play the way he wanted us to play."

Little did they know, but the chaos and distractions of the season were just beginning as the Blue Devils would drop from a nationally ranked 9–3 team with a head coach having won two of the last five national championships to losing 15 of their next 19 games and finishing 13–18 overall, missing the NCAA Tournament for the first time in 12 years.

As time passed Mickie Krzyzewski was revealed as a key player in the decision to go on indefinitely without their head coach. The wife and closest confidante of Krzyzewski, she had watched her husband go through the pain and misery of back problems, the surgery, and then the precipitous return to his regular routine of being a "workaholic" college coach.

Married more than 20 years with three young daughters, her ultimatum seemed like an idle threat that couples can throw at each other. But those close to Mickie knew how tough she was, what a force she had become behind the scenes of Duke basketball, and when she said something, she meant it.

By now she was much more worried about her husband, Mike, than the basketball coach at Duke. Butters had become an early ally in Krzyzewski's leave of absence, rebuffing the coach's offer to resign and telling him to get better and then they would discuss the future. Butters might have done more as the season spun out of control, but he seemed resolved that it was a lost year and even went on a golf vacation to Florida in February. "[Krzyzewski] was in trouble," Butters said. "He didn't know why. I didn't know why. He offered to resign, and I said that was crazy. Let's find out what is wrong, assess the situation, and see what to do from there."

What became worse than the defeats—five in a row after Coach K left the bench and three more three-game losing streaks—were the rumors that Krzyzewski had a mental breakdown and was walking away from the game. It was not only a major distraction at Duke, but also to the entire world of college basketball. Everyone had their version of why Krzyzewski was missing the season.

The reason was simple but not very well articulated by anyone at Duke. He came back too early from back surgery and was exhausted, and a few weeks off was not going to miraculously make him better. He needed to fully recover, and Duke University was more than willing to give him all the time he needed.

• • •

No one heard a word from Krzyzewski until Duke released a statement on January 16 that the coach would remain "out for an indefinite period of time expected to last several weeks." That actually stoked the speculation because a back injury wouldn't keep him from doing an interview even if lying in bed. It gave new life to the rumors about what was really ailing the coach who had become a national name almost overnight.

Recruiting had to go on, though, and when highly touted Vince Carter made his visit to Duke on Saturday, January 14, he visited Krzyzewski at his home. Carter was the only person outside the Duke basketball program known to have seen the head coach during his absence. Asked about it years later, Carter said Krzyzewski was lying down but otherwise seemed to be fine.

Coach K's secretary Donna Keane made occasional trips to the house, bringing correspondence and tapes, but Mickie carefully monitored how much contact her husband had with his assistant coaches and players. She demanded he have complete rest and was miffed when she caught him on the phone late at night talking to Brey or Gaudet.

Finally, Butters and the Krzyzewskis agreed that the coach would not return that season and released the news to the media without any quotes from Coach K or his doctors. That sent the speculation soaring again, as the team blew a number of early leads and lost some close games—all the signs of a wayward ship with no captain.

A closer look at the results showed that Duke wasn't playing bad basketball, losing only once by more than 10 points. After winning at Notre Dame to break the six-game losing streak, the Blue Devils nearly stunned eighth-ranked Maryland at College Park. Behind Parks, their senior center averaging nearly 20 points and 10 rebounds, they seemed ready to turn their season around. And the second-ranked Tar Heels were coming to Cameron for the first game in February for both teams.

Even with all the turmoil surrounding the Blue Devils, they still found a way to play an incredible basketball game against their heavily favored archrival, one that lives on in the annals of Duke-Carolina—and perhaps the ultimate proof that regardless of the team records going in, anything can happen in this rivalry.

The Tar Heels were loaded with the forward tandem of Stackhouse and Wallace and a three-guard lineup of McInnis, Donald Williams, and Dante Calabria. They were 16–1, having just beaten No. 16 Wake Forest in Winston-Salem. By comparison Duke had lost seven of its last eight but had played far better in the win at Notre Dame and the two-point loss at Maryland just five days earlier.

Still, this did not set up as a regular Duke-Carolina game. Smith vs. Gaudet didn't have the same sting as Bubas vs. Smith or Smith vs. Krzyzewski.

Strangely, this made the game unusually appealing to many in the national media. They knew that when Duke and Carolina played basketball, it was bound to be a good show. And this bizarre circumstance might make it even better.

For the first time ever, there were two telecasts of a game from Cameron Indoor Stadium by the ACC Network and ESPN2, the second cable station for the so-called "World Wide Leader" that had been launched the year before on the strength of subscriptions sold to a nation that wanted to see the ballyhooed No. 1 vs. No. 2 match-up in Chapel Hill.

Mutual Radio broadcast the game worldwide. Print writers included Alex Wolff and Tim Crothers from *Sports Illustrated*; Dick Weiss of the *New York Daily News*; Malcolm Moran, *The New York Times*; Ivan Maisel, *Newsday*; Skip Myslenski, *Chicago Tribune*; Bill Connors, *Tulsa World*; Larry Donald, *Basketball Times*; Jim O'Connell, New York Associated Press; and Curry Kirkpatrick, who was filing for *Newsweek*.

Krzyzewski's absence loomed, but once the ball went up at 9:07 PM, it was just another Duke-Carolina game. And what a game it was with wild runs by both teams and numerous lead changes throughout both halves. Before the game Gaudet had joked about the 9:00 prime-time start and predicted, "We'll still be in overtime by midnight." Early in the game with Cameron packed and the temperature sweltering,

UNC's Smith made the unconventional move of taking off his suit jacket and rolling up his shirt sleeves.

The attending media, a national TV and radio audience, and the 9,000-plus squeezed into Cameron Indoor Stadium witnessed an unforgettable basketball game with regulation ending in an 81–81 deadlock.

Most ironic about this game was that Duke rallied from eight points down with 17 seconds remaining in the first overtime. "Eight points and seventeen seconds" is a legendary phrase in the rivalry, referring back to Carolina's comeback in the 1974 game in Chapel Hill. The Blue Devils trailed 94–86 in this one with 28 seconds showing on the clock.

Freshman Trajan Langdon ignited the comeback by hitting a three-pointer from the right wing. UNC's McInnis hit a free throw at the other end for the Tar Heels, and Capel answered with a drive and a free throw to make the score 95–92 with five seconds to play. Capel then fouled Carolina reserve Serge Zwikker, who missed the first free throw, and Smith called a timeout with four seconds on the clock to calm his big Swedish center and, if he missed again, set up something to defend a three-point shot to tie. "In the timeout Coach Brey diagrammed a play," Capel explained. "We had Trajan and Chris [Collins] in the corners. We felt like there was going to be pressure and we would kick the ball up. But there was no pressure. They were really concentrating on Trajan and Chris."

The actual pressure was on Zwikker. If he made the second free throw, the game would be over, but it rattled out, and Parks grabbed the rebound, passed it quickly to Capel, who took two long dribbles as he crossed midcourt and let loose a 35-footer while Tar Heel Ed Geth raised both arms high, trying to run at him as a distraction.

The most enduring memory of the game is the nearly half-court shot by Capel ripping through the nets to force overtime as Cameron erupted over the tie score and a second overtime. It looked like the Devils would finally have their own miracle finish to talk about.

"What was it, four seconds on the clock?" Parks asked. "That's a long time. People don't realize it. I was standing about 10 feet behind Jeff when he threw it up and I thought it had a great chance of hitting something. If there had been somebody pressuring, it could have taken a couple of seconds to find someone, but there was no one there, so I just gave it to him, and he was able to get as close to the bucket as he could."

"Fluke things happen to us all the time," Stackhouse said, "so it ain't like anything we haven't seen before. I felt like Capel's shot was going in as soon as it left his hand."

Gaudet was smiling in the huddle as the teams prepared for another extra period, perhaps remembering his offhand comment that the game would go to double overtime and last past midnight. Both predictions came to pass.

After Carolina survived by outscoring Duke 7–5 in the second overtime, which ended with a missed jumper from freshman guard Steve Wojciechowski, Tar Heels students rushed Franklin Street, set bonfires, and partied into early Thursday. All for beating a team that fell to .500 for the year and 0–8 in ACC play. "If you don't like that, you don't like college basketball," a still sweating Smith said afterward. "That's the best team we have played based on that game."

"I've always said it doesn't matter what the records are," said Parks, who was playing in his eighth Duke-Carolina game. "Both teams could be 0–20, both teams 20–0. It doesn't matter. Everybody's always up for the game. It's always going to be a good game regardless."

The epic struggle would be a high mark for this Duke team—a sad commentary when a loss is the highlight of a season. Without Krzyzewski at the helm, the Blue Devils would finish up by falling again to Wake Forest in the ACC Tournament, as Duke nemesis Randolph Childress led the Deacons to the championship over UNC and winning MVP honors.

Three days before the ACC Tournament in Greensboro, the world had finally gotten a glimpse of Krzyzewski, who had been recovering at his home since early January except for a visit with his players to tell them he would not be returning to coach that season, a day before the school released its statement.

• • •

It was March 6, and Cameron Indoor Stadium was set up for one of the most anticipated press conferences in years. Approximately 120 media members were in attendance with local ABC affiliate WTVD carrying the presser live along with the Duke Radio Network.

Krzyzewski looked rejuvenated in a gray suit and a blue and silver tie. "I'm doing great, absolutely doing great," he said. "I'm doing great because I'm taking proper care of myself and I've gotten the proper advice from my doctors. I got the proper advice and great care in October. I just didn't do well with it. My anxiety to get back and work with the team overshadowed my good sense. I couldn't ever balance the rehabilitation, rest, coaching my team, and finally my back wasn't getting as good as it should be. I got unbelievably exhausted at one point where I couldn't get much sleep. I had never had that feeling in my life, and you can be damn sure I never will again."

Krzyzewski had been slipping back into coaching at his own pace the last two weeks of the season. On February 22 he met with the team again prior to the Florida State game in Cameron and gave his famous "draw a line in the sand" speech, where whatever happened prior to that date was over, and it was a new season. The Blue Devils won 72–67. But they lost their last three games to UCLA, Maryland, and at North Carolina, all ranked in the top 10.

After beating N.C. State in the embarrassing ACC Tournament play-in game and the loss to Wake Forest, Brey remembered saying to himself as he boarded the bus for Durham, "Thank God it's over." The nightmare of a season had finally ended.

Brey had been considered a hot coaching prospect during Duke's run of Final Fours. Sensing changes were coming, he jumped at the Delaware head coaching job when offered. Gaudet resigned, citing problems with the NCAA limit on restricted earning for the so-called "part-time assistant" on each staff. Ironically, Gaudet remains the only "part-time" assistant with a head coaching record of 4–15, as those 19 games were excluded from Krzyzewski's career mark.

Insiders knew that Krzyzewski and Gaudet had crossed on whom to play at point guard. Gaudet went with senior Kenny Blakeney while Krzyzewski wanted freshman Wojciechowski, who would go on to become one of Coach K's favorite players and eventually a trusted assistant coach. The atmosphere around the program had deteriorated so much that Gaudet expected Krzyzewski to eliminate all the remnants of the season.

Gaudet remained at Duke, teaching in the physical education department. Even with the rescinding of the restricted earnings rule, due to a class action suit against the NCAA won by a group of assistant coaches, he never returned to Duke basketball, and his longtime friendship with Krzyzewski ended over the lost season. Coach K had recovered and had been planning drastic changes when he returned.

One of the clear problems with the entire 1995 debacle was the lack of direction from the administration. With Krzyzewski out the reigns of the team fell to Gaudet, the oldest and only former head college coach on the staff. It is not hindsight to say that was a mistake. Gaudet, truly one of the great tacticians in college basketball, saw the game differently and could break down film of another team and produce the exact keys needed to winning the next game.

Krzyzewski's motivational speeches and intensity alone hadn't gotten him to seven Final Fours in nine years. It took more than that, even more than the great players Duke had recruited. Gaudet's knowledge of the game, much like that of Dean Smith's most trusted assistant Bill Guthridge, was an important cog in the victory machine Duke basketball had become.

Gaudet would have been okay as interim coach for a few games, but he was much better at spending his time breaking down film and game-planning for the next opponent, and that was minimized. It resulted in the Blue Devils failing to hold numerous late leads in 1995.

The Duke brass should have seen the problems and known more about the essential elements of his basketball program—the crown jewel of the athletic department and for many believers the crown jewel of the entire university. Yet, they sat back and watched as the 1995 team imploded, saying it was Krzyzewski's basketball program and he would do whatever the head coach decided.

Brey, the older of the two other assistants, would have been the logical head coach with Gaudet continuing to break down film and Amaker out recruiting and reassuring prospects that Coach K would be back the following season.

But that didn't happen, and the collapse of the program reinforced what might have been taken for granted—just how valuable Krzyzewski was to Duke basketball. Without his presence and leadership, the Blue Devils lost their leader and their edge and needed a new start.

With his return came other departures besides Brey and Gaudet. Gone was Keane, his loyal administrative assistant, and gone was the weekly call-in radio show where Krzyzewski was losing patience over taking questions from local yokels. If not directly impacting the Duke basketball team, it was removed from his desk. Things would continue to change. His time was now controlled by Mickie and former sports information director Mike Cragg, whose sole responsibility soon became Duke basketball and "handling" Coach K. "He was a different person when he came back. It was a sad thing," Keane said of her old boss. "It was such a disappointment to see that person fade away and see someone else in his body."

Besides changing the losing atmosphere, Krzyzewski had to rebuild the program, and the only way was through recruiting. That would take time, and there were still a few more speed bumps to negotiate.

He began the resurrection by hiring two young assistants to replace Brey and Gaudet. Tim O'Toole, who had worked the past four years as a volunteer and restricted earnings coach for Jim Boehiem at Syracuse, was the first hire. Next came former player Quin Snyder, a popular figure who had graduated in 1989 and was very familiar with the program.

Snyder served as an administrative assistant for basketball while he worked toward his MBA and JD at Duke. He completed both degrees in the summer of 1995 and moved into the role of assistant coach. Snyder became one of the best hands-on teachers of all the Krzyzewski aides. His hiring was very important to this team. He still played pickup games with the Blue Devils in Card Gymnasium during the summer and preseason and got to know the makeup of the team.

He was instrumental in the handling of rising sophomore Wojciechowski, whose fragile freshman season not only included losing the college coach who had recruited him, but also the death of his high school coach over Christmas break.

The 1995–96 season would be about recovery on the court and in recruiting, which had slipped for almost three years with Krzyzewski's overloaded schedule that included working as an assistant to head coach Chuck Daly with the USA Dream Team at the 1992 Olympics.

With Krzyzewski back in charge, the Blue Devils rolled out to four straight wins that included upsetting No. 23 Indiana and No. 10 Iowa

in Anchorage at the Great Alaska Shootout. The trip had been scheduled as a homecoming for Langdon, an Alaska native, but a knee injury
forced him to miss the entire season.

Duke jumped back into the national rankings at No. 12, almost a
year since it had dropped out of the top 20 in January of 1995. With
a confidence-building tournament title in their hands, the Blue Devils
returned home to defeat UNC-Greensboro for their 95th straight home
win against a non-ACC team.

Four days later that streak ended.

It had been 12 years since Duke lost to a non-conference foe in
Cameron Indoor Stadium, falling to Louisville 91–76 on January 12,
1983. The villain this time would be the University of Illinois, handing the Blue Devils a 75–65 defeat. Adding insult to injury, two players that Duke had recruited hard and failed to land, Richard Keene
and Jerry Gee, scored 14 and 13 points, respectively, with Gee pulling
down 12 rebounds for the Fighting Illini.

The first Duke-Carolina game of that season was in Chapel Hill
with the Blue Devils again unranked after having lost four straight
to Clemson, Georgia Tech, Wake Forest, and Virginia. They did win
dramatically at N.C. State on a shot by senior Collins that hit every
part of the orange rim before dropping through the basket in the final
seconds.

The team was guard heavy with Collins, Price, and Capel. Collins
was becoming the leader as he went from one of the best long-range
shooters in college basketball to a driver and disher of the ball.

The Blue Devils were facing the No. 8 ranked Tar Heels, who
replaced early NBA departures Stackhouse and Wallace with highly
touted freshmen Vince Carter and Antawn Jamison. UNC had won
15 of its first 19 games, but ACC teams that would see Carter and
Jamison for a second time learned how to better defend Carolina.
Despite the difference in records and ranking, the Blue Devils took
the Tar Heels to the final seconds of the game before Dante Calabria
tipped in a shot, and Price missed a jumper at the buzzer to seal UNC's
73–72 victory.

Even Dean Smith knew he got away with a close win, and the future
of Duke basketball was bright with the two players on the bench in
Langdon and Roshown McLeod. Langdon was redshirting with the

knee injury, while McLeod was sitting out his transfer year from St. John's. Before the game Smith told reporters that with Langdon, "The Blue Devils could be undefeated at this point in the season."

It would be Langdon who helped bring the Blue Devils out of the darkness of seven consecutive losses to Carolina, but it wouldn't be until the next season and after another defeat from the Tar Heels on Senior Day in Cameron. After this Duke team put together a late run with consecutive wins over Virginia, N.C. State, Florida State, Maryland, and No. 16 UCLA, the regular season finale arrived with now No. 19 UNC on March 3, 1996.

In the first half of his senior day at Duke, Collins had 11 points and looked to be playing a solid game. Then with 13:55 remaining, he went out with an injury to his right foot, and the Blue Devils suffered a contentious 84–78 defeat. "I was coming off a screen and I got tangled up with Shammond Williams and I just kind of rolled my foot over," Collins lamented after the game. "I thought I had just turned my ankle, but the more I tried to put pressure on my foot, the more it hurt. I tried to play but was hurting the team more than helping them."

The intense pressure of the rivalry blew up at one point after McInnis hit a three-pointer and turned to say something to Collins, resulting in one of two technical fouls of the day on the impetuous Tar Heel guard. The second came, along with automatic ejection, when McInnis shoved Duke walk-on (and soccer star) Jay Heaps into the press table, as Smith reprimanded McInnis while players and coaches from both teams barked at each other.

Nevertheless, Duke's losing streak to the Tar Heels now stretched to seven in a row.

For Collins, one of the more emotional and visible players on the Duke team, the defeat in his last game as a player at Cameron was difficult. He had tasted victory over the Tar Heels only once in his college career, the first time they met in 1993, his freshman season. "It's very disappointing," he said, sitting in the gym one afternoon, following the end of the regular season. "This is a game you look forward to being a part of your whole career."

At respective press conferences prior to the 1996 ACC Tournament, the bitterness of the last game lingered on. Both Smith and Krzyzewski fired salvos at each other. Smith's first comments were about Duke student behavior and how McInnis was treated and yelled at following his second technical and ejection from the game. "We talk about role models," Smith said. "The coach is a role model, and the players are. How about the students? I think the Duke students should be role models. They were chanting, calling McInnis names. The esteemed Duke faculty has to be embarrassed. There were many high school kids watching on television. It's ridiculous. The schools have to do something, the ACC office has to do something. It won't happen here. I don't think we have had any obscene language by our students. Our faculty and our student body in fact would probably be upset."

Krzyzewski fired back on media day at the ACC Tournament in Greensboro. "I take offense to that," he began. "Our fans have been terrific this year. If there is a problem, it is out there on the court, not in the stands. The problem was definitely not in the stands. I'm speaking up for the fans. They have been great. I am going to stick up for them. I have nothing against Dean, and Dean and I are pretty good friends. But when I don't like some of the things some people in my family do, I tell them about it. Our crowd reacted to what they thought was unsportsmanlike play. That's their reaction. That kind of thing has happened in every arena we've played in. Not that you like it, but it happens. I don't like it either."

There were implications from the Tar Heel camp that ACC official Steve Gordon stalked McInnis and was looking to assess him a technical. "Jeff walked away, and Gordon followed him," Smith had said earlier in the week.

Krzyzewski was quick to respond to this as well: "It is bad when you start saying an official is stalking somebody or following somebody around. What that does is put officials in a position where there is pressure on them not to do anything with a particular player. I think that is uncalled for."

The two rival coaches even went off the basketball reservation to take verbal jabs at one another, a veiled reference to Krzyzewski's role in the Bud Light TV commercials. "Can you believe there is still beer advertising on the game?" Smith asked. "What about those role models? You have to lie, you have to tell someone you are going to marry them in order to get their beer. And you have to steal. Remember that beach ad where the girl comes up and cons the guy into putting sand on him, and she steals his beer. We all laugh. But talk about our role models. The ACC office is supporting beer ads during the day for my grandchildren to watch and be smart and say 'Yes, I am' [referring to Krzyzewski's parody spot for CBS prior to the 1994 Final Four]. The whole idea for these role models is to cheat and lie."

And, of course, the Blue Devils' head coach had a comment when asked about Smith's reference to the ACC and beer ads. "If you are going to set a precedent on that, you have to take care of your own house. On the Tar Heel Network, they have beer commercials. Our ACC office has done a magnificent job of promoting this basketball league for my 16 years here."

Smith chafed at Krzyzewski pointing out the conflict of interest. After the season he told athletic director John Swofford that he wanted UNC's contract with Coors cancelled. And it was.

For Duke what Krzyzewski would call the "Bridge Year" ended with two more losses—to Maryland in the quarterfinals of the ACC Tournament and then to Eastern Michigan in the first-round NCAA game. The final record stood at 18–13 with no national ranking for the second straight season.

For Carolina the season ended much the same with the loss in the ACC Tournament to Clemson on a last-second dunk by Greg Buckner and going out to Texas Tech in the NCAA Tournament, a 21–11 record, and a final ranking of 25th in the nation.

Not much to celebrate about the greatest rivalry in college basketball for this subpar season for both programs, one trying to get back into contention for ACC and national championships and the other facing the approaching retirement of its iconic coach.

As Krzyzewski continued to rebuild his team, he welcomed the return of sharpshooter Langdon and the addition of McLeod, his first transfer, along with freshman forward Mike Chappell. Even more excitement was created by two freshmen, tough and gritty Chris Carrawell and Nate James, whom Krzyzewski would rely on to reestablish Duke as an ACC and national power.

With Langdon and McLeod starting, plus the highly touted freshman class, the Blue Devils began the 1996–97 season ranked 10th. They were 10–2, including an early ACC victory over Florida State by the time conference play began in earnest. While Duke stumbled to a

2–2 ACC record, Carolina was losing its first three league games and started 2–4.

The rivalry games have long been measuring sticks for both Duke and Carolina, and with the Blue Devils having lost seven in a row, this one presented a great opportunity. Duke was ready to turn the corner, cross the Krzyzewski "Bridge," and get back to being a one of the nation's best programs. But the records never mattered much going into these games.

Behind Langdon, whom Smith said would have had Duke undefeated coming into the Carolina game the year before, the Blue Devils weren't unbeaten, but the "Alaskan Assassin" hardly proved Smith wrong.

The night before, Krzyzewski met with a supportive student body that had been camping out in the aptly named Krzyzewskiville tent city. More than 170 tents were in place for this year's big game, and both Capel and Wojciechowski spoke to the students along with the head coach inside Cameron.

Later, Krzyzewski and Capel talked about Capel returning to the starting lineup. He would replace junior Price, who was shooting under 40 percent and making almost twice as many turnovers as assists. "I told Coach I wanted to start," Capel said. "I felt like I was ready to be the leader of this team. Personally, I really wanted to beat Carolina for the first time in my career. I felt like we deserved it, and our fans deserved to experience a win in Cameron, especially the seniors."

Unknown to most observers, this game with the Tar Heels had been building inside Langdon throughout his season on the bench without Coach K as he helplessly watched two wins over UNC slip away. "Playing against Carolina is special anytime, but when you watch the team play them twice a year and the intensity is so high, when you come back you want to do anything you can to win," Langdon said, "especially when you haven't beaten them in seven straight games."

In this first meeting, Langdon came through with the best game of his college career, scoring 28 points and hitting seven three-pointers, including the dagger that secured the 80–73 victory and halted the losing streak to the Tar Heels. Smith, whose defense dogged Langdon the entire game, renewed his praise for the Alaskan Assassin.

Capel responded to the starting role with 19 points as the Blue Devils and their fans got a chance to celebrate a win over Carolina. Most of the student body had not been in school for the last such celebration back in 1993.

The Blue Devils were back. The bridge was complete. Even with an eighth loss to Carolina in the last nine regular-season meetings, they finished ahead of the Tar Heels in the ACC standings and made it to the second round of the NCAA Tournament before losing to Providence in Charlotte.

The resurrection of Duke basketball was about to be completed as Krzyzewski added perhaps the greatest recruiting class in the history of the program—the ballyhooed "Killer Bs"—Shane Battier, Elton Brand, and Chris Burgess, along with Will Avery, who would lead the Blue Devils back to the top of the college basketball mountain. Only two years before, it was unclear whether Krzyzewski would ever coach again. Now he was on his way to becoming arguably the greatest coach in the history of the game.

Chapter 10

Heroes

*T*he 1991–92 Duke basketball team took the term "sports heroes" to a new level. Rather, call the Blue Devils, who would go on to win their second straight national championship, rock stars. Since the suffocating media coverage after winning the 1991 NCAA title, they were treated more like celebrities than college athletes.

Everywhere the team went, fans wanted to see them, touch them, get their autographs, and speak to them—or, in the case of teenage girls, squeal like the Blue Devils were the latter day Beatles. On almost every road trip, the Duke managers had to come up with an exit strategy.

Although the players weren't particularly close off the court, the two biggest rock stars on the team were Christian Laettner and Bobby Hurley, who received fan mail into the thousands and could barely walk through a hotel lobby or between the team bus and the arena.

I saw it firsthand several times—nowhere worse than the unlikely town of football-crazy Clemson, South Carolina, on March 4, 1992. Duke had rallied from a halftime deficit to defeat the Tigers 98–97 behind 23 points from Laettner and Hurley's eight assists and a career high of 30 from Brian Davis. One would think that most Clemson fans left Littlejohn Coliseum devastated.

After the game I went out the back door of Littlejohn toward my car and had to go back in and get head trainer Dave Engelhardt. He stuck his head out the door and saw hundreds of fans—most dressed in *orange—surrounding the Duke team bus. We surmised the Blue Devils would never make it on board.*

Engelhardt found the bus driver, who backed the bus down through the elephant doors and inside the bowels of Littlejohn, where Laettner, Hurley, and the rest of the rock band...uh...basketball team got on safely. As they pulled out of the tunnel, dozens of fans, mostly young girls, were screaming and banging on the side of the bus. Elvis had left the building.

On another road trip—this one to Notre Dame in 1991—there were so many fans outside the back door from the Duke locker room that the shy Hurley wanted no part of it and was stashed inside a large duffel bag and carried out by two managers. Once safely on the team bus, Hurley popped out of the bag undetected. Sometimes heroes have to take desperate measures.

—JM

DECADE OF DOMINANCE

Between 1997 and 2006, when Duke won either the ACC regular season championship and/or the ACC Tournament for 10 consecutive years—unmatched or even closely approached in the history of the conference—the Blue Devils played 160 ACC games and lost only 27 for a winning percentage of .831. They finished first in the ACC seven times and won seven ACC Tournament titles. They won both in five of those 10 years, plus brought home their third national championship in 2001 and reached two more Final Fours in 1999 and 2004.

Undoubtedly, Duke ruled the ACC during the 1998, 1999, and 2000 seasons like no other basketball team ever has—going 15–1, 16–0, and 15–1 while becoming the first and only team to go undefeated over a 16-game schedule. Duke had gone 14–0, 13–1, and 11–3 from 1963–65, finishing first three straight years, capturing two ACC Tournament crowns, and making two Final Fours under Vic Bubas (who added a third Final Four in 1966) and behind stars Art Heyman and Jeff Mullins. The 1967, '68, and '69 North Carolina Tar Heels followed by winning three straight ACC regular season (posting three consecutive 12–2 records for a winning percentage of .857) and ACC Tournament titles, reaching the Final Four each year.

After winning national championships in 1991 and 1992, the Blue Devils had taken a step back from 1993 to 1997 while losing eight out of 10 games to the Tar Heels. Not until the signing of perhaps Duke's greatest class of all time did the Blue Devils gain true, extended dominance in the series. Will Avery, Shane Battier, Elton Brand, and Chris Burgess led Duke to one of the strongest teams in its hoops history.

The 1999 Blue Devils completed the coveted "Triple Crown" by winning three games against the Tar Heels in one season for the first time since 1988 and 1966. North Carolina, meanwhile, had pulled off the "Triple Crown" four different times since 1957, the last coming in the 1976 season.

Duke basically spent the entire '99 season ranked as either the No. 1 or No. 2 team in the nation. The three games against North Carolina were won by an average of 18.3 points, increasing the winning margin from 12 points to 20 in the home-and-home games and to 23 in the ACC Championship Game in Charlotte, avenging a disappointing loss to the Tar Heels the year before in Greensboro. "I don't remember a team dominating the league the way they have," North Carolina head coach Bill Guthridge said of the 1999 Duke juggernaut.

The Blue Devils rolled through the regional portion of the NCAA Tournament, winning by a ridiculous average of 30 points in their first four games to advance to the Final Four in St. Petersburg, Florida. After the Blue Devils arrived, their bus crossed over the bridge to St. Petersburg Beach. Visible from the bridge was the beautiful pink hotel, the Don CeSar, which when it opened in 1928 at the height of the Jazz Age had quickly become known as the Gulf Coast playground for America's pampered rich. With its long, elevated entrance way lined with tall palm trees, a pool overlooking the Gulf of Mexico, and luxurious rooms, it was a hotel fit for a national championship basketball team. The Duke bus pulled into the Don CeSar with every bit of that intention.

With wealthy donors and celebrities such as Kevin Costner checking into the hotel, this Final Four had a feel like no other. The team had a walk-through in the spacious, immaculate ballroom, which had been laid out to resemble a basketball court. Everything seemed set for Duke to wear its first national crown in seven years—since the rock star team of 1992.

The top-ranked team in the nation carried a 31-game winning streak and 36–1 record into the Saturday semifinal against No. 2 Michigan State. The Spartans confused Duke with a second-half zone and hung in there before losing 68–62. While it was another victory, the Blue Devils' lowest scoring output of the season created concern heading into Monday night's national championship game against Connecticut, which had reached its first Final Four under veteran coach Jim Calhoun. "I don't think it was a bad game for us," sophomore Shane Battier said. "We had a heck of a game defensively and on the boards. We're never going to judge ourselves on whether or not our shots go down."

Two nights later against No. 3 UConn, Krzyzewski would judge one bad shot not going down as a determining factor in the game. Midway through the first half, freshman Corey Maggette took a turn-around, fall-away jumper from the lane that missed badly. Krzyzewski was furious; wild shots weren't part of the Blue Devils' motion offense.

Maggette was immediately pulled and had been on the bench for several minutes when assistant coach Quin Snyder suggested to Krzyzewski to get the best athlete on either team back in the game. Struggling for weeks with a painful hip that would be replaced after the season, Krzyzewski was on edge, trying to make it through the national title game. Still upset about his whirling dervish of a shot, he said, "Fuck, Maggette," to Snyder.

Maggette sat out most of the second half and played only 11 total minutes, as UConn's Rip Hamilton kept the Huskies in the game and would not allow the Blue Devils to pull away despite 15 points and 13 rebounds from Brand, 25 points from Trajan Langdon, and 11 points, five assists, and only one turnover by Avery.

With Duke trailing by one, it was Langdon's late turnover in the closing seconds that allowed UConn to win its first national championship 77–74. Of the three NCAA title games Duke has lost under Krzyzewski, this one was the most painful in more ways than one.

Following the game, Krzyzewski needed a golf cart to take him to the press conference. He had the hip replaced a few days later and then faced the first underclassmen departures of his coaching career. National Player of the Year Brand, who had missed 15 games of his freshman season, was expected to leave. Then without Krzyzewski's blessing, sophomore Avery and a miffed Maggette announced they

Duke High Draft Picks (Round)

Dick Groat, 1952 (1)	Trajan Langdon, 1999 (1)
Art Heyman, 1963 (1)	Corey Maggette, 1999 (1)
Jeff Mullins, 1964 (1)	Will Avery, 1999 (1)
Jack Marin, 1966 (1)	Chris Carrawell, 2000 (2)
Gary Melchionni, 1973 (2)	Shane Battier, 2001 (1)
Tate Armstrong, 1977 (1)	Jason Williams, 2002 (1)
Jim Spanarkel, 1979 (1)	Mike Dunleavy, 2002 (1)
Mike Gminski, 1980 (1)	Carlos Boozer, 2002 (2)
Gene Banks, 1981 (2)	Dahntay Jones, 2003 (1)
Vince Taylor, 1982 (2)	Luol Deng, 2004 (1)
Johnny Dawkins, 1986 (1)	Daniel Ewing, 2005 (2)
Mark Alarie, 1986 (1)	Shelden Williams, 2006 (1)
Danny Ferry, 1989 (1)	J.J. Redick, 2006 (1)
Alaa Abdelnaby, 1990 (1)	Josh McRoberts, 2007 (2)
Phil Henderson, 1990 (2)	Gerald Henderson, 2009 (1)
Christian Laettner, 1992 (1)	Kyrie Irving, 2011 (1)
Brian Davis, 1992 (2)	Nolan Smith, 2011 (1)
Bobby Hurley, 1993 (1)	Kyle Singler, 2011 (2)
Thomas Hill, 1993 (2)	Austin Rivers, 2012 (1)
Grant Hill, 1994 (1)	Miles Plumlee, 2012 (1)
Antonio Lang, 1994 (2)	Mason Plumlee, 2013 (1)
Cherokee Parks, 1995 (1)	Ryan Kelly, 2013 (2)
Erik Meek, 1995 (2)	Jabari Parker, 2014 (1)
Roshown McLeod, 1998 (1)	Rodney Hood, 2014 (1)
Elton Brand, 1999 (1)	

were entering the NBA draft. Brand went No. 1 to the Chicago Bulls, Maggette No. 13 to the Orlando Magic, and Avery No. 14 to the Minnesota Timberwolves. With senior Langdon going 11th to the Cleveland Cavaliers, it marked the first time that any college team had four lottery picks in the same draft. "When they all decided to leave, it hurt my feelings a little bit," Krzyzewski admitted. "I was sorry to see them go because you can't establish as strong a relationship in one or two years as you can in four. I could understand Elton's situation. He had missed a lot of time as a freshman with a broken foot, and the risk of something like that happening again was hanging over him."

UNC High Draft Picks (Round)

Lennie Rosenbluth, 1957 (1)

Pete Brennan, 1958 (1)

Joe Quigg, 1958 (2)

Lee Shaffer, 1960 (1)

York Larese, 1961 (2)

Doug Moe, 1961 (2)

Billy Cunningham, 1965 (1)

Bill Bunting, 1969 (2)

Charles Scott, 1970 (1, ABA)

Robert McAdoo, 1972 (1)

Dennis Wuycik, 1972 (2)

Bobby Jones, 1974 (1)

Mitch Kupchak, 1976 (1)

Walter Davis, 1977 (1)

Tom LaGarde, 1977 (1)

Phil Ford, 1978 (1)

Dudley Bradley, 1979 (1)

Mike O'Koren, 1980 (1)

Al Wood, 1981 (1)

James Worthy, 1982 (1)

Michael Jordan, 1984 (1)

Sam Perkins, 1984 (1)

Brad Daugherty, 1986 (1)

Kenny Smith, 1987 (1)

Joe Wolf, 1987 (1)

J.R. Reid, 1989 (1)

Rick Fox, 1991 (1)

Pete Chilcutt, 1991 (1)

Hubert Davis, 1992 (1)

George Lynch, 1993 (1)

Eric Montross, 1994 (1)

Jerry Stackhouse, 1995 (1)

Rasheed Wallace, 1995 (1)

Jeff McInnis, 1996 (2)

Serge Zwikker, 1997 (2)

Antawn Jamison, 1998 (1)

Vince Carter, 1998 (1)

Shammond Williams, 1998 (2)

Brendan Haywood, 2001 (1)

Joseph Forte, 2001 (1)

Marvin Williams, 2005 (1)

Raymond Felton, 2005 (1)

Sean May, 2005 (1)

Rashad McCants, 2005 (1)

David Noel, 2006 (2)

Brandan Wright, 2007 (1)

Reyshawn Terry, 2007 (2)

Tyler Hansbrough, 2009 (1)

Ty Lawson, 2009 (1)

Wayne Ellington, 2009 (1)

Ed Davis, 2010 (1)

Harrison Barnes, 2012 (1)

Kendall Marshall, 2012 (1)

John Henson, 2012 (1)

Tyler Zeller, 2012 (1)

Reggie Bullock, 2013 (1)

P.J. Hairston, 2014 (1)

Krzyzewski was also smart enough to know that if certain players from UNC hadn't left early the Blue Devils may not have become as dominant. "If Antawn Jamison and Vince Carter don't leave North Carolina early, there's no way Elton's picture is on all those preseason magazines," he said. "Kids are widely publicized before they've had a chance to do very much. None of our kids expected to be gone after one or two years. But when they're talented and have had extreme success like we had, they feel like it might be the best time to take advantage of their notoriety and move to the next level."

Three veterans remained: Chris Carrawell, Nate James, and Battier, who were joined by freshmen Jason Williams, Carlos Boozer, and Mike Dunleavy. The 2000 season would find the Blue Devils stretching their win streak over North Carolina to five with an overtime win in Chapel Hill and a record-breaking victory in Cameron when Battier nailed six three-pointers. Duke easily dispatched UNC on Senior Day for Carrawell, who won ACC Player of the Year to complete the Blue Devils' second 15–1 record around the 16–0 gem. But Duke was not a deep team and tired after winning its second straight ACC Tournament. It lost to Florida in the Sweet 16 to finish 29–5 and completed the three most dominant seasons in ACC history without winning a national championship. Duke would win it all the next season.

AT&T—DUKE KILLERS

Antawn, Tyler, and Ty loved playing basketball for Carolina but never more so when they took on Duke. Their combined record against the Blue Devils was 11–4.

Other Tar Heels had their special moments against Duke—Larry Miller and Charlie Scott in the ACC Tournament championship games, Phil Ford's fabulous 34 on his Senior Day, Dudley Bradley's dunk on Mike Gminski, King Rice's battles with Bobby Hurley, Eric Montross' blood game, the highlight reel slams by Jerry Stackhouse and Rasheed Wallace at Cameron Indoor Stadium in 1994 and '95, and Sean May's 26 points and 24 rebounds (not to mention Marvin Williams' three-point play) in 2005.

But Jamison, Hansbrough, and Lawson made careers over their performances in the blue blood rivalry. In seven games against Duke from 1996–98, Jamison had five double-doubles, including games of 23 points and 14 rebounds, 33 and 11, 35 and 11, 23 and 13, and 22 and 18 (for an average of 27.2 points and 13.4 rebounds). He made 69 of 99 shots against the Blue Devils, which is a hair under 70 percent. ESPN kept a clock on Jamison during the February 5, 1998, game in Chapel Hill and determined that he had shot 20 times (making 14) in 52 seconds with the ball in his hands. "I just went out there and constantly moved without the ball," Jamison explained. "The quick release separated me from the rest of the guys. I'm always moving and thinking ahead, whether I have the ball or not. That's the biggest key. I'm a headache for big guys. They'd rather push all day."

Jamison capped his college career against Duke by yanking down 18 rebounds despite a sore groin in the 1998 ACC Championship Game at the Greensboro Coliseum, an 83–68 win over the Blue Devils that gave the Tar Heels the No.1 seed in the NCAA East region with the Sweet 16 scheduled back in Greensboro. It was a home-court advantage that helped Carolina advance to its second straight Final Four and fifth in the 1990s.

Tyler Hansbrough's record against Duke in four years was 6–2, one win better than Jamison's 5–2. But Hansbrough's distinction, of course, is that his two losses came at home to Duke, meaning he won all four years at Cameron Indoor Stadium. And he sealed the first and last of those four with long three-pointers—not exactly the best part of the inside banger's game. But with the shot clock winding down both times, Hansbrough connected from the top of the key and the right wing.

The 2006 dagger capped a second-half comeback that gave Hansbrough 27 points (and 10 rebounds) for the game and ruined Senior Night for Duke star J.J. Redick, who missed 15 of his last 16 shots, as the Tar Heels outscored the top-ranked Blue Devils 46–38 in the second half. Besides the big three-pointer, Hansbrough hit two late free throws and said that's when he realized, "We just beat Duke over here. Nothing feels better than this."

"After he won there the first time," Roy Williams said, "he went over there with the attitude that we are not losing. And it rubbed off on the team."

It sure did. In 2007 Hansbrough was held to three rebounds at Duke, but freshman Brandan Wright came through with 19 points and nine rebounds while senior Reyshawn Terry had 10 and 10. Duke led by five at the half, but again the Tar Heels stormed back with a 79–73 victory.

In 2008 Hansbrough had 16 points and 15 rebounds at Cameron, and Carolina staved off a Duke rally by scoring the last 10 points of the game. Danny Green chipped in with 18 points, including his famous flying facial dunk of Duke's Greg Paulus, which remains a repeatedly viewed YouTube clip. The 76–68 win avenged an earlier loss to the Blue Devils in Chapel Hill, when Ty Lawson missed the game with a sprained ankle (which left him 5–0 in his career vs. Duke).

Lawson was healthy for the first game of the 2009 season in Durham and scored 21 of his 25 points in the second half as Carolina erased an eight-point halftime deficit and outscored Duke 57–35 in the second half. Again, Hansbrough hit a key three, and the Tar Heels paraded to the foul line to make the final margin a misleading 101–87.

When the Blue Devils arrived in Chapel Hill for the 2009 regular season finale, they had a chance to tie the Tar Heels for first place in the ACC. Carolina had won two straight ACC championships and were gunning for a third, but those plans were jeopardized when Lawson injured his toe in practice two days before the game. Ty's toe became the big story, and Lawson had to play with a larger shoe equipped with a metal plate.

Lawson did not start but came off the bench in heroic fashion, fighting off the pain to finish with 13 points, nine assists, and eight rebounds as the Tar Heels won their third straight ACC regular season. After the game Lawson's toe swelled up so dramatically that Roy Williams thought he might have hurt his team's chance to win the national championship by playing Lawson against Duke.

Williams held Lawson out of the ACC Tournament in Atlanta, which Duke won, but got his point guard back for the last five games of the NCAA Tournament, as the Tar Heels won six consecutive games by double figures on the way to cutting down the nets at Ford Field in Detroit. Hansbrough and Green graduated, and Lawson and Wayne Ellington turned pro. The next time Carolina went to Cameron, fourth-ranked Duke won 82–50. "They played like they were trying to make up for the last four years in one night," Roy Williams said, "and to me it felt like they did."

HEROES ALL

The 2001 season would be among the most interesting in the rivalry. The Blue Devils and Tar Heels were both preseason top 10 teams, even though the Dean Smith era had effectively ended with the retirement of Guthridge and (when Roy Williams elected to stay at Kansas) the hiring of former Tar Heel player Matt Doherty from Notre Dame.

Duke spent the first half of the season ranked No. 2 or No. 3 in the nation, and when Carolina visited Cameron on February 1, it was No. 2 versus No. 4. That was typical of the Krzyzewski-Smith rivalry but somewhat unexpected with Doherty taking over and the Tar Heels getting off to a 3–2 start in non-conference games.

But this game was anything but typical for the Blue Devils, who had two ACC losses over the last three-and-a-half seasons. They shot an ice-cold 39.7 percent from the floor and missed 14-of-27 free throws. It, however, was still a tie game when senior Shane Battier made a fresh-man mistake by fouling UNC's Brendan Haywood 15 feet from the basket in the closing seconds. Haywood, who as a freshman in 1998 had missed two critical free throws at the end of Duke's comeback win in Cameron, stepped to the line as a senior, and the future first-round draft pick nailed both foul shots for the 85–83 victory. "The obvious thing is that we just couldn't make any shots," said sophomore Dunleavy, experiencing his first loss to the Tar Heels. "We played with a lot of emotion and worked hard, but we just couldn't make any of our shots go down."

"We looked like we were ready to play," Krzyzewski said, referring to the tough practices the prior two days in which his perimeter players drained 168 three-pointers in five minutes—the nylon swishing repeatedly as shot after shot zipped through. The next day they made 190 threes in the same drill. The Blue Devils literally might have shot their way out of the Carolina game before it ever tipped off. And now they had to wait until the season finale in Chapel Hill to even the score.

For Doherty the upset win looked like a springboard to a success-ful coaching career at Carolina. Students chalked his name on the campus sidewalks, and some began calling themselves "Doherty's Disciples," making up T-shirts to sell with that slogan. Far different from Smith and Guthridge, Doherty was flamboyant and open. He tried to loosen up his team late in the game with his infamous remark that, "Duke still has the ugliest cheerleaders in the ACC." Afterward, when hugged by his father, Doherty facetiously downplayed the win, "This definitely doesn't suck." But the stunning victory would turn out to be the highlight of his short stay at UNC.

Duke had lost one other ACC game, by two points at Virginia, heading into Battier's Senior Night against Maryland. The Blue Devils had defeated the Terrapins in overtime earlier in the season in what was dubbed the "Miracle Minute" when Jason Williams hit two three-pointers and a layup to force the game into overtime. Duke went on to win 98–96 in College Park, silencing a raucous Cole Field House crowd that thought it had won.

Battier, who had his No. 31 retired, and fifth-year player Nate James were the only scholarship seniors left on the roster after Will Avery and Elton Brand turned pro as sophomores and Chris Burgess transferred to Utah.

A 23–7 run to end the first half gave the Blue Devils a 50–43 advantage, and it looked like Battier's Cameron swan song was going off as planned. Suddenly, with 14:32 left in the game, Duke center Carlos Boozer came off the floor limping. Trainer Dave Engelhardt worked to get Boozer back on the court, but Boozer was in too much pain.

His replacement, sophomore Casey Sanders, picked up four quick fouls, and a Maryland team that was headed for the Final Four won going away 91–80. And now the bitterly disappointed Blue Devils had to go to UNC without their starting center and beat Carolina to force a tie for first place in the ACC standings. Even though the Tar Heels, who had won 18 straight and briefly were ranked No. 1, had slumped and lost two of their last four games, they were still a favorite to defeat the depleted Dukies.

X-rays showed that Boozer had suffered a fracture to a non-weight-bearing bone in his foot and would be lost for at least three weeks, maybe longer. After the Maryland press conference and shaking a few hands, Krzyzewski summoned his coaching staff to their private locker room. They all changed into warm-ups, preparing for an all-nighter to devise a plan not only for Carolina but how to play the ACC Tournament without their starting center. That way if Boozer made it back for the NCAA Tournament, it would be a bonus.

The 2001 Blue Devils were one of the strongest teams in the school's history, even though they did not always play up to that level. And perhaps without Boozer's injury, they might have never raised their level of play to be national champions. But Battier and sophomores Dunleavy and Jason Williams, plus highly recruited freshman Chris Duhon, still gave Duke a formidable lineup. How they would replace Boozer was the key.

Now undersized the Blue Devils figured to go with Sanders in the middle and hope for the best. Sanders was a 6'11" prep All-American from Tampa, Florida, who came to Duke after a very stellar high school career, recording 26 double-doubles and being named Mr. Basketball in Florida and a McDonald's All-American. To that point in the season, Sanders had played in 26 games, averaging eight minutes, 1.5 rebounds, and 2.3 points per game.

But going with Sanders for extended minutes was never a consideration. Krzyzewski was yet to believe in Sanders, thinking he was still too soft. During Sanders' freshman year, the veterans snickered whenever the coaching staff called him "Pussy" Sanders to try to get him to be more aggressive. His four quick fouls against Maryland did not demonstrate aggressiveness as much as it did stupidity.

Speed and confidence were what Krzyzewski and his coaches came up with. When they walked into practice on Thursday, he told them, "If you do what I say, we'll win the national championship."

The plan was to move Duhon to the point, start Sanders, and run. They would use their speed to try to get a lead and their superior defense to win the game. But Sanders got into quick foul trouble, and Krzyzewski was left with putting in the 6'5" James and going with one of their smallest lineups—but also one of the quickest with Duhon at point guard—ever.

Sanders played only 11 minutes before fouling out, and James came through with 27 hard-nosed minutes, taking turns guarding UNC's Haywood, Kris Lang, and Julius Peppers.

It was a classic team effort by the Blue Devils. Although Duhon shot poorly in the first half, missing all four of his attempts, he went 5-for-7 in the second half. With Duhon running the point, Williams was free to create and shoot the ball. He knocked down seven three-pointers for a total of 33 points in the game. And the defense was led by Battier, of course, as Duke swarmed the ball and totally disrupted the taller Tar Heels' plan to go inside.

With 16:45 left in the game, Carolina's Joseph Forte stole the ball from Dunleavy at the top of the key and took off down the floor for what looked like a sure two points. But coming from behind, the 6'8" Battier caught Forte and forced him to jam the ball against the front of the rim. As Dunleavy grabbed the rebound, he dished it out to Williams, who headed down court and nailed another three.

The five-point swing expanded Duke's lead to eight, and the game was essentially over with Carolina knowing its own plan had failed and Duke's had succeeded. Williams led all scorers with 33 points, but Battier had a typical Battier night with 25 points, 11 rebounds, five blocked shots, and four steals.

In the coaches' locker room following the game, Krzyzewski smiled and said, "Wow, how about the game Battier played?"

He was far more composed and matter of fact in the press conference, not wanting anyone to think he was surprised that his team won without Boozer. "You still have to beat Duke," he said.

The 95–81 victory gave the Blue Devils a share of the ACC regular season title for a record fifth straight time and started them on a roll of 10 consecutive victories that included edging Maryland and crushing Carolina in the ACC Tournament in Atlanta.

Coming off the bench as to not destroy the chemistry that had been rebuilt in his absence, Boozer returned for the last four games of the NCAA Tournament, but he nevertheless restored perhaps Duke's best lineup ever (four first-round draft picks and two second-rounders). Duke rolled to the Final Four in Minneapolis, winning four games by an average of 20 points.

In the national semifinals, the Blue Devils had an improbable fourth meeting of the season with Maryland and trailed by 22 points in the first half before Krzyzewski called a timeout and screamed at them, "What the fuck are you afraid of? Just play basketball!" They cut the deficit to 11 by halftime and ran away from the Terps in the second half to win 95–84. Boozer regained his form with 19 points and four rebounds.

In the National Championship Game against Arizona, Boozer had a double-double (12 and 12), but it was Dunleavy's barrage of threes in the second half that sent Duke to its third national championship—10 years after the Blue Devils had won their first.

Groat's 'Greatest Game'

One of the first true heroes in the Duke-Carolina rivalry was Richard Morrow Groat, better known as Dick Groat. At 5'11", 185 pounds, the Swissvale, Pennsylvania, native was a supremely gifted athlete. The talented baseball and basketball player could do it all. He had a star-studded baseball career and an incredible basketball career. "Baseball was always like work for me," Groat explained. "Basketball was the sport that I loved."

His tireless work at baseball paid off very well. He was the 1960 National League MVP, winning the batting title with a .325 average and leading the Pittsburgh Pirates to the 1960 World Series title from his shortstop position. In his 14-year major league career, he was named an All-Star five times and was on the 1964 World Series Champion St. Louis Cardinals as well.

But ask about his final game in Duke Indoor Stadium against North Carolina, and he will say it is his finest sports memory. "You had never played anywhere growing up like Duke Indoor Stadium," he said of the barely 10-year-old building. "No one had a palace to play basketball like it. I remember saying to myself the first time I walked in there, 'Wow, this is where I get to play basketball.'"

His final game in his basketball palace didn't start off so great. "My father fell on the way to the game. My mother and sisters were with him, and they delayed the start of the game until they returned from the hospital," Groat said, wondering if TV would allow for that today.

Groat pumped in 17 points in the first half as Duke opened up a huge halftime lead. When Carolina rallied to close within eight points in the second half, Groat promptly hit eight straight shots to regain control of the game. "When Carolina made a run at us, I started shooting, and it seemed like everything I shot went in the basket," he said. "Shooters know when they get that hot hand. It's so strange. As a senior in high school, I had the most points I ever scored in my last game. At Duke it was the most I had ever scored in college. Once you got going, it seems like everything would go down, a wonderful feeling."

Groat finished with 48 points, then a school and Southern Conference record, hitting 19-of-37 field goal attempts and 10-of-11 from the free throw line. In the fourth quarter, he was removed from the game with 15 seconds left to a prolonged standing ovation. When the teams left the floor, the fans carried him off on their shoulders.

Groat broke down in tears in the locker room as he accepted congratulations from his teammates. He returned to the court and spoke to the fans about their marvelous support. After he left the court with his uniform still wet with sweat, the physically and emotionally drained star sat in the Duke locker room. Then the Carolina players came in to shake his hand, and each Tar Heel congratulated him on an incredible performance. "I was sobbing in the locker room and I didn't even know my dad was standing beside me. He said to me, 'Christ, Richard, you didn't even want to come down here and now you don't want to leave.'"

Groat has lived in Pittsburgh all his life and still does color on the Pitt Panther radio network. Even after 60 years of home runs, World Series rings, and all those baseball accolades, he says that his 48 points against the Tar Heels remain one of his most cherished memories. The 48 points by Groat still stands as the most points ever scored by a Duke player against North Carolina.

CUNNINGHAM AND THE EFFIGY

Dean Smith's first truly great player at UNC was Billy Cunningham, the 6'5" lefty jumping jack nicknamed "The Kangaroo Kid" by former UNC sports information director Bob Quincy, who went on to become a brilliant columnist in Charlotte.

Seven-foot Rusty Clark holds the single-game rebounding record at UNC with 30 against Maryland in 1968, but Cunningham has the next three best rebounding games at 28, 27, and 25. Lennie Rosenbluth also had two games in which he pulled down 25 rebounds. All of those dominating performances were against losing ACC teams in an era when only the Big Four schools really cared about basketball, and, frankly, there were a lot more missed shots to rebound.

But Cunningham is the only Tar Heel among their eight career rebounding leaders who played just three seasons because freshmen were still not eligible. Thus, his astonishingly consistent career average of more than 15 rebounds per game is almost five better than the next highest per-game average. The Kangaroo Kid could really jump.

Voted ACC Player of the Year by a landslide in 1965, when he led the league in both scoring and rebounding, Cunningham had his legacy hurt slightly by having never played in an NCAA Tournament. Nevertheless, he was good enough to be the fifth pick in the 1965 draft by the Philadelphia 76ers, where he began with a $12,500 salary and $2,500 bonus. (Today's comparable draft pick is guaranteed $7 million with a three-year team option that could mean $12 million more.)

Cunningham's Irish family back in Brooklyn wanted him to forget basketball and go to law school. But The Kangaroo Kid both played for and coached NBA championship teams in Philadelphia and is one of nine UNC alumni in the Naismith Hall of Fame. The awkward kid, who blushed over compliments from his college professors, cared more about winning than anything else, and what he did not win at UNC he made up for in the NBA.

As a Tar Heel hero, Cunningham is known for an off-the-court act early in the 1965 season. The fourth team of still embattled head coach Dean Smith had returned to campus after a 22-point drubbing at Wake Forest, Carolina's fourth consecutive loss, giving the Heels a 6–6 record. (They were already 0–2 in the ACC.) As the team bus droned to a stop in front of Woollen Gym, a group of wise-ass students hovered around a tree across the street. Suspended from a limb was an effigy of Smith, who at the time was hanging on as Carolina's coach.

Smith long claimed that he did not see what happened, but everyone else on the bus—including *Daily Tar Heel* sports writer and eventual Hall of Fame journalist Peter Gammons—watched in awe as Cunningham jumped off the bus, bolted across the street, and used his pogo stick legs to pull down the dummy and chase off the practical jokers. Distraught at first, Smith found comfort with some close friends that night and admitted, "The hanging did help me give my best pep talk of the season before our next game."

Smith's own Hall of Fame career was jump-started three days later at eighth-ranked Duke, when the Tar Heels slowed the game down, and Cunningham limited Blue Devils All-American Jack Marin to nine shots in the 65–62 upset, Smith's first win over Duke as a head coach after seven losses. Cunningham and sophomore scoring sensation Bobby Lewis combined for 43 of the team's 65 points.

This time when the UNC bus returned to Chapel Hill, a happy crowd of students and townsfolk had gathered along the sidewalk, chanting "Go to Hell, Duke!" They wanted Smith to say something as he stepped off the bus, but he could only remark sarcastically about being unable to speak because something was choking his neck. Cunningham laughed at his coach's zinger, and seven weeks later, the Tar Heels swept the now No. 5 Blue Devils with a 71–66 in Woollen. Carolina went on to a 10–4 record and a three-way tie for second behind Duke. UNC never finished lower than third in the ACC standings for the next 37 seasons.

Smith not only survived, but he also retired 32 years later with the most victories of any major college basketball coach.

THE MISSOULA MOUNTAIN

One of the most beloved Duke players was big Mike Lewis from Missoula, Montana.

At 6'8", 235 pounds, Lewis was a big man who fit right into the Blue Devils' offense of shooters like Bob Verga and Jack Marin.

But Duke had never recruited a player from Montana and had no idea what it would be like having a guy from the land of cowboys and cattle drives visit their campus. "I was flattered by their interest in me being from Podunk Montana," Lewis said. "I had watched Duke in the 1964 Championship Game against UCLA on television, and it was incredible they were talking to me. I came to Duke for my visit in the spring on Joe College Weekend, and it was awesome. I was from Montana. *What the hell was this all about?* I saw Ike and Tina Turner in concert, when they were young."

With Lewis as a sophomore center on the No. 3-ranked team in the country, Duke rolled through the regular season with just two losses and defeated Carolina 88–77 in Chapel Hill and 77–63 in Durham.

In the semifinal of the ACC Tournament in Raleigh, Duke would face the Tar Heels again but not the *same* Tar Heels. With the Blue Devils averaging more than 88 points a game, Carolina coach Dean Smith thought it would be a good idea to hold the ball and try to force the Blue Devils out of their 2–3 zone. Duke never came out and trailed for most of the game until rallying late in the second half.

With the game tied at 20 and just seconds remaining, Lewis held the ball at the foul line with the fate of his team's season in his hands. Duke had to win the ACC Tournament to get back to the NCAA Tournament it had missed the prior year. He had two shots and needed to make one. "I had made a move in the low post and got fouled," Lewis recalled. "There wasn't a lot of time left, so I'm standing on the free throw line, and Verga comes by and says, 'No problem, do it just like in practice.' That was the last thing I needed to hear because I didn't make many in practice. I missed the first free throw so badly I could have been blindfolded and gotten it closer. But I took a deep breath with my knees knocking and I made the second one."

Carolina then jumped out of bounds and inbounded the ball. Lewis stole the pass. Well, sort of stole it. "Steal is probably the wrong word to use. They threw it right to me," Lewis said with a laugh. "It wasn't like I made some phenomenal defensive play. I just happened to turn around, and there was the ball."

Duke won the famous 21–20 slowdown game, defeated N.C. State the next night, and eventually reached its third Final Four in four years. The Blue Devils lost to Kentucky in the semifinals with Verga playing sick. Had they won and faced talented Texas Western (now UTEP) for the national championship, Duke might have been the team that lost to the first all-black starting five. That fate fell to Kentucky in coach Adolph Rupp's last trip to the Final Four.

What Lewis remembers most about his years at Duke is the discipline and care his coach, Vic Bubas, showed him. "After I graduated, that didn't end my relationship with him," Lewis said. "I have called him for advice in my career after basketball. He is just one of those people that I value for his advice and I valued for the example he set. Of course, there were times I could have killed him when I was playing. I thought I knew everything. I was a big hot shot and didn't like some things he did. Five of us got suspended for drinking. We got caught, we knew it was against the rules, he didn't give us another chance, and he kicked our ass off the team for a game. It was on the front page of the paper in Missoula for my parents to see. The guy had rules. If you want to be here, then you play by the rules. So later in life when I had to discipline my own kids, I thought about that. It made an indelible mark on me. There are a lot of things that I admired about Coach, but that one really made a mark on me."

MILLER TIME

In the more than 100 years of basketball that has been played on the UNC campus, Larry Miller has been just about as quintessential a hero on the court and legendary off the court as any other player. The 6'3" lumberjack handsome brute created quite a stir. His hair flopped down as he raced up the court, and a medallion bounced around his neck. When he wheeled into the Granville Towers parking lot in his red convertible, coeds risked their lives, hanging out of high-rise windows waving and squealing at No. 44. "He was a lot like Joe Namath," Dean Smith said. "When he made up his mind to do something, he would do it and do it well."

"In the clutch the guy was incredible," Duke's Vic Bubas added.

After his team lost to Carolina in the 1967 Far West Classic, Oregon State coach Paul Valenti said of Miller, the tournament MVP, "I've seen a lot of college teams that couldn't beat Larry Miller and four girls."

Ah, the girls. They were never far away from Miller. After playing an afternoon game at Carmichael Auditorium, Miller had his pick of fraternity parties and he usually arrived with his arms full—a comely Carolina coed under one and a six pack of Pabst Blue Ribbon under the other. Legend was Larry could reverse the natural order of things, party all night, and still get 20 and 10 the next day.

He was a schoolboy hero in Catasauqua, Pennsylvania, but also a strong boy who ran with a weighted vest his father made from a hunting jacket and often worked out with ankle weights to improve his jumping ability. As a teenager he played with grown men in the old Eastern semi-pro league and more than held his own. No wonder he did not care that UNC hadn't won anything under the 33-year-old Smith when he picked the Tar Heels over Duke. Miller was going to change all that and he did, leading the Tar Heels to back-to-back ACC championships and Final Fours, winning ACC Player of the Year each season.

Miller's 13-of-14 shooting in the 1967 ACC Championship Game against Duke is part of UNC lore, but how he did it only added to his legend. First, he told his parents not to come down for the tournament because they would make him too nervous. Years later he was outed by Smith who smiled and said, "Larry probably wanted to sell his tickets." Next, with Smith fretting over a close game in the second half of what would be his first ACC title, Miller dribbled by the Carolina bench and said, "Coach, don't worry, we got it."

As a sophomore, Miller had emerged as a star by scoring 12 of UNC's final 14 points when the unranked Tar Heels stunned Ohio State in Columbus. As a senior, Miller had 20 points in the Final Four to lead Carolina over Ohio State in the semifinals. The week before, he had perhaps his greatest college game with 27 points and 16 rebounds in the Sweet 16 to knock off previously unbeaten and third-ranked St. Bonaventure with All-American center Bob Lanier.

Miller opted for the new ABA and the Los Angeles Stars, hoping to also land an acting career. A few game show appearances were as far as that went, but Miller did set the league's single-game scoring record of 67 points with the Carolina Cougars in 1972.

More than anything, Miller loved to tangle with Duke, the team for which he nearly played. Not only did he beat the Blue Devils three times as a junior to help secure Carolina's first ACC championship in 10 years, he always held Bubas in the highest regard after tearfully telling him that he was going to Chapel Hill. In fact Miller could not open the letter he received from Bubas shortly thereafter until he had played his final college game, hoping Duke wouldn't be mad at him for picking UNC.

Left sealed for four years, Bubas' letter wished Miller the best of luck in his career at Carolina, which was indeed a fortunate one. Miller averaged 21.8 points and 9.2 rebounds and was a two-time All-American as one of UNC's ultimate and enduring heroes.

TRIPLE OVERTIME

For older Carolina fans, the name Fred Lind might still bring a jaw-clenching scowl to their faces, while the same name to an older Duke fan will bring a slight smirk and a glimmer in the eye. March 2, 1968, was just another day in Duke basketball history that let you know there were actual magical powers within the rock walls of the Indoor Stadium.

After four consecutive ACC regular season titles from 1963–66, three ACC Tournament championships, and three Final Four appearances, the Blue Devils had fallen behind the tall and talented Tar Heels of Dean Smith and North Carolina.

They made an NIT appearance in 1967 but the following season had moved back into the national rankings behind the play of All-American center Mike Lewis. Senior Day at Duke would find Lewis facing North Carolina's own star center in Rusty Clark. The third-ranked Tar Heels were loaded with other great players like Charlie Scott, Larry Miller, and Bill Bunting and would end the year losing to UCLA 78–55 for the national championship.

But this day would belong to a seldom-used Duke junior named Fred Lind and a couple of other Duke players, who may not have been carried off the floor like Lind but were the real reasons the Blue Devils emerged victorious after three grueling overtime periods.

It all happened because Duke head coach Vic Bubas recognized that he might need Lind, who had played a total of 19 minutes all season. "Coach Bubas told me Friday to be ready, and I thought, 'Yeah, sure," Lind said. "I knew it would take something big happening like Mike fouling out for me to get in the game."

The Blue Devils figured they would play some man-to-man against the Tar Heels, who had a history of holding the ball against zone defenses, and if so, that increased the possibility of foul trouble. "We needed height to match the Tar Heels on the boards and would look to Fred in case Mike got in foul trouble," Bubas said. "So in our practice sessions during the week, we kept telling Fred to be ready. As it turned out, the young man more than met the challenge. We couldn't have won without his contributions."

"Coach was doing what good coaches do and have everyone ready," Lewis added. "We played a lot of different defenses against them. As a veteran player, I should have never gotten into foul trouble. But I did, and Fred was given the opportunity and he just maximized it. It was very difficult to sit there and watch when you have been a three-year starter and played the majority of minutes. And who knew it was going to go three overtimes, and I'd end up sitting for basically another half of a game. I was going crazy."

Before Lewis fouled out in regulation with 18 points and 18 rebounds, Lind had scored just 12 points the entire season. He hadn't played a minute against Carolina since scoring 20 points against the Tar Heel freshman team three years earlier. He wound up playing 31 minutes, scoring 16 points, and pulling down nine rebounds in what became a legendary performance.

After Lewis fouled out with 3:54 to go, Lind went the rest of the way. He hit a pair of foul shots at the end of regulation to force overtime and then knocked down a tying 18-footer with seven seconds left in the first overtime. He came up with key rebounds to help send the game into triple overtime.

Lind's biggest moment came in the final overtime, when in the space of seconds he blocked Clark's layup from behind, looped in a left-handed shot to give Duke the lead, and then blocked a shot by Tar Heel Dick Grubar. "I just saw an opening," he said of the clinching basket. "I'm right-handed, but it called for a left-handed shot. I didn't hesitate."

When the horn sounded and Duke had finally won 87–86, students, who had waited for Lind to emerge from the locker room, carried him on their shoulders around the court.

Lind's career wasn't over. As a senior he joined Bubas' regular rotation and averaged 10.6 points. Again he saved his best for last against the Tar Heels, who were ranked No. 2 in the country when they arrived at Duke for the regular season finale. The Blue Devils, who were also playing their last home game for retiring coach Bubas, were a .500 team. But Lind scored 18 points and grabbed 10 rebounds as they shocked Carolina again 87–81.

SCOTT AND THE PROTEST

Charles Scott was a hero in so many ways to not only UNC and the Duke-Carolina rivalry but to college basketball in the South. He was an 18-year-old pioneer, a black youngster in a still very racist region of the country, trying to make it at a predominantly white, state university, playing for a coach whose goal was to integrate the UNC basketball program with the right test case.

Scott was the first African American scholarship athlete at Carolina and almost 50 years later he is a hero to those who watched him play or now study sports history. But few can identify with just what a hailstorm he stepped into when, after attending prep school in Laurinburg, North Carolina, where he was valedictorian, Scott could have gone back to the Northeast and joined any number of college basketball teams with black players.

It was the spring of 1966, and Dean Smith dispatched assistant coach Larry Brown to see Scott, who had committed to Davidson and coach Lefty Driesell but was still talking to other schools, among them Duke. Brown had already been to Lebanon, Indiana, to see high school legend Rick Mount play and was shocked after watching Scott scrimmage. "Coach, Scott is better," he said to Smith.

"No, no, better?" Smith replied

"Better," Brown said.

Smith called Laurinburg coach Frank McDuffie and inquired about Scott, the student, as well as the player. No. 1 in his class and serious about getting an education, Smith was told. On the court he was skilled beyond belief and yet very unselfish. Smith said he wanted to invite Scott to Chapel Hill for the annual spring Jubilee Weekend, where The Temptations and Smokey Robinson and The Miracles were performing. The town appeared liberal and welcoming.

Scott had fun but also took the weekend seriously. He attended Sunday morning services at the integrated Binkley Baptist Church, and Smith introduced him to both white and black professors and prominent Tar Heel alumni. On Sunday afternoon before Scott went back to Laurinburg, he walked the campus and Franklin Street alone, where no one knew who he was. He said he found friendly people. No wide eyes or snickers and certainly nothing like the long looks he had encountered when visiting conservative Davidson.

Scott committed to UNC and eventually signed to play for the Tar Heels, telling Driesell, "I love you Lefty, but Chapel Hill is just a better place for me." Smith had the player he knew was good enough to star in the ACC, smart enough to excel in the classroom, and, he hoped, tough enough to endure the bigotry he would face on the road in the ACC.

Scott won a gold medal at the turbulent 1968 Olympics in Mexico City, supported a protest by black cafeteria workers on campus, made All-ACC and All-American teams, and played in two Final Fours. But he is best remembered for two games in his junior season.

Scott went wild for 28 points in the second half against Duke in the 1969 ACC Championship Game in Charlotte (he scored 40 in all) and led the Tar Heels to their third straight ACC Tournament title. "I've seen Charles play some great games," Smith said after Scott hit 12 of his 13 shots in the second half, "but I've never seen him on a streak like that."

It continued the next week in College Park, Maryland, against Davidson and the coach he nearly played for and where Driesell would become the new Maryland coach the next season. Scott had contemplated not playing in that regional final to protest five voters leaving him off the first-team All-Conference ballot when he was unquestionably one of the 10 best players in the ACC, if not *the* best.

As Smith briefed the team that Scott might sit out the Davidson game—and he had every right to protest what he believed was racial prejudice in the All-ACC voting—Scott drove around College Park with UNC assistant coach John Lotz, who would become best man at Scott's wedding. Together they decided Scott's best answer would be to play and make fools of the voters who had left him off their ballots.

To get Carolina to a third consecutive Final Four, Scott had to hit a top of the key jumper as the clock ran out. He finished with 32 points in the 87–85 thriller that Driesell has long called his most disappointing defeat at Davidson.

At the Final Four in Louisville, Scott faced Purdue and Mount, the player whom Brown said wasn't as good as the Tar Heel pioneer. It was Mount's night, scoring 36 points as the Boilermakers routed the Tar Heels 92–65. Scott managed just 16 against the tough Purdue defense. But he went on to be Rookie of the Year in the old ABA and win an NBA championship with the Boston Celtics. Scott's son, Shannon, plays for Ohio State.

BOBBY AND SWEET D

Bobby Jones and Walter Davis were both All-ACC players and then NBA All-Stars, but they will never be forgotten for two games against Duke in the 1974 season when the nationally ranked Tar Heels had to rally twice against the Blue Devils, who would finish last in the ACC standings.

The first game came two weeks after Carolina had dispatched Duke by 10 points for third place in the Big Four Tournament at the Greensboro Coliseum. The Blue Devils of interim head coach Neill McGeachy were 6–5 and had a 1–1 record in the ACC after losing at Virginia and defeating Clemson in their conference home opener. With senior Chris Redding; juniors Bob Fleischer, Kevin Billerman, and Pete Kramer; and sophomore Willie Hodge in a veteran starting lineup, plus freshman sharpshooter Tate Armstrong coming off the bench, Duke was a solid team early in the season.

The Tar Heels were ranked No. 5 and 11–1 with their only loss coming to eventual national champion N.C. State in the Big Four. Carolina was tall inside with the 6'9" Jones, 6'9" Mitch Kupchak, and 6'10" Ed Stahl but still struggling to score from the perimeter with juniors Ray Harrison and Brad Hoffman and Davis, a freshman who was improving steadily. Confident Duke took a 38–32 lead into halftime, and Cameron was going crazy.

Although Carolina made its typical second-half run, Duke still had the ball with the game tied in the final seconds. McGeachy had called a timeout at midcourt and figured the worst that could happen was overtime. But Paul Fox's inbound pass intended for Billerman hung in the air long enough for the cat-quick Jones to pick it off in full stride and race toward the winning basket. He laid it up, looked back to make sure the ball went in, and kept running toward the visitors' locker room. "He stole the ball, took a couple of long dribbles, and laid it in off the wrong foot," teammate Kupchak marveled after the 73–71 victory.

Duke lost five of its next seven games and by the rematch in Chapel Hill on March 2, rumors were rife that Duke would hire a permanent coach to replace McGeachy. The Blue Devils were 2–9 in the ACC (10–14 overall) and were looking to salvage the season by beating the still fourth-ranked Tar Heels they had taken to the wire in Durham. This time with only seconds to play, Duke led by eight points behind five starters in double figures and Billerman dishing out 14 assists to stun the Carmichael Auditorium crowd, most of which had already headed for the exits.

Duke led 86–78 with 17 seconds left in the game before Jones made two free throws, and Carolina converted two stolen inbound passes into baskets by Jones and freshman John Kuester to cut the lead to two points. Kramer was fouled with three seconds remaining but missed the first of a one-and-one, and Dean Smith called his last timeout.

UNC had a play called "513," which was to throw a football pass to the point guard (1 man) at halfcourt and call a timeout. But with no timeouts remaining, Smith said in the huddle, "513 but skip the 1" which meant the pass from 5 man Kupchak was going directly to the 3 man Davis. Smith told his freshman small forward he had "plenty of time" to catch the ball, drive hard to the basket, and shoot a 20-footer to send the game into overtime. The play worked imperfectly.

Kuester set a screen for Davis, and Kupchak hit him with the pass. Davis was so anxious to shoot that he took a couple of loping dribbles and let fly from about 35 feet. The ball was off to the right but long enough to hit the backboard and carom right through the hoop. The crowd, which had scrambled back to its seats, erupted, and some fans rushed the court, though the game was still going into overtime. The Tar Heels won 96–92, and Davis finished with 31 points and Jones with 24. The legend of "8 points in 17 seconds" was born.

The following Monday in practice, Carolina tried the same play with the same time left on the clock—and Davis shot an air ball, as all the Tar Heels broke up laughing. Clearly, that moment in time could not be recaptured.

DENNARD AND BANKS—SO LONG AND THANKS

Standing outside Cameron Indoor Stadium in the afternoon of early March, a number of students were wearing white T-shirts with two sketched-out faces and the words: "Dennard and Banks—So Long and Thanks." It was Senior Day 1981 at Duke for two of the greatest characters to ever don a Duke uniform.

The first three years of their career had been an almost Cinderella-like journey, playing for the national championship, being ranked No.1, gracing magazine covers, and being the subjects of numerous national and local interviews. Things changed in their final year.

At the end of their junior season, they had watched the coach they came to play for walk away from the program. Bill Foster had taken the job at South Carolina. In stepped a one-time Captain in the U.S. Army as their head coach, a guy who not only coached at the Military Academy but played there as well. He was coming from a job where discipline both on and off the court was a part of the game.

Discipline was not the first word that came to mind when describing Banks and Dennard, who were among the most charismatic players in college basketball but not necessarily the most predictable. All-American Banks had missed several practices over the years traveling back to Philadelphia to take care of family and had even been investigated for involvement with drugs at one point in his career. "Tinkerbell," as he was known, was his own man.

Dennard appeared on the cover of *Tobacco Road* publication nude with only a basketball covering his private parts. The 6'8" player once left after the end of the season and drove out of the Duke campus with his head out the sun roof, heading for Florida for his spring break.

Reverse dunks and windmill dunks and over-the-head passes were much more the language of these two than any words used by members of the U.S. Army. But they did have one ingredient that the young head coach from Army could relate to—they knew how to win. When they played the game, it was at one speed—full.

So Mike Krzyzewski knew he needed them and vowed he would make it through one year. "One year," he would say on several occasions. The 34-year-old had just one season to make it work with them. In Krzyzewski's first game against North Carolina in the last Big Four Tournament, the Blue Devils fell by two points 78–76 and they lost the next meeting in Chapel Hill 80–65.

The season wasn't an entire loss; there were wins over No. 19 Clemson and No. 13 Maryland at home. The Blue Devils entered the regular season finale with a 14–11 record against the No. 11 Tar Heels, who went on to play in the 1981 Final Four.

This day would belong to Banks and Dennard. It was only fitting that the shot that sent the game into overtime and the eventual winning basket involved the most unlikely duo to ever play together.

Banks was the Mr. All-Everything from the big city of Brotherly Love. Dennard hailed from King, North Carolina. Only North Carolinians may have heard of King and known where it was located. But the two struck up a relationship as soon as they arrived on campus. The magic between Banks and Dennard developed in the summer prior to their freshman year. "We were both in Durham that summer," Dennard recalled. "Gene was in a pre-college summer school program, and I was working odd jobs around town. We played every night in the intramural building because they were tearing up the original floor in Cameron Indoor Stadium that summer."

The IM Building was just a basic gymnasium with a rubber floor and metal girders sticking out of the pre-fabricated walls. "Some of the greatest pickup games I ever played in were in that old building," Dennard said. "Gene and I would light each other up, playing incredibly hard against each other, having a ball just playing basketball, and gaining a great deal of respect for each other's game. We battled as competitors and became blood brothers, dark blue brothers to this day."

Four years later it was their Senior Day.

With Carolina as the opponent and Banks and Dennard playing what was probably their last home game in Cameron (Duke did eventually play two NIT games there), there couldn't have been more people packed into the building that day. Banks, who had come to know almost everyone in Durham, couldn't say no to anyone who asked him for a ticket to this game. When Banks ran out of tickets, most of his fans still found a way to get in.

In those days the seniors were introduced and ran off the bench as the spotlight in the darkened gym shone on midcourt. Banks had brought a box of roses into the locker room. But he did not bring them out when he took the court for the seniors' ceremony. "Where are the roses?" One of the Duke staffers asked him.

"You really think I should do it?" He replied.

"If you want to, Tink. It's your senior day," the staffer said.

"They're back in my locker."

A manager ran to the locker room to get the long stems.

Dennard was introduced and basked in the spotlight for longer than he was supposed to, covering for his compatriot. Finally, the manager returned, scurried around behind the players on the bench, and gave the white box to Banks.

Krzyzewski had no idea what was going on but knew something was up because he had that furrowed brow that Dennard and Banks had given him throughout the season.

As Banks was introduced to thunderous applause, the star player ran to all four corners of the court and tossed roses to the fans and then went to midcourt, where he grabbed his teammate Dennard and gave him a big hug.

Dennard, grinning the whole time, reminded Banks that he was full of shit and returned the hug. So it was no surprise that the two would hook up on one of the most famous shots in Duke basketball history.

"Two seconds to go—tie game at 56," Dennard said. "Sam Perkins at the line—we have only one timeout. No matter what happened with the free throws, whether Sam made them or missed them, Coach K told us to call our last timeout. He made both of them, and before I could call timeout, Dean Smith called one for Carolina, which gave us an extra timeout and turned out to be a rare tactical error by Smith. We go into the huddle, and Coach said to get the ball to halfcourt and call timeout. We would not have had that opportunity if Dean hadn't called timeout to set up his defense. I threw it to Tommy Emma at midcourt, and he quickly called timeout."

Banks and Dennard have laughed for years over what happened in the Duke huddle. "K called the play for Chip Engelland because everyone thought I would be going to Gene, so we used Gene as a decoy," Dennard said. "Chip was a great shooter, but he was a sophomore, and this was our senior night, so Coach drew the play up, and Gene was supposed to set a pick down the baseline, and Chip came around it and hit the corner jumper. When we broke the huddle, I looked at Gene, he looked at me, and we really never had to talk. But I did say, 'You know what to do, come to the top.' It was a magical play. You are in a zone and not really sure what is happening, you just do things on instinct. The key to making it work was that I led him to where he had to turn and shoot; it wasn't something I did consciously. If I had thrown it directly to him, he wouldn't have time to catch, turn, and shoot. By leading him to the open spot he was able to catch it and shoot."

Banks got the shot off just over Perkins' outstretched arm. "The ball went in, and the place went crazy. It was the loudest I've ever heard the building for over a minute," Dennard said, recalling the moment with glee. "All you had were goose bumps. It was an incredible experience."

Krzyzewski hadn't called *that* play. But fully aware of the difficulty controlling Dennard and Banks, the holdover seniors, he wasn't surprised. The Dennard-Banks hookup in his first season as the Duke head coach, though, allowed him to beat North Carolina, which he did not think was possible right away. After all, the Tar Heels were going to two straight Final Fours and would win the national championship in 1982.

It seemed inevitable that somehow Duke would find a way to win in overtime.

And they did when Banks rebounded, scored, and took over the game. Strapping the Blue Devils to his back, he scored on six of the eight shots in the extra session with the final two coming with 12 seconds left to seal the 66–65 win.

For Duke students and fans, February 28, 1981, may well have been the perfect day. The combo factor of great things happening was incredible. A win over nationally ranked Carolina on Senior Day in Cameron followed by a one-hour drive to the Greensboro Coliseum and the Bruce Springsteen Concert. It also ruined Dean Smith's 50th birthday.

HUBERT DAVIS—THE LONG RIDE HOME

The U.S. Olympic Team had just won the 1976 Gold Medal in Montreal, beating Yugoslavia and avenging the controversial loss to Russia four years earlier in Munich, the first time the Americans had not won the gold medal in men's basketball since the sport was introduced in 1936 and breaking their 63-game winning streak.

Oklahoma State's Henry "Hank" Iba had been the Olympic coach in 1964, 1968, and 1972 and, having already retired at OSU in 1970, said that Munich would be his last assignment with the U.S. men's team. He was succeeded by UNC's Dean Smith, who agreed to do it for one Olympiad and believed that a different coach should get the chance every four years.

Smith held Olympic tryouts in the late spring of 1976 in Chapel Hill and Raleigh, looking to put a team together that was not only talented but would have the smallest learning curve for playing together in the short span of practice time. He chose Scott May and Quinn Buckner off Indiana's 1976 undefeated NCAA championship team and seven players from the ACC, including four Tar Heels—Walter Davis, Phil Ford, Mitch Kupchak, and Tom LaGarde. The other ACC players selected were Duke's Tate Armstrong, Maryland's Steve Sheppard, and N.C. State's Kenny Carr. The team's leading scorer turned out to be Notre Dame All-American Adrian Dantley.

Smith said it was the only team he ever coached where winning was the clearly stated priority. He wanted players who understood that and would not have to be bound by curfews or any other requirements except bringing the gold medal back to the United States. It was a family affair, and many of the players' parents and relatives traveled to Montreal to cheer the team on to victory. Among those family members were Walter Davis' older brother, Hubert, and his wife, Bobbie, and their six-year-old son, Hubert Jr. Together with Phil Ford, they all drove from Big Hubert's home in Virginia up the East Coast, across the Canadian border, and into Montreal.

After the gold medal ceremony on the night of July 27, 1976, the same five people piled into Big Hubert's car and headed home. Hubert Jr. spent most of the 16-hour drive sitting on the laps of his Uncle Walter and Ford, playing with their gold medals.

When Walter was in prep school in Delaware before enrolling at UNC, he had spent weekends at his brother's home. After Tar Heel assistant coach Bill Guthridge had driven up to visit Walter and have dinner with the family, he wrote a thank you note to the Davises and added the aside, "At this time we want to officially begin the recruitment of Hubert Jr."

Hubert Davis grew into a heralded three-sport high school star in Burke, Virginia, while crying himself to sleep for months after Bobbie died of cancer when he was 16. He remained determined to make his parents proud of the way they raised him and spent many lonely and sorrowful hours shooting at the old rim in his backyard. He became what Dean Smith and Guthridge believed was a mid-major college basketball prospect.

When Hubert and his father visited Chapel Hill, Smith was very direct with them. He was offering Hubert a scholarship because he was family but wanted him to think about attending a smaller school where he might get more playing time. The two Huberts did not have to think it over. Hubert Jr. wanted to follow his Uncle Walter to Carolina and see what happened.

After the first day of practice on October 15, 1988, Guthridge was asked how things went. He smiled and said, "Hubert Davis is a lot better than we thought."

Davis played in all but two games his first two seasons and became a starter midway through his sophomore year. He averaged 13 points as a junior and was turning into a deadly shooter, making 52 percent from the floor and 49 percent from the three-point line. That's when the chant of "H-u-u-u-u-bert" became so popular in Chapel Hill.

As a senior Davis finished fourth in the ACC in scoring with his 21.4 average, one-tenth of a point behind ACC Player of the Year Christian Laettner. Yet Davis only made second-team All-ACC. Many of the voters who had already cast their ballots probably wanted to take them back on Laettner's Senior Day, when Davis scored a career-high 35 points while draining 6-of-8 three-pointers. The game was tied at halftime, and Davis made the Duke students who had begun the game mockingly chanting "H-u-u-u-u-bert! H-u-u-u-u-bert!" so nervous late in the second half that they were yelling at him to stop shooting. Fortunately for them the Blue Devils went on to win 89–77. "Everybody seems to think we hate each other, and on the court I guess we do," Davis said. "But we do respect each other."

Hubert Davis was drafted by the New York Knicks in the first round and went on to have a distinguished professional career, playing for six teams over 12 seasons, and remaining the second best three-point shooter in NBA history with a .441 percentage. After seven years as an ESPN broadcaster, Davis joined Roy Williams' coaching staff in 2012—completing that long ride that began in 1976 with the trip to Montreal.

SWEATING IT OUT

It was only fitting that Mike Krzyzewski would call Steve Wojciechowski's Senior Day at Duke, "one of the greatest one-point performances in the history of basketball."

Krzyzewski loved Wojo. They were kindred spirits. Krzyzewski grew up on the tough side of south Chicago while Wojo grew up in Baltimore, where his father was a worker on the docks. Wojo was the epitome of what Krzyzewski wanted in a player. He was tough, hard-nosed, and intense. He wasn't blessed with natural talent. He had to work his way to being a great basketball player. He took on every possession like it was the last play of the game. Wojo was the essence of Krzyzewski on the court.

It had been a long journey for Wojo, whose four years in college must have seemed like a lifetime. He began his college career in the tumultuous 1994–95 season, starting his fourth game as a freshman, then tumbling through the Christmas death of his high school coach and mentor, and soon after losing his coach at Duke and his starting position. "It was a nightmare," he recalled, heading into his final game in Cameron. "That's the best way that I can describe it. It seemed like everything that could possibly go wrong for me went wrong. I didn't handle it as well as I could have or as well as I would have if it happened to me now. But that was all part of the maturation process."

Wojo was a major part of a rebuilding job that included winning the ACC regular season championship and reclaiming the No. 1 ranking, but as he headed into his senior game against the Tar Heels, he had been on the winning side of this rivalry just once.

On February 5, 1998, Duke and Carolina had clashed in Chapel Hill as the top two teams in the nation, only the second time in the history of the rivalry that had happened. The top-ranked Blue Devils came in with a 20–1 record with the lone loss at Michigan back in December. The No.

2 Tar Heels were 22–1, losing at Maryland and trailing Duke by a game in the ACC race.

The game would pull incredible numbers on the ESPN2 national broadcast and the Raycom regional network and was viewed in more than 1.6 million households. The power of Duke-Carolina even affected NBA attendance. The Charlotte Hornets had sold 21,984 tickets for their home game against the Vancouver Grizzlies, but barely 14,000 fans, the smallest crowd to that point in the history of the franchise, showed up. What's more, Hornets coach Dave Cowens had a very brief postgame press conference, lasting just two minutes and ended it by saying, "All right guys, let's go watch the game."

More than 33 percent of the televisions in the Charlotte market were tuned to the game, which garnered a 24.3 rating in the Queen City. What the fans in the arena and on television watched was the *Antawn Jamison Show*. Carolina didn't need much else as Jamison exploded for 35 points and 11 rebounds in the 97–73 rout of the Blue Devils, who trailed at halftime (50–34) for the first time all season. "If he's not the national player of the year, I don't know who is," said Duke sophomore Chris Carrawell.

"He deserves every accolade he gets," added freshman Shane Battier. "He's so tough. Once you think you have him defended, he spins around to the other side of the lane, catches the ball, and scores."

"You've really got to give him a lot of credit," Wojciechowski said. "He has an uncanny ability to score under the basket."

As the final seconds ticked off the clock, the Carolina student body stormed the court and celebrated once again beating their rivals, taking their top ranking this time. "They are the real deal. They are a heck of a team," said Krzyzewski after the game. "It's obvious in their celebration how much they wanted to beat us and how happy they were. The game meant a lot to them, which it should."

Walking out of the Smith Center, Carrawell said, "I'm going to remember this night, and my teammates will also. We're going to play them again and we'll be ready. They were ready for us tonight, and we'll be ready for them the next time we meet."

The next time came on February 28, the regular season finale on Senior Day at Duke with the ACC regular season title up for grabs. The Blue Devils were 14–1 and the Tar Heels 13–2, having lost a second conference game to N.C. State. But sweeping Duke would give Carolina first place by virtue of the tiebreaker.

On a sweltering Saturday afternoon in Cameron Indoor Stadium due to the 70 degree weather outside, the Tar Heels ran out to an 18–4 lead and did not let up. It looked like the Blue Devils would not only lose for the 10th time in their last 11 games to their archrivals, but also their seniors would get blown out in their final home game.

At the half with spectators trying to catch their breath in the crowded concourse, the Blue Devils trailed 42–30. Krzyzewski had already sweated through his white dress shirt and when he returned to the floor for the second half he had put on a Nike polo-style shirt under his dark jacket. "It was all wet," he said of the sopping dress shirt about an hour later. "I was so mad that we were playing so poorly and working to try and get us back in the game. It was just all wet, so I decided to go with my cool look—as cool as you can look at 51."

The new look didn't seem to help much, and with 11:39 left in the game, the Blue Devils trailed by 17 points. But over the last 11 minutes, Duke mounted perhaps its greatest comeback in the history of Cameron, considering the opponent and the stakes. Carolina's goal—to sweep Duke and lock up the No. 1 seed in the NCAA East region before the ACC tourney—began slipping away.

Behind Wojciechowski's defensive intensity, Elton Brand's strong inside play coming off the bench, and Roshown McLeod's key buckets, the Blue Devils suddenly came alive. Senior McLeod and freshman Brand began to pound the tiring Tar Heels inside, as Duke scored 10 of its last 13 field goals in the paint and held Jamison to just one tip-in and a free throw over the last 11 minutes. Duke scored on 15 of its last 18 possessions while holding Carolina to just two field goals in the final 11:39 of the game.

The comeback began when freshman Will Avery drove inside for a bucket and made two free throws. Brand, playing in just his third game since having a cast removed from his broken foot, scored eight points in three minutes to make it a seven-point deficit. Avery's three-pointer made it anyone's game, and McLeod finished off a 23-point performance with six in the last three minutes, including a driving layup that gave Duke its first lead of the entire game with 59 seconds left. McLeod also made two big defensive plays at the end by stealing a lob pass and tying up Vince Carter for a jump ball to give Duke possession.

Still, the biggest key to the win was the play of Wojciechowski, who with the instruction of assistant coach Johnny Dawkins from the bench, began feeding the ball to Brand on the low post where he could power inside and score.

On each Blue Devils possession late in the second half, Wojo had the ball in front of the Duke bench as Brand set up in the low post. Dawkins screamed, "Now!" when he wanted Wojo to get the ball to Brand. It worked to perfection.

Wojo scored just one point, but his 11 assists and leadership on the court were the largest contributors to the 77–75 win and the Blue Devils' second straight ACC regular season title. As the game ended, the emotions of four years at Duke and what Wojo had learned from his head coach swelled over. Instead of hugging his teammates, Wojo ran straight to Krzyzewski, pushing players out of the way to give his coach a huge hug.

Krzyzewski was asked directly about Wojo after the game. "With all of it on the table—everything at stake today and Senior Day and all that kind of stuff—for him to get 11 assists and one turnover and play great D, it was the best one-point performance ever here," he said.

Chapter 11

Leaders and Teachers

*I*t was 2004, and the Blue Devils were in San Antonio, Texas, for the Final Four and another shot at the national championship. Alex Wolff, writing for Sports Illustrated, walked up to me and asked if I had any good story ideas for him. "Not really," I said. "You know most of the angles with this team—Redick shooting, Deng playing great on both ends of the court."

"What about that nickname you guys used to have for Mike?" he asked.

"You mean Captain?" I said. "We still call him that, and it may be more appropriate now than any other time."

"Why's that?"

"He is the captain of the team," I explained. "Look at how they turn back to him for every play during the game and how he has their undivided attention in huddles. He is the captain of this team."

—JM

TRAINED TO LEAD

Mike Krzyzewski not only spelled his name to everyone in attendance at his introductory press conference at Duke, but he also told everyone how to pronounce it. Was it with a silent K, like "shu" or was it a hard K? He wouldn't be called "Coach K" for a number of years; "Special K" was the first promotional material put out on the former Army player and coach.

But looking for a good nickname, the people within his inner circle at Duke came up with the most appropriate one available—Captain. Since he was a Captain in the Army, it just fit him. So for years he was either called Captain or Mike.

Being "Captain" or a leader has always been a natural fit for the kid from south Chicago. "Growing up, I was always the leader of my group. There were just instinctive things you do as a leader," he explained. "Looking back, the people I admired were leaders, whether it was my coach in high school or my college coach. I gravitated toward wanting to know what leaders did."

Krzyzewski also grew up with a love for the game of basketball. He played at the all-boys Archbishop Weber High School in Chicago. "I loved playing basketball from the time I was in the seventh grade," Krzyzewski said. "I fell in love with basketball and I played all day with my buddies. I shot a lot by myself and imagined that my team always won. My high school coach, Al Ostrowski, made me better. He pushed me to be a better player and he helped me to understand the nuances of the game."

In the Captain's junior season, Ostrowski had to light a fire under Krzyzewski to get him to shoot more. He finally told him he would have to run laps every time he didn't take an open shot. In the next game, Krzyzewski lit up the scoreboard for 30 points and ended up leading the Catholic League in scoring that year, getting an early taste of what leadership and belief can do for a player. "I always thought the basketball was my friend, and it would never let me down," he said. "It's been my friend my entire life."

After high school Krzyzewski headed for the best leadership school in the world at West Point—the United States Military Academy. "You take that desire or instinct to lead and now you are taught how to lead," Krzyzewski explained. "After West Point being in the service you are around a lot of leaders—good leaders, medium leaders, and not so good leaders. So you start developing your own leadership style."

During his active duty, he coached service teams and served for two years as head coach at the U.S. Military Academy Prep School at Belvoir, Virginia. After resigning from the service with the rank of Captain in 1974, Krzyzewski worked as a graduate assistant for his old Army coach, Bob Knight, at Indiana University.

Krzyzewski always wanted to teach. His ambition in high school was to be a high school teacher and coach. But he was now more than a teacher. He was a leader. "The thing I loved the most—and still love the most about teaching—is that you can connect with an individual or a group and see that individual or group exceed their limits," he said. "You feel like you've been a part of them. You become something bigger than yourself."

He got his first head coaching job at his alma mater and served there from 1975–80, putting together a 73–59 record and one trip to the NIT—not very impressive credentials to take over a Duke basketball program that played for the national championship in 1978 and had spent most of the next two seasons ranked among the top 10 teams in the nation. But here he was recruiting high school kids to play against two of the top collegiate programs, UNC and N.C. State, and not making much progress. He missed on several top recruits before hitting the jackpot with his freshman class that entered Duke in the fall of 1982 that included Johnny Dawkins.

In those days Krzyzewski wasn't known so much for being a leader; he was a defensive coach—a belly-button-in-your-face, help-side defensive coach. This was a world of change for most of the players and all the fans who had gotten used to zone defenses in this area of the country. North Carolina was one of the top multiple-defense teams with its coach Dean Smith being a great teacher of zones to change the pace of the game from his traditional man-to-man.

It took time and a lot of mistakes to get Duke's pressure defense down. But by the Blue Devils' first NCAA Tournament appearance under the Captain in 1984, their man-to-man defense was becoming part of the fabric of college basketball. One of the strongest rules in teaching this man-to-man, help-side defense was faith in the system. And Krzyzewski, with his leadership background, was able to use belief as the lighting rod that made his defense effective.

In taking that leadership and teaching mantra to heart, Krzyzewski has developed into one of the finest college basketball coaches in the history of the game. A 12-time National Coach of the Year, he has also been voted the ACC Coach of the Year five times, second on the all-time list. In 1991 he was inducted into the National Polish American Sports Hall of Fame. *The* (Raleigh) *News and Observer* named Krzyzewski the best coach in ACC history in celebration of the league's 50th anniversary in 2002–03. The *Sporting News* named Krzyzewski their Sportsman of the Year in 1992, making him the first college coach to receive the honor. In a postgame ceremony on November 17, 2000, the Cameron Indoor Stadium playing floor was named Coach K Court.

As part of a joint venture, *Time* magazine and CNN named Krzyzewski "America's Best Coach" in 2001. "No college hoops coach has won more in the past two decades, and Krzyzewski has accomplished all this with a program that turns out real deal scholar athletes—kids who go to class, graduate, and don't mind telling everyone about it," *Time*'s Josh Tyrangiel wrote.

On October 5, 2001, Krzyzewski was inducted into the Naismith Basketball Hall of Fame. He became the youngest recipient of the Distinguished Graduate Award at the United States Military Academy in 2005 and in September of 2009 he was inducted into the Army Sports Hall of Fame. In 2011, along with Tennessee women's coach Pat Summitt, he was named the "Sportsman of the Year" by *Sports Illustrated*. In 2013 he received the Chicago History Museum "Making History Award" for distinction in sports.

Beginning in 2005 Krzyzewski's success led to a slew of endorsements including TV commercials for Chevrolet (and an endorsement deal with GMC), All-State and State Farm Insurance companies, and a series for American Express that was shot in Cameron Indoor Stadium and looked more like an infomercial for Duke than a spot for AmEx. "I don't look at myself as a basketball coach," he said in one of the spots. "I look at myself as a leader who coaches basketball."

It was part of the "My Life, My Card" campaign, which also featured Ellen DeGeneres, Tiger Woods, Robert DeNiro, and surfer Laird Hamilton. American Express spokesperson Rosa Alfonso said the commercials were not a pitch for Duke—rather the university was just a central part of Krzyzewski's story. "It's the reflection of his life and the story he has to tell as with all the individuals we feature," Alfonso said. "The reality is that he is an inspiration to many people, and he affects a lot of people personally off the court."

Since missing most of the 1995 season with back and other health issues, Krzyzewski's non-basketball life has been carefully managed by a team led by his wife, Mickie, and Duke senior associate athletic director Mike Cragg, who also heads up the Legacy Fund, a foundation for men's basketball that raises money to endow player scholarships and coaching salaries and improve capital facilities. The minimum gift for Legacy Fund donors is $1 million.

The Krzyzewski brand has grown exponentially along with the Duke basketball brand. And it has been the perfect partnership between a wealthy private university that can pay him anything it wants and a coach who desires his personal brand to be known beyond basketball—*literally and figuratively*. Krzyzewski has a weekly hour-long SiriusXM satellite radio show titled *Basketball and Beyond* in which Coach K converses with leaders from other sports and all walks of life.

He has other ways to impart his brand on a carefully targeted audience. After working at Flight School, Michael Jordan's fantasy camp in Las Vegas, Krzyzewski brought the concept back to Durham and developed the K Academy. Now in its 12th year, the K Academy touts team-building techniques into a once-in-a-lifetime weekend fantasy camp for business leaders who are also rabid college basketball fans. Campers, who average about 35 years old, spend five days playing in Cameron Indoor Stadium—where they go from opening day tryouts to a draft of teams to Sunday's championship tournament. The cost for this experience is $10,000 with a portion of the proceeds going to the Emily K Center, a Durham non-profit named for Krzyzewski's late mother, which helps underprivileged academically focused children prepare to further their education.

• • •

His success has also made him a very rich man with reports of his annual earnings exceeding the $10 million mark and averaging well over $7 million. Those estimates come from Coach K's tax returns because Duke, as a private school, discloses nothing about its employees that they don't want known.

What is very public about Krzyzewski, from his PR team to his own website, Coachk.com, is that he has won more games than any major college coach—983 (entering the 2014–15 season) with the 1,000-victory milestone imminent. Passing his old adversary Dean Smith (879) and his own mentor Bob Knight (902) along the way, it is a record that undoubtedly will never be approached because today's college coaches don't start as young as Krzyzewski did (28) and don't last nearly as long (2015 will be his 40th season as a head college coach).

Understandably, Krzyzewski has been wooed by a number of college and pro teams—from UCLA, Arkansas, and Kentucky to the Boston Celtics and Los Angeles Lakers—to leave Durham. At the time a minority owner of the Miami Heat, former Carolina star Billy Cunningham sat in Krzyzewski's living room talking to him about his future in the late '80s.

Following the 1990 season, the Celtics offered Krzyzewski their coaching position, but after meeting with Celtics chairman (and long ago Duke assistant coach) Red Auerbach in Washington, he soon declined because Auerbach told him pro basketball franchises are businesses, not families. In 1994 the Portland Trail Blazers came close to landing Coach K, but after a weekend at the beach with his family, he turned down that offer as well.

After winning a third national championship in 2001, Duke offered and signed Krzyzewski to a lifetime contract in order to seal the bond with its iconic coach. The agreement mandated that Krzyzewski serve as head coach until at least 2011, which of course he has already exceeded, and bound him to conclude his career at Duke. It covered the rest of his coaching career and beyond, taking him through the university retirement age of 65, which he has since surpassed. It also gives him the title of special assistant to the president, a position Krzyzewski says he intends to hold after he retires from coaching.

But that didn't deter other pro offers. In 2004 the Lakers came calling, looking to replace high-profile coach Phil Jackson. Krzyzewski was given a formal offer from Lakers general manager and former UNC star Mitch Kupchak reportedly for five years, $40 million and part ownership of the team. But again Coach K turned down the NBA—much to the relief of new Duke president Richard Brodhead.

In 2010 the New Jersey Nets offered him between $12 million and $15 million a year, and in 2011 the Minnesota Timberwolves came with a better offer. Both were politely declined. With all the victories and accolades, Krzyzewski has been able to turn his coaching success into much more than just wins and losses. "My profession has stayed exciting because—as my world has expanded—the core of that world is coaching basketball," Krzyzewski said of all his outreach programs. "Basketball gives me a platform to do other things. I love the game of basketball. I'm not just using it; I love it. As a result it gives me a chance to do some really good things with the V Foundation for Cancer Research, the Emily K Center, the Duke Children's Hospital, the opportunity to speak on leadership all over the country, including at my alma mater, West Point. There is more meaning than I just scored more points than you did. If that was the only thing that drove me, I would have moved on years ago."

His leadership plan is simple.

"The single most important quality of a leader is to be trustworthy. He has to be believable," Krzyzewski said. "He has to have the courage of conviction and the courage to do the right thing at the right time. Forget about the consequences; do the right thing. A leader has to have energy. You need to be enthusiastic, you can't show weakness, you have to be strong. Strong is how you look and how you act. And a leader has to be able to listen—not just to words but listen to the language of the people he is leading. Listen to the environment."

Dallas Cowboys head coach Jason Garrett has taken advantage of the access Krzyzewski provides to his coaching peers. "I have been able to study the atmosphere that is created, what the program stands for, how you see the relationship between coaches and staff, relationships with the players, and how they all communicate. All of that is universal to any team, and they do it better than any program I have been around," said Garrett after spending the weekend of the Duke-Carolina game with the Blue Devils. "I leave here saying I have a long way to go because they do it so well. I take a lot of notes and when I get back to Dallas I share them with my staff. We can only get better because of this experience."

Players and family members alike have all felt Krzyzewski's leadership. "When we were struggling my freshman year, we lost two in a row and we were really down," said Blue Devils assistant coach Jon Scheyer, a senior on the 2010 National Championship team. "He told us in a team meeting that if we keep doing what we were doing, we would win a national championship—and my senior year we did."

"He's gotten a grasp on the fact that leadership isn't a singular thing," explained his wife, Mickie. "You have to have people who want to be led, who want to be part of something, and take them where they want to go. It has to be a group effort."

"He's successful because he understands his audience and he understands how to adapt. He's a great communicator," said Lakers star Kobe Bryant, who played for Krzyzewski on two U.S. National Teams in the Olympics Games. "He's very passionate about his message, very passionate about the game."

"He has been able to adapt to so many different eras," offered former Duke star J.J. Redick, who plays for the L.A. Clippers and is one of 17 former Krzyzewski players currently in the NBA. "His players feel he never has an off day or a bad day. You can feel it every day in practice, in games, in the huddle, or in meetings. You are getting his best. You know you are getting his absolute best."

"Every day I watched him attack life," added Jason Williams, another former Duke All-American and now an ESPN broadcaster. "He was always proactive, not reactive."

"The biggest thing with him is strength," echoed Gerald Henderson, who left Duke after the 2009 season and now plays for the Charlotte Hornets. "You never see a weak moment when things are going bad or not like you planned. He is always strong and thinking of ways to dig himself out of a hole."

Krzyzewski was named head coach of the USA Basketball Men's National Team in October 2005 and over the next seven years led Team USA to a bronze medal at the 2006 FIBA World Championship and gold medals at the 2007 FIBA Americas Championship, 2008 Beijing Olympics, 2010 FIBA World Championship, and the 2012 London Olympics.

Krzyzewski became the first coach of multiple American Olympic teams since Henry Iba in the 1960s and 1970s. After announcing the 2012 Olympics would be his last as coach of Team USA, he changed his mind the following May and decided to stay on from 2013–16, hoping to qualify for the 2016 Summer Games and pull the gold medal hat trick in Rio. But even with all the leadership accolades,

Krzyzewski was still missing something he needed, which he couldn't find on the basketball court. "In my own sport, once you get to a certain level people aren't going to share much with you," he explained. "You are the one that talks about basketball at clinics. Where do *you* get ideas from? How do *you* keep learning? So I have gone outside my field to keep learning from leaders in other fields."

His mentors have become Wall Street tycoon John Mack, former chairman and CEO of Morgan Stanley; Las Vegas entertainment and hotel entrepreneur Steve Wynn; and one of his former West Point players, a three-star general, Lt. General Bob Brown, Commander of Combined Arms Center and Fort Leavenworth. "Since I was at Duke and we started winning, I was able to do speaking engagements to major companies and be around leaders in other fields," Krzyzewski said. "If I am speaking to a company, I get to study that company and pick up some things they are doing in leadership. It's a bonus for me."

It is reported that Krzyzewski gets a guarantee of $1 million a year from the Washington Speakers Bureau and works with Creative Artists out of Los Angeles as his marketing agency.

And he has stepped into the political ring only sparingly—once with a fund-raiser in 2002 held at the Washington Duke Inn that he and Mickie hosted for Republican senate candidate Elizabeth Dole, a Duke graduate. It probably caught more attention than most political fund-raisers because her Democrat opponent was former UNC president Erskine Bowles, who was backed very publicly by Dean Smith. Dole won the senate seat for North Carolina in the 2002 election, succeeding longtime North Carolina senator Jesse Helms.

In 2004 the Fuqua/Coach K Center on Leadership & Ethics, a premier academic center, was established by the university's Fuqua School of Business in collaboration with Duke University athletics and Kenan Institute for Ethics. Krzyzewski serves as an executive-in-residence at the center, teaching and writing on leadership and ethics during the basketball offseason.

The Polish kid from Chicago had used his leadership abilities to win national championships, gold medals, and not only represent one of the most prestigious universities in the country, but also become the very face of the school as a basketball coach—and leader.

Dean Smith had his rules and pet peeves, but loyalty to his players, coaches, and Carolina basketball program trumped all. He was a punctuality freak, saying if you are late for any appointment, it meant your time was more important than the person you were meeting. One day I had an 11:00 AM interview scheduled with him and showed up at his office at 10:55. He emerged at 11:30, apologizing because he was speaking with a former player.

I kiddingly asked him whose time was more important than mine— his or his former player's. He smiled before making his priorities quite evident by saying, "Let's cut this short. I have to meet Coach Guthridge for lunch at noon."

—AC

Born To Teach

Like Mike Krzyzewski knew from an early age he wanted to be a leader, Dean Smith's DNA was to teach. And when he gravitated to coaching like his father, Smith treated an empty gymnasium as his personal classroom. He turned into what legendary UCLA coach John Wooden called "the greatest teacher of basketball."

It started as a child in a home with two schoolteacher parents. Smith's father, Alfred, was a three-sport coach in Emporia and Topeka, Kansas. Smith went to practice with his father as a toddler and wound up doodling plays on a piece of paper to show his dad. As a child Smith was given Chip Hilton books by his mother, Vesta, who wanted her son to read and understood his early love of sports. Smith also attended church services twice a week, where his father was a deacon and his mother played the organ. He joined the family at the Red Cross shelter, putting together care packages for the troops overseas. He saw his father weep over the news that one of his former students or players had died in WWII.

Smith watched his father fight to keep a black player on the Emporia team when the school principal wanted him to remove Paul Terry because of pressure being exerted by the Kansas High School Athletic

Association. Alfred Smith refused, risking his job. That imprint helped turn Dean Smith into a liberal Democrat from a Republican state and led to his integrating the UNC basketball program with the signing of Charlie Scott in 1966.

After attending Kansas and warming the bench for legendary Jayhawks coach Phog Allen, Smith's path included a ROTC stint in the Air Force coaching basketball teams (similar to Krzyzewski) overseas in Germany. It led to his serving his last two years of active duty as an assistant coach to the inventive Bob Spear at the Air Force Academy and eventually being hired by Frank McGuire at UNC, where he was an assistant for three seasons.

Smith became the quiet tactician to McGuire's fire and brimstone. The players hated it when McGuire went off recruiting and left Smith to run practices, which turned much tougher with more drills and fundamentals than merely scrimmaging. Smith also tutored players in math and made sure they went to class. He even organized McGuire's records and receipts when the NCAA investigated UNC's program in 1960.

After McGuire resigned under pressure in the summer of 1961, the 30-year-old Smith was the only choice to succeed McGuire, the flamboyant Irishman.

UNC chancellor Bill Aycock hired Smith with a mandate to clean up a program McGuire had let spin out of control after winning the 1957 National Championship. Aycock had seen Smith operate and believed he was the man to teach the Tar Heels discipline and put a renewed emphasis on academics. Despite UNC's lean records two of his first three seasons, Aycock continued to back his coach even after the chancellor returned to teaching at the UNC law school.

It is uncanny how Smith's career preceded Krzyzewski by 14 years with eerily similar paths. Both grew up with more modest ambitions than becoming internationally known icons and Hall of Fame coaches. Both got their lifetime jobs as unknown coaches whose selection was questioned and criticized. And both were very nearly fired after four seasons before being saved by the athletic directors who hired them. Krzyzewski's champion was athletic director Tom Butters, who turned out to hire and not fire the coach that led Duke to unprecedented heights, as Smith had done at UNC.

As the sport they coached grew in popularity and stature, they built college basketball programs that were known—a decade apart—as America's Team. Smith came first in the 1970s and '80s when his longtime teachings that were studied by many of his peers became a national phenomenon and eventually a controversy that changed the rules of the game.

Smith had a point guard named Phil Ford, who wasn't the first Tar Heel player to run the Four Corners spread offense but clearly the most famous. Ford was a scoring point guard unlike any other Smith had before, and when the Tar Heels held the ball with a lead late in the game, the warring fans reacted with either excitement or trepidation.

Four Corners was invented almost accidentally in Smith's third season as head coach of the Tar Heels while preparing to play Duke, a team that usually employed a zone defense. "In the last game, Duke played a halfcourt zone press, and a typical strategy against it was to send four men to the corners with a center at the foul line," Smith wrote in his book, *A Coach's Life*. "But we did something slightly different. Looking to score out of this set, we put our best ballhandler, Larry Brown, at the foul line instead of a big man. I huddled the defense and told them to show the zone press and then switch into man-to-man. I wanted to see if Larry would recognize the change and go to our man-to-man delay game as he was supposed to do...Larry didn't recognize it, but he did know a scoring opportunity when he saw one. He drove right by his man and passed to a teammate for a layup. I told them to do it again.

"It dawned on me that we could use this offense against a man-to-man defense...It would work against any defense for that matter. In fact, it would be an especially effective strategy if you had the lead. We would call it Four Corners."

It became a high-percentage play with Ford because he was such a superb ball handler, learning how to dribble low to the ground on dirt courts in his hometown of Rocky Mount, North Carolina. It was very difficult—almost impossible—for one man to take the ball away from Ford. So when the trailing team ran two men at Ford, he was also a deft enough passer to find the open man. If the open man was out on the court somewhere, Ford would give up the ball and go get it right back, running valuable time off the clock. Occasionally, Ford would make a move toward the goal, drawing a double team from a defender underneath. That left the open man near the basket, and Ford would hit him for a layup.

When Carolina played Virginia and 7'4" All-American Ralph Sampson in the 1982 ACC Championship Game, Smith was content to hold the ball with a slight lead if Sampson refused to come away from the basket where he would get every rebound. So the Tar Heels ran large chunks of time off the clock in the nationally televised game and won 47–45. The criticism was so strong that a shot clock was implemented in the ACC the next season. That, too, was okay with Smith, whose high-scoring teams were among the best in the nation at fast breaks. In fact, Smith had long lobbied for the shot clock and the three-point shot. Until they entered the college game, Smith just played by the old rules better than any other coach.

He taught sound basketball principles. For example, he emphasized being in position to see the man you were covering and the ball at the same time and the unselfish passing game offense that tired defenders to the point where they gave up an open shot or lane to the basket. Smith, however, was better known as one of the great innovators of the game. Besides creating the Four Corners, his players were the first to use a tired signal to take themselves out of the game when they became winded. They had the right to put themselves back in by saying, "Coach, I'm ready." Carolina's tired signal was raising a fist to the bench. Other teams use different signals, such as tugging at their uniform jerseys or raising their hand. But the idea originated with Smith.

Smith also wanted assists to be included in the official game statistics and kept throughout the season. His statisticians did it, but he wanted more recognition for his players so they would consider passing the ball more important than shooting it. As a result Carolina players who scored pointed to the man who passed them the ball, a gesture that is used at all levels of basketball today. It became so prevalent with the Tar Heels that their fans would point at the passer from the stands.

Other so-called "Deanovations" were springing trap defenses on opponents like the run-and-jump or the scramble, which was a surprise double team on the ballhandler geared to forcing a turnover. Smith popularized changing defenses in general to keep the opposing team off balance. Primarily a man-to-man coach, Smith would have his Tar

Heels press fullcourt on one possession, then fall back, pick up their men on the next possession, and force the man with the ball against the sideline or into the corner with a double team. Smith later incorporated zones into his defensive strategy, changing from one kind of a zone to another during a game.

After a foul sent a player to the free throw line, Smith was also the first coach to have his teams huddle, easily allowing the point guard to call the next play or the next defense. And of course he was best known for saving his precious timeouts until the end of the game, so his team could stop the clock after scoring and make seconds seem like minutes while trying to mount a comeback. A lesser known innovation was the use of wristbands, which Smith got from watching tennis players who wore them to keep their hands from sweating. *Basketball players' hands sweat, too*, Smith said to himself.

From Frank McGuire, Smith adopted how to dress himself and his team. He wore a coat and tie to every game (something Roy Williams says he will always do because Smith and McGuire did it) and was on the cutting edge with his teams' uniforms and apparel. He broke out Carolina blue Converse sneakers in the 1970s and in the late 1980s asked Chapel Hill native and well-known designer Alexander Julian to change the UNC uniforms and warm-ups. After three years of tinkering with colors and patterns in his studio, Julian unveiled the new unis with a blue argyle stripe, which has become a trademark symbol of not only UNC basketball but other Tar Heel sports as well. Once a season the end zones in Kenan Stadium are painted argyle.

In his practice gym/classroom, which was always closed to the public and where visitors needed a special pass to watch from halfway up in the stands, Smith tried to teach life as well as basketball. He began every practice with a thought of the day that ranged from his favorite philosophers to current events. His practice plans were developed in meetings with his staff earlier in the day and typed out by his secretary. Every activity was scheduled to the minute. He was as concerned with his players' emotions as much as their execution. On certain days when he thought they needed it, he instructed his assistants to instill confidence or be tough on them.

No one taught loyalty better than Smith, and those in the sacred Carolina basketball family know that was his greatest strength and

sometimes could be his greatest weakness. He pushed former players or coaches for jobs when he might have known in his heart they
weren't the best candidates. He never wanted anyone to leave his program unhappy and would always be there for them. He told friends
and acquaintances who asked him for recommendations that they
could not come at the expense of a family member who was seeking
the same opportunity. Even his golden rule of punctuality could be
compromised if it was for the family. Not quite *The Godfather*...but
pretty close.

Although Smith could be a taskmaster in practice or in the privacy
of a closed huddle, his teaching philosophy was built around positive
reinforcement. He would stop practice and praise a screen set by a
player, and that often carried over to other players trying to set the same
screen. He asked his players to recognize their mistakes, learn from
them, and then forget them. Personally, Smith tried to adhere to the
Serenity Prayer principles: accept what can't be changed, change what
he can, and know the difference. He respected individual rights, and
when his players wanted to, for example, march in a Vietnam protest
in the early '70s, he reminded them that they were representing themselves, their personal families, their basketball family, and their school.

Most of them thought twice about doing it.

Smith's success was mostly attributed to the great players he
recruited, but his emphasis on academics and honesty sometimes cost
him a high school star or two. It, though, helped him at times, too.
When he told Phil Ford that he might have to play junior varsity for
a year, Ford's parents admired that kind of candor in a coach when
others were promising their son a starting position and instant star-
dom. But later in his career, he lost players who had already become
highly coveted through publicized recruiting ratings and wanted to be
assured they would play when they arrived in Chapel Hill.

Despite becoming a national figure, Smith—unlike Krzyzewski—
stayed away from most commercial endorsements and appeared only
on public service announcements to support certain charities and
causes. He was probably making $1 million when he retired in 1997—
nothing compared to what coaches have been earning over the past
10 to 15 years. And he was generous with what money the enterprise
did make—like his summer camp that was run by his staff and at

Duke Head Coaching Trees

(Listed are players who played for or assistants who worked for these coaches)

Under Eddie Cameron
- Gerry Gerard: Duke
- Horace Hendrickson: Elon

Under Gerry Gerard
- Red Auerbach: Washington Capitals, Tri-Cities Blackhawks, Boston Celtics

Under Harold Bradley
- Lefty Driesell: Davidson, Maryland, James Madison, Georgia State
- Fred Shabel: Connecticut

Under Vic Bubas
- Tony Barone: Bradley, Creighton, Texas A&M, Memphis Grizzlies
- Hubie Brown: Kentucky Colonels, Atlanta Hawks, New York Knicks, Memphis Grizzlies
- Chuck Daly: Penn, Cleveland Cavaliers, Detroit Pistons, New Jersey Nets, Orlando Magic,
- Jeff Mullins: UNC-Charlotte
- Steve Vacendak: Winthrop
- Bucky Waters: West Virginia, Duke

Under Bucky Waters
- George Krajack: Xavier
- Jim Lewis: George Mason (women), Washington Mystics (WNBA), Georgetown (women)
- Neil McGeachy: Duke
- Sonny Moran: West Virginia, Morehead State
- Ron Righter: Wilkes College, Clarion College
- Jack Schalow: Morehead State, Seattle University

Under Bill Foster
- Bob Bender: Illinois State, Washington
- Kevin Billerman: Florida Atlantic
- Lou Goetz: Richmond
- Dick Lloyd: Rutgers
- Scott Sanderson: Mobile, Lipscomb
- Steve Steinwedel: Delaware
- Bernard Tomlin: SUNY College at Old Westbury
- Jim Valvano: Iona, N.C. State
- Bob Wenzel: Jacksonville, Rutgers

Under Mike Krzyzewski
- Tommy Amaker: Seton Hall, Michigan, Harvard
- Mike Brey: Delaware, Notre Dame
- Robert Brickey: Shaw
- Jeff Capel: VCU, Oklahoma
- Chris Collins: Northwestern
- Johnny Dawkins: Stanford
- Mike Dement: UNC-Greensboro, SMU
- Bobby Dwyer: Sewanee
- Danny Ferry: Cleveland Cavaliers, Atlanta Hawks (GM with both)
- Pete Gaudet: Army, Duke
- David Henderson: Delaware
- Bobby Hurley: Buffalo
- Billy King: Philadelphia 76ers, Brooklyn Nets (GM with both)
- Billy McCaffrey: St. Bonaventure (interim)
- Tim O'Toole: Fairfield
- Quin Snyder: Missouri, Utah Jazz
- Chuck Swenson: William & Mary
- Steve Wojciechowski: Marquette

North Carolina Head Coaching Trees

(Listed are players who played for or assistants who worked for these coaches)

Under Frank McGuire:

- Dean Smith: UNC
- Ken Rosemond: Georgia
- Donnie Walsh: (President) Indiana Pacers, New York Knicks

Under Dean Smith:

- Larry Brown: Kansas, UCLA, SMU, two ABA teams, and nine NBA teams
- Scott Cherry: High Point University
- Billy Cunningham: Philadelphia 76ers
- Matt Doherty: Notre Dame, UNC, Florida Atlantic University, SMU
- George "Butch" Estes: Palm Beach State College
- Eddie Fogler: Wichita State, Vanderbilt, South Carolina
- George Karl: Denver Nuggets, Milwaukee Bucks, Seattle SuperSonics, Golden State Warriors, Cleveland Cavaliers
- John Kuester: Boston University, George Washington, Detroit Pistons
- Mitch Kupchak: (GM) Los Angeles Lakers
- Jeff Lebo: East Carolina, Auburn, Tennessee Tech, Chattanooga

- Doug Moe: Denver Nuggets, Philadelphia 76ers
- Buzz Peterson: UNC Wilmington, Coastal Carolina, Tennessee, Tulsa, Appalachian State
- King Rice: Monmouth
- Tony Shaver: William & Mary
- Roy Williams: Kansas and UNC

Under Matt Doherty:

- Doug Wojcik: Tulsa, College of Charleston

Under Roy Williams:

- Matt Doherty: Notre Dame, North Carolina, FAU, SMU
- Neil Dougherty: TCU
- Blake Flickner: Dallas Baptist
- Jerry Green: Oregon, Tennessee
- Ben Miller: UNC Pembroke
- Steve Robinson: Tulsa, Florida State
- Kevin Stallings: Illinois State, Vanderbilt
- Mark Turgeon: Jacksonville State, Wichita State, Texas A&M, Maryland
- Jerod Haase: UAB
- Wes Miller: UNCG
- Jacque Vaughn: Orlando Magic
- Rex Walters: FAU, San Francisco

which Smith made only token appearances. It drew more than a thousand campers every summer with no advertising and was called the Carolina Basketball School to emphasize the teaching elements for campers as well as the games they would play. And every morning in gyms all over Chapel Hill, it was drills, drills, and more drills before the kids could play games in the evening.

Smith's office and gym were always open to former players and coaches and even colleagues, who wanted to visit or sought his guidance on matters both personal and professional. Every fall just before practice started, he convened a coaches' clinic limited to only his staff and college and NBA coaches with direct ties to the UNC program. They would share ideas and strategies, play golf, and enjoy dinners at Smith's home and private rooms in local restaurants. He never considered running an academy or fantasy camp for business leaders like Krzyzewski has at Duke.

That wasn't Dean Smith at all.

Ironic to the academic scandal that dogged UNC athletics long after his retirement, Smith was most proud of his graduation rate, which was listed in the UNC media guide as in the high 90s percentile. Whether players left school for personal reasons or to play professionally, he emphasized returning to graduate, and most of them did. In fact, he had many NBA general managers put bonuses into the contracts of UNC rookies they signed for completing their degree work. The academic standing of players was always held in the utmost privacy, and Smith only occasionally varied from that, like when he redshirted Kevin Madden in 1987 for poor class attendance or got into a squabble with Krzyzewski over the SAT scores of two black UNC players (J.R. Reid and Scott Williams) compared to two white Duke stars (Danny Ferry and Christian Laettner), which was prompted by what Smith considered a racial slur toward Reid by Duke students.

Krzyzewski was equally proud of the academic record of his players but also went public when they screwed up such as the time he refused to hang the 1990 Final Four banner until two seniors on that team, Phil Henderson and Alaa Abdelnaby, came back to graduate. Smith despised the NCAA requirement that teams had to arrive at the tournament site a full day before their games to practice and meet with the media. Those days almost always caused players to miss class, and Roy Williams has continued voicing Smith's objections over the years.

Although Williams is clearly his own man, his mentor's teaching is all over his work. He recruits top talent, his teams play among the fastest tempos in college basketball, and with his nearly .800 winning percentage he joined Smith in the Naismith Hall of Fame in 2007. In reaching 700 career victories faster than any coach in history besides Kentucky's Adolph Rupp, the 64-year-old Williams has been National Coach of the Year seven times and Big 8/Big 12 and ACC Coach of the Year nine times. Smith was National Coach of the Year four times and ACC Coach of the Year eight times.

Smith led the USA team to the gold medal in Montreal in 1976 and afterward said it was time for another coach to take over. Besides the Naismith Hall of Fame, Smith was named Sportsman of the Year by *Sports Illustrated* and one of the five all-time greatest American coaches of any sport by ESPN. In 1998 he won the Arthur Ashe Courage Award, which was presented at the annual ESPY Awards, and was moved to tears when several of his former players surprised him by coming on stage to congratulate him. He owns more records for consistency than any other coach in history, including 27 consecutive seasons with 20 or more wins, 13 straight trips to the NCAA Sweet 16, and 23 bids to the NCAA Tournament in succession from 1975 through 1997, his last season. Besides winning two NCAA championships in 1982 and 1993, Smith took 11 Tar Heel teams to the Final Four.

On November 17, 2006, Smith was recognized for his impact on college basketball as a member of the founding class of the National Collegiate Basketball Hall of Fame. He was one of five, along with Oscar Robertson, Bill Russell, John Wooden, and Dr. James Naismith, selected to represent the inaugural class. In 2007 he was enshrined in the FIBA Hall of Fame and in 2011 received the prestigious Naismith Good Sportsmanship Award. He rarely lost his cool, forever biting his lip while considering what to say. "I always tell the truth, but I don't always say everything I am thinking," Smith liked to say.

Williams is more candid than Smith and occasionally gets himself in trouble by saying too much. Often that comes with trying to shield his players from the extra attention that follows winning two national championships (2005, 2009) and taking five other teams to the Final Four. Over time Williams has gotten even more Smith-like in protecting his players.

Smith, in fact, kept his program away from the general athletic department academic support and tutoring programs. He employed tutors like longtime favorite Burgess McSwain to help those players who needed it. That practice has also been called into question in recent years since the administrative assistant (Deborah Crowder) to the deposed former chairman of the old African American studies department has been the longtime partner of former Tar Heel player Warren Martin, a highly respected public school teacher in Chapel Hill for more than 30 years.

Smith, who developed progressive cognitive dementia after undergoing knee replacement surgery in 2008, was not capable of answering questions and charges against his program as the scandal unfolded. Certainly, Smith helped all of his players with their academic and professional progress and was very controlling in doing it, but for a coach who clearly put education ahead of basketball, it would be foolhardy to believe he broke any law or violated any NCAA or university policy.

On November 20, 2013, the great coach, the humanitarian, and the son of rural Kansas teachers was awarded the Presidential Medal of Freedom for his off-the-court work fighting segregation, nuclear warfare, the North Carolina speakers' ban, and the death penalty, among other causes.

His wife Linnea, members of his family, and close friends were at the White House to accept the Medal of Freedom—the highest civilian honor in the United States—from President Obama, and people whose lives Smith touched for more than half a century sent in their congratulations and well wishes. Among them was his adversary from Duke he competed against for 17 seasons and 38 games, who admittedly learned a lot from the teacher eight miles down the road. "He used the platform he attained as a coach to have an influence on other areas of our society. That's what we should all do," Krzyzewski said in an interview with WCNC-TV in Durham.

Krzyzewski said Smith's stance on equality would force those who admired him to recognize issues they might otherwise oppose. "Some people who were against that [social equality] weren't against him. So it made those people look at it because they wouldn't challenge him," Krzyzewski said.

Smith holds a 24–14 advantage over Krzyzewski in head-to-head competition. Their elite coaching escalated the Duke-UNC rivalry to a national audience. "The basketball gods were good about bringing us together," Krzyzewski said. On December 20, 2010, the night Krzyzewski earned his 879th career victory to tie Smith, he had this to say about his old rival, who had been retired for 15 years: "It was as intense as any game you've ever been in," Krzyzewski said. "If you think today's game is intense, the '80s and early '90s were something else. Not as many guys went pro early. As a coach you had to become good…or go into TV.

"Dean's never been in TV. Look, we competed really hard against each other. But the ultimate thing a competitor can say about one another is that he respects him 100 percent. When two teams go after it that are coached by guys this competitive, you've got to make each other better. No one's done a better job in the ACC by far than Dean. What he did was set a standard that you had to adopt or else you dropped by the wayside. He was one of the great pioneers, and that doesn't even describe it. He built a program when most people didn't even know what the hell a program was. He built one hell of a program at a great school. He recruited unbelievably great kids, developed great relationships with them, and they played a brand of basketball where they showed up every night. We've done a lot like that in our own way. So that's produced some really good basketball.

"When Dean left the game, he could have [stayed and] won more games if he lingered. Somebody like him or somebody like me will not linger because we didn't get in this to linger. We got in it to go for it. For Dean to be that competitive for that length of time is unbelievable…just unbelievable. I would hope that as long as I am coaching, I will be as competitive as I can be. And not linger. Dean has really been something special for the game of basketball. And to share something with him for this moment is a good thing, a really good thing."

Acknowledgments

A rt Chansky is a 1970 UNC graduate who has followed and covered the Carolina-Duke rivalry since arriving in Chapel Hill. He was the sports editor of *The Daily Tar Heel* and later the *Chapel Hill Weekly* and *Durham Morning Herald*. He has written and published seven books on UNC basketball, including *March To The Top*, 1982; *Return To The Top*, 1993; *The Dean's List*, 1996; *Dean's Domain*, 1999; *Blue Blood*, 2005; and *Light Blue Reign*, 2009.

Chansky drew from more than 40 years of his own research, interviews, and writings, plus *ACC Basketball, An Illustrated History* (Ron Morris, 1988); *Carolina Court* magazines, 1986–2002; *Sports Illustrated* (March 6, 1995); UNC media guides from 1967; *A Coach's Life* by Dean Smith (2000); and archives of every major newspaper in North Carolina, plus *The Washington Post*, *The Atlanta Journal-Constitution*, and *The* (South Carolina) *State*.

He is most grateful for the time and friendship of UNC senior associate athletic director for media relations Steve Kirschner, basketball sports information director Matt Bowers, interviews granted by former UNC athletic director Dick Baddour and chancellor James Moeser and UNC alumni Larry Brown and Roy Williams and archived interviews with Dean Smith, Frank McGuire, and too many of their former players to list.

Chansky cherishes the support of his wife Jan, stepson Ryan, and Dukie father-in-law Harold Bolick for understanding his weird hours and other quirks.

Johnny Moore is a 1977 graduate of Guilford College and a life-long Duke fan. He joined the Duke information staff in May of 1977 and worked under Tom Mickle as assistant and associate sports information director, then served as director of promotions and marketing for the Blue Devils until he started his own communications company and purchased the rights to the Duke Radio Network and the Duke coaches' radio and TV shows. Through those mediums and publishing *Blue Devil Weekly* for 18 years, Moore has interviewed hundreds of Duke players and coaches.

He is especially grateful to the late Mickle and former Duke athletic director Carl James for hiring him and to his invaluable associate John Roth for the last 35 years of working together and developing some truly outstanding publications, radio broadcasts, and television shows. Thanks to John for editing so many of Moore's stories and making them look good.

To John and Margaret Moore, parents who taught Johnny firsthand about the Duke-Carolina rivalry.

To Amy McDonald, assistant university archivist and the staff of the Duke University Archives at the Rubenstein Rare Book & Manuscript Library in Perkins Library for all their tremendous support and being the keepers of the "Holy Grail"—the files of past Duke basketball games. To *Durham Morning Herald*, *The Durham Sun*, *The Duke Chronicle*, *The Raleigh News and Observer*, *The Raleigh Times*, *Greensboro Daily News*, *Fayetteville Times*, *The Charlotte Observer*, *Richmond Times-Dispatch*, and all the writers who penned wonderful stories contributing background and insight into this book.

To the guys at Duke, Art Chase, Matt Plizga, and Mike Sobb, who have always provided incredible support and help in all of our endeavors with the Blue Devils over the years.

Among Moore's biggest supporters and best friends are Barbara and Sammy Rigsbee, Jim Pomeranz, Scott Yakola, Charlie Smith, Tommy and Betty Saunders, cousin Terry Moore, Rev. Brian Gentle, Rev. George Johnson, Tim Kent, Anthony Dilweg, Will Hedgecock, Charles Woody, Tom Drew, and Dr. Jim Urbaniak.

Moore has been a Duke basketball "insider" throughout the coaching careers of Bill Foster and Mike Krzyzewski and is grateful for the private interviews granted by both over the years. Thanks also for the time from former coaches Vic Bubas and Bucky Waters, along with Blue Devils from every decade back to the 1950s, including Dick Groat, Fred Lind, Mike Lewis, Mike Gminski, Jim Spanarkel, Gene Banks, Kenny Dennard, Johnny Dawkins, Shane Battier, and Jabari Parker. Special kudos to the Duke Basketball Database link on GoDuke.com, which is the best and most easily accessible aggregation of season and player records on any college website.

Special thanks to Jay Bilas, who has been a part of this rivalry for more than 30 years as player, coach, and broadcaster, for agreeing to write the foreword.

After producing hundreds of radio broadcasts, awarding-winning TV shows and specials, and articles for *Blue Devil Weekly* and GoDuke.com, Moore has (co-) authored his first book.

• • •

Art and Johnny both would like to thank Noah Amstadter and Jeff Fedotin of Triumph Books for believing in the project and making it happen.

Chansky and Moore got to know each other in the late 1970s, particularly as "insiders" on the firing of Duke football coach Mike McGee and have been friends and gentle adversaries ever since. *The Blue Divide* is believed to be the first book co-authored by writers representing opposite sides of a rivalry as historic as Duke-Carolina basketball. At the basis of this book are what Chansky and Moore have seen and heard that few others have.